Odyssey of a Child Survivor

*From Latvia
through the Camps
to the United States*

Odyssey of a Child Survivor

*From Latvia
through the Camps
to the United States*

George David Schwab

Odyssey of a Child Survivor

From Latvia through the Camps to the United States

George David Schwab

Published in the United States by
George David Schwab

ISBN 978-0-578-75610-3

Design and artwork, Glen Powell Graphic Design
Printed and bound by IngramSpark

For My Sons

Clarence Boris, Claude Arkady, Solan Bernhard

Grandchildren
Eleonora Cara, Zachary Eli, Michael Adrian,
Jonah Eric, Noah Alexander, Ava Eleana

Daughters-in-law
Pamela, Diana

Partner
Sheila
and

In Memory of
Arkady Jacob Aron (Father), Klara (Mother),
Bernhard Boris (Brother), Eleonora (Wife),
Adrian (Son)

Comment on The Chosen People

Queen Victoria once asked her Prime Minister Benjamin Disraeli:

"What proof can you give me that God really exists?"

Disraeli answered:

"The survival of the Jewish People."

On History

"The past is never dead. It is not even past."

William Faulkner

CONTENTS

FOREWORD
Wendy Lower

Of the estimated six million Jews murdered in the Holocaust, about 1.1 million were children. Memoirist George Schwab was born in 1931 to an interwar and wartime generation of Jewish youth whose odds of survival were the slimmest in Europe and perhaps in all of European history. How could parents have imagined and their children, innocents, comprehend the world they entered into under Nazi rule that sought to destroy, as Hitler stated in summer 1941, "every Jewish family in Europe," root and branch. In this brave, lucid even at times witty account of survival, Schwab offers readers something very rare and precious—the view of a child who experiences the Holocaust as distinct blows: the arrival of the German military; the murder of his father; loss of home; rejection of non-Jewish classmates; loneliness; confusion; separation from his protective brother and resourceful mother; physical deprivation to the point of complete helplessness and near-death. Like many published memoirs of survival, the postwar period provides that rejuvenating story of renewal, love, family, and professional success in America. Yet this "return to life" narrative should not be read as normal, certainly not expected. It must confound us as a contrast to the wartime ruptures and losses.

This is one autobiography with multiple chapters. One can relate to George's tales of "starting out" in New York as a non-tenured professor with a heavy teaching load, high rent, and new family, indeed triplets in a one-bedroom apartment! Schwab is honest with his reader. Reading about his postwar triumphs and often humorous exploits among the aspiring and elite in Manhattan, Europe, and South Africa, one detects the persistent pangs of sadness about his disrupted childhood and the absence of loved ones in his otherwise abundant life. Schwab embodies that survivor spirit and so his life story keeps unfolding—entering into new realms, relationships, and a steadfast commitment to scholarship and diplomacy on a grand scale. He embraces life, perhaps as he stated to "repress" those earlier times and bad memories of growing up during the Holocaust.

In the vast documentation of the Holocaust, Nazi discourse and policy-making on Jewish children specifically as a target group appears at critical junctures in the radicalization of the "Final Solution." With the Nazi occupation of Poland in September 1939, Jewish children were subjected to persecutory measures. Those above the age of 10 years old were forced to be marked as Jews, subjected to reduced rations, and then ghettoized with their families. Forced labor was imposed on teenage boys and girls.[1] Schwab was eight years old when the war started. Many Jews in Central Europe and Poland fled eastward to the Soviet zones where George lived in Latvia, and brought news of Nazi policies and the rampant anti-Semitism. George overheard the adults speaking about Jews in Vienna who had to wipe with their coats the cars of Nazi officials, and was reassured by his disbelieving father that the Germans were too cultured to behave so despicably. They did not know that in the months that followed the life of a Jewish child had been reduced to a "useless eater." Death rates from famine-related illnesses soared in the Warsaw and Lodz ghettos as of autumn 1940.[2] Or perhaps Schwab's parents learned this but shielded him. In those days, in the bourgeois household that George enjoyed, adult conversations were just that, a separate event intended to protect the children.

Everything changed irrevocably after June 22, 1941, when the Nazis and their allies invaded the Soviet Union and occupied George's hometown of Liepaja/Libau (about 121 miles southwest of Riga on the Baltic Sea) on June 29, 1941. During these fateful summer months when Hitler and Himmler began to push for the mass murder of all Jews, the issue of Jewish children was raised as both a hindrance and a justification. Lower-level perpetrators were reluctant to kill babies and toddlers. Overriding what seemed to be expressions of moral revulsion, Himmler argued that the kids must be killed otherwise they would grow up and avenge the murder of their parents. In early July 1941, a member of reserve police battalion 105 wrote home to Bremen that "Jews are free game. . . . One can only give the Jews some well-intentioned advice: Bring no more children into the world. They no longer have a future."[3] As one Wehrmacht general concurred in August 1941, that "brood must be stamped out." Perhaps this was the cumulative effect of eight years of Nazism and anti-Semitism. It is deeply troubling to realize that moral inhibitions to mass murder women and children seemed to dissipate in a matter of a few weeks. Nazi leaders and their more fanatical supporters in the SS-police and military, who believed that the war against the Soviet Union was a existential battle against Judeo-Bolshevism, escalated the murder of Jews from men in state and party positions to entire communities and families who were shot in ravines, meadows, public parks in broad daylight across Ukraine, eastern Poland, Belorussia, and the Baltic States. George's father, an accomplished and well-known doctor, was among the first victims of the Holocaust in Liepaja. After being brutally tortured, he was shot in the sand dunes of the Baltic coast, a few miles from George's childhood home.

The German hunt for Jewish children intensified during the war. SS and police routinely scoured orphanages, searched for them in hiding, examined the captured boys to see if they were circumcised, tested the girls knowledge of the church if they pretended to be Christian. Those whose identity could not be confirmed faced numerous fates: death, the camp system, adoption, or auctioning off to an impoverished family in Eastern Europe. The odds of survival were slim for a child, and the many who lost their entire families also lost their Jewish identity.[4]

This is one of the several reasons this remarkable memoir is of great value. It cuts against the Nazi drive to destroy and erase the most vulnerable. It restores life and dignity to the Schwab family through George's vivid childhood memories. It shows us in a candid, informative, and often gut-wrenching prose. Schwab recalls the odyssey he endured of the ghetto and camps, and a death march on a barge in the icy waters of the Baltic Sea. Yet having experienced this trauma as a child, he recollects the experiences not as a logical, detailed story, rather as memory shards and flashbacks remembered in conjunction with moments of deep loss and physical suffering, as the time when his father was murdered, when he felt severe hunger, and when he was separated from his brother and mother.

George's liberation was not a moment of jubilant triumph. He and other Stutthof prisoners had been tugged on barges in the Baltic westward, not fed for a week and abandoned in the sea. Little George had to be dragged to the shore. The prisoners were assembled at a German submarine training center. The morning before the British arrived, German naval soldiers were shooting half-dead prisoners. And then suddenly they laid down their weapons in the afternoon. One German told George, "why don't you go over there to that soldier, that American [it was a Brit] and he will give you something to eat." Deliriously famished, George bit into a bar of soap that he thought was bread.

At war's end, George was among eleven million refugees trying to find something to eat and wear, shelter, and reunite with family. Remarkably, he found his mother in 1946 in Germany, and by way of a letter of inquiry that was sent from a relative in the USA. The postwar chapters are not presented in an abbreviated way. We see how his childhood resonated into adulthood. George chose to pursue an academic track at Columbia University and to write a dissertation on the controversial legal theorist Carl Schmitt, which brought him back to Europe and Germany for his research. What was it like for him as a Jew to return to the continent and to deeply engage with Schmitt, who had ingratiated himself with the Nazis and produced anti-Semitic texts in the mid-1930s? George's father had taught him about German Kultur, and it was part of his upbringing in the upper-class German-speaking Jewish community in Latvia. Now George had to reckon with his acculturation and personal hatred of the Nazis. In his new American home of New York City, George befriended other survivors, including Elie Wiesel and joined a movement to memorialize, research on, and educate about the Holocaust. Starting in 1986, he served on various committees that had been formed to build the U.S. Holocaust Memorial Museum, and he has been actively guiding research and educational programs at the Museum since it opened in 1993. Schwab's videotaped oral history is in the Museum's collection, available on the internet, and offers an interesting comparison to this written account.

Schwab's postwar career is a success story. After receiving his doctorate at Columbia University, he became a professor of history at the City University of New York and a distinguished scholar as a co-founder and president of the National Committee on American Foreign Policy (early 1990s-2015). He was a self-identified Cold Warrior, a political realist guided by a mission of peace that he pursued as Track I½ and Track II diplomacy, especially in the bridges he built as a mediator in the Northern Irish Peace Process, the lessening of tensions between the United States and China, and détente between China and Taiwan. George returned to Latvia in 1990, and reached out to the president, Vaira Vike-Freiberga, to help secure the country's entrance into NATO. To honor his late wife and promote education in Jewish history and the Holocaust in Latvia, Schwab established the Eleonora Schwab Library (with more than 14,000 publications) in the center of Riga at the historic Jewish cultural center. He realized the importance of speaking at many of the commemorative ceremonies in Riga, which are held annually on July 4th (the date when the massacres of Jews began in 1941). He and his partner Sheila Johnson Robbins supported the campaign to memorialize the Jews killed in Liepaja as well as a few local rescuers. George continues to guide scholars and lead visitors through the town, telling his story, which in his sharing has become ours to remember and tell others.

When the Nazis occupied Liepaja there were 8,000 Jews living there. One hundred and seventy five survived the war. The survival rate for children who were George's age and younger was 0%.[5] Reading this memoir you will learn about survival against all odds not as a miraculous redemption, but as luck, street smarts, determination, love of family, and a fellow prisoner, Jule Goldberg, who chose to help at critical moments. You will learn about a life lived to the fullest in spite of all.

Dr. Wendy Lower, *John K. Roth Professor of History at Claremont McKenna College and Chair of the Jack and Morton Mandel Center for Advanced Holocaust Studies at the United States Holocaust Memorial Museum, Washington, D.C.*

Notes

1. See major works on children during the Holocaust by Patricia Heberer, *Children during the Holocaust* (Lanham MD: Altamira Press in association with the U.S. Holocaust Memorial Museum, 2011); Nicholas Stargardt, *Witnesses of War: Children's Lives under the Nazis* (New York: Vintage, 2007); Deborah Dwork, *Children with a Star: Jewish Youth in Nazi Europe* (New Haven: Yale University Press, 1991).
2. By war's end, 15% of Warsaw's Jews (60,000 men, women, and children) had died of starvation. See Martin Dean, volume editor. *Encyclopedia of Camps and Ghettos, 1933-1945, Ghettos in German Occupied Eastern Europe*, Volume II (Bloomington: Indiana University Press, 2012), 360.
3. Christopher Browning with Juergen Matthaeus, *The Origins of the Final Solution: The Evolution of Nazi Policy*, September 1939-March 1942 (Omaha/Jerusalem: University of Nebraska Press/ Yad Vashem), 260-61. On lost identities, Jewish children in Poland, Joanna Beata Michlic, "Jewish Children in Nazi-Occupied Poland, Early Postwar Recollections of Survival and Polish-Jewish Relations During the Holocaust," *Search and Research*, Volume 14, Yad Vashem Studies, 2008.
4. On lost identities, Jewish children in Poland, Joanna Beata Michlic, "Jewish Children in Nazi-Occupied Poland, Early Postwar Recollections of Survival and Polish-Jewish Relations During the Holocaust," *Search and Research*, Volume 14, Yad Vashem Studies, 2008.
5. Martin Dean, volume editor. *Encyclopedia of Camps and Ghettos, 1933-1945, Ghettos in German Occupied Eastern Europe*, Volume II (Bloomington: Indiana University Press, in association with the US Holocaust Memorial Museum, 2012) Liepaja entry, p. 1013.

INTRODUCTION
Carol Rittner

Why do we read memoirs written by Holocaust survivors? Because we are curious, curious about how a human being, destined for annihilation, not only defeated death, but embraced life. George Schwab's memoir, *Odyssey of a Child Survivor: From Latvia through the Camps to the United States* is a book about a young boy who survived the Holocaust, thus defeating Hitler and the Nazis. *Odyssey of a Child Survivor* is the memoir of a pampered, rich, indulged, naïve, "momma's boy" from Latvia who against improbable odds endured the Holocaust with all of its horrors. After the end of World War II, George lived in liberated Europe for a year before being reunited with his mother, who also survived the Holocaust. They emigrated to the USA, where George finished high school, went on to university, and subsequently became a well-known scholar and teacher, not to mention a beloved husband and father, and the respected leader of the National Committee on American Foreign Policy in New York City.

Why do we read memoirs written by Holocaust survivors? We read them to try to understand the survivor, to gain insight into what makes a Holocaust survivor "tick," what enables him or her to choose life rather than to embrace death. Learning about the Holocaust is not only a matter of learning facts, although reliable information is of great importance.

Why do we read memoirs written by Holocaust survivors? We read these memoirs so we can reflect on comments like this one written by Raul

Hilberg in his 1961 magnum opus, *The Destruction of the European Jews*: "No obstruction stopped the German machine of destruction. No problem proved insurmountable. . . . The old moral order did not break through anywhere along the line."

What did Raul Hilberg mean when he said that nothing stopped "the German machine of destruction," that "The old moral order did not break through anywhere along the line?" I think he meant that the system of obligations in European society that is a central dimension of Western culture, that is, those behaviors that define and organize the proper relations among individuals and groups in a community failed to prevent the Holocaust. One of those obligations is our ordinary expectation of **neighborliness**, that is, the expectation we human beings have that other human beings will extend help to us in our extreme need.

How can one read George Schwab's memoir, *Odyssey of a Child Survivor: From Latvia through the Camps to the United States*, without reflecting on the unanswerable question **Why?** *Why* were George and his family, indeed, why were the Jews in Nazi German-occupied Europe during World War II and the Holocaust denied the benefit of **neighborliness?** *Why* did so many people avert their eyes from what was happening to them and simply go about their daily lives in the midst of a ghastly dictatorship? George Schwab's memoir makes me think about **neighborliness**—and about **bystanders.** Who were these bystanders? Where were they? Why did they do nothing to stop "the German machine of destruction?"

Cynthia Ozick, the American Jewish author, writes that "Of the great European murder of six million Jews, and the murderers themselves, there is little left to say. . . . Of the murder and the murderers everything is known: how it was done, who did it, who helped, where it was done and when and why."[1] We know about the murder and the murderers. And we know about the victims as well: six million Jews and millions of others. We know what we think about the murders and murderers. We are not at a loss about how to regard them.[2] But, what about the **bystanders?** What about the people who looked, but refused to see, who noticed but did not acknowledge what was happening to their neighbors, Jews, of course, but so many others as well?

INTRODUCTION

The expectation of help, the certainty of help—*neighborliness*—especially in a time of extreme need when one's life is at stake is one of the fundamental expectations of human beings. It is what "trust in the world" is all about. "Trust in the world" includes all sorts of things, including the certainty that by reason of written or unwritten social contracts the other person will spare me—more precisely stated, that he will respect my physical, and with it also my metaphysical being.[3] But, as George Schwab and his family discovered, and as millions of others during the Nazi era and the Holocaust were to discover, "trust in the world" breaks down at the first blow. It breaks down when "The other person, *opposite* whom I exist physically in the world"[4] strikes the first blow, seeking to destroy me.

Bystanders were neither perpetrators nor victims. They were ordinary people. In Nazi Germany during the 1930s and '40s, and in occupied Europe after September 1, 1939, there were so many bystanders that **they** set the norm. When a whole population takes on the status of bystander, the victims are without allies; the criminals, unchecked, are strengthened. "[B]ystanders . . . because there were so many of them—defined what was . . . exceptional and what was unexceptional," what was ethical and what was not. Their behavior raises troubling questions about human nature and about the very foundations of human ethics and morality.

For more than 40 years as a scholar and teacher, I have confronted the Holocaust and other genocides and mass atrocities. Human failure is something with which I am familiar, having pondered it for many years. George Schwab's Holocaust memoir makes me think about what my friend Professor John K. Roth from Claremont McKenna College in California calls "the failure(s) of ethics, the multiple shortfalls and shortcomings of thought, decision, and action that tempt and incite us human beings to inflict incalculable harm" on others.[5]

Ethics involves what is *right* and *wrong, just* and *unjust, good* and *evil.* Ethics arguably is civilization's keystone, just as **neighborliness**—the expectation that human beings have that other human beings will extend help to them in their extreme need—is a central dimension of community. Without the overriding of moral sensibilities, if not the collapse of ethical traditions during the Nazi era, the Holocaust could not have happened.

The Holocaust confirms that the singular failure of ethics is that ethics has not made us human beings better than we are. ***What happened to neighborliness?*** Where were the Schwab family's neighbors? Why didn't they try to stop "the German machine of destruction?" What happened to "Do unto others as you would have them do to you?"

Whether they were committed Christians or not, I think the argument can be made that for hundreds and hundreds of years, millions of people in Europe had been baptized in Christian—Roman Catholic, Protestant and Orthodox Christian—churches; acculturated, influenced, and educated in Christian homes and schools; that they celebrated the Christian holidays of Christmas, Easter, as well as other religious holidays. Their parents and grandparents, their teachers and clergy taught them the Ten Commandments, including the commandment, "Thou shalt not murder." That they were influenced, formed, educated as Christians, even if they were not regular church members, is undeniable. And yet, during the Nazi era and the Holocaust too many people closed their eyes, turned their backs, and ignored the Schwab family, the entire Jewish community in Latvia, and Jews throughout Nazi German-occupied Europe.

We human beings are often far from being what should make us proud to be human because of the abuse we human beings inflict on each other, including inaction and indifference in the face of such abuse. In these instances when we fail to live up to the best of our ethical traditions, ethics seems fragile and weak, unable to do what we hope, at least in our better moments, ethics can accomplish: that is, to enable us not just to know right from wrong, good from evil—but to embody that knowledge in our humane action on behalf of those who expect our help in their extreme need.

Forty years ago, Elie Wiesel was the Chairman of President Jimmy Carter's Commission on the Holocaust. In a letter he wrote to President Carter, Elie Wiesel had this to say:

> The most vital lesson to be drawn from the Holocaust era is that Auschwitz was possible because the enemy of the Jewish people and of [hu]mankind—and it is always the same

enemy—succeeded in dividing and separating, in splitting
human society, nation against nation, Christian against Jew,
young against old. And not enough people cared. In Germany
and in other occupied countries, most spectators chose not
to interfere with the killers; in other lands, too, many persons
chose to remain neutral. As a result, the killers killed, the
victims died, and the world remained world.[6]

The enemy to which Elie Wiesel was referring is *indifference*—and in
the case of the Nazi era and the Holocaust, I think he was referring to the
passivity of bystanders and to their lack of **neighborliness** toward George
Schwab and his family, not to mention their lack of neighborliness toward
Jews in general during World War II and the Holocaust.

Why do we read Holocaust memoirs like George Schwab's *Odyssey of a
Child Survivor: From Latvia through the Camps to the United States?* I suggest it
is to encourage us to think about **then**—think about and reflect on events that
happened to the Jewish people—and to non-Jews too—between 1933 and
1945 in Nazi Germany, in Latvia, and in the ghettos, and the concentration
and death camps in Nazi German-occupied Europe. But, it also should cause
us to think about **today** as well. Are **we** *bystanders* to the horrors that others
are suffering and that we witness every day in the media and through the
internet—in Syria and Iraq, on the U.S. Border with Mexico, in Palestine and
Gaza, in the refugee centers and in the cities and towns across Europe as wave
after wave of desperate human beings seek refuge, acceptance, shelter—safety,
seek life, seek a **neighborly** response from us and from our governments?

We must read the memoirs of Holocaust survivors if we are to cultivate
empathy and sensitivity to those who endured the horrors they endured.
George Schwab not only endured the horrors, he survived to embrace life
in all its complexity.

Dr. Carol Rittner, RSM, *Distinguished Professor of Holocaust & Genocide
Studies Emerita, and Dr. Marsha Raticoff Grossman, Professor of Holocaust
Studies Emerita, Stockton University, New Jersey, USA.*

Notes

1. Cynthia Ozick, "Prologue" in Gay Block and Malka Drucker, *Rescuers: Portraits of Moral Courage in the Holocaust* (New York: Holmes and Meier Publishers, Inc., 1992) xi.
2. Ibid.
3. See Jean Amery, *At the Mind's Limit: Contemplation of a Survivor on Auschwitz and Its Realities* (Bloomington: Indiana University Press, 1980).
4. Ibid.
5. My comments about ethics and its failures come from notes, correspondence, and discussion with (and from) John K. Roth.
6. Elie Wiesel, "Letter to President Jimmy Carter" in *Report to the President: President's Commission on the Holocaust* (Washington, DC: President's Commission on the Holocaust, 1979) ii.

PREFACE

After four years spent in a ghetto and in Nazi concentration and work camps, I was liberated in May 1945 at the age of 13½. With my family destroyed and childhood gone, I began a new life. Now, I am the father of triplet sons—Clarence, Claude, and Solan—and grandfather of six grandchildren: Michael, Jonah, Zachary, Eleonora (Ellie; named after my late wife), Noah, and Ava. I have at last decided to record my story on paper so that my family may connect to their past. Why so late in life?

Liberation came with four years of horrific memories that, subconsciously at first, I tried to repress by escaping into the world of pleasure. Pleasures were superseded upon my entering college and graduate school, where challenging intellectual adventures gradually captured my mind.

Still, with few exceptions, I would rarely speak about those horrifying years—except with my mother with whom I had been reunited in 1946. From time to time, I would speak about my experiences under the Nazis when I accompanied my mother to gatherings of survivors. Otherwise, when pressed, I would say: "I went through the war years in Europe." Full stop.

The turning point came in 1982. As a teacher was preparing my sons for their bar mitzvah in our dining room, she turned to me and asked that I briefly relate to my sons some of my wartime experiences, which I did—something I had not even shared with my wife.

How did I—a child survivor who had lost his father, brother, did not know the fate of his mother and relatives—learn to cope with and speak about my dismal past? In high school, college, and graduate school in New York, I learned from teachers and readings that wars are a constant in the history of mankind. This implied, of course, merciless killings of perhaps hundreds of millions, life-threatening injuries, and families torn to shreds. Looking at history from that perspective, I rationalized that my case was far from unique and that I was unable to do much about it. In response, I began to confront reality and unhesitatingly began to speak about the horrible past.

Further, the Holocaust, which had been planned to eliminate an entire people, added a new dimension to warfare. Aggressive behavior is innate in humans, but the Holocaust could not have been conceived or carried out without anti-Semitism. As anti-Semitism is associated with Jesus, who is widely believed to have been born into a religious Jewish family and died as a religious Jew, I concluded that an anti-Semite is a Jesus killer. As anti-Semitism is a mental disorder, it can be cured by way of education.

Emotionally less constipated at last, I accepted Elie Wiesel's invitation in 1986 to join him in his efforts to build the United States Holocaust Memorial Museum in Washington, D.C. In 1988, I also accompanied him on a trip to Auschwitz-Birkenau, which preceded by one day the Paris conference of Nobel laureates titled "Facing the 21st Century"—where I served as his adviser on disarmament and peace. I even began to write short pieces about the war years, and, in 1990, I visited Latvia, which I had vowed never to do. Finally, in the new century, I, at Elie Wiesel's entreaties, began to slowly write a historical account of my checkered life.

While working on my story, I began to accept invitations to speak about my experiences. At Oxford University, I spoke about my war years—as I did at Stockton University. At the National Catholic Center for Holocaust Education at Seton Hill University, I spoke about my life as a street boy immediately following the war. I was also extensively interviewed by the Holocaust Museum in Washington, D.C.; in 2018, I was the subject of a documentary, *Zockele*, filmed in Latvia, which was directed by Dr. Wendy Lower under the auspices of the Museum. I was also the subject of a 2010 Prix-Europe- winning novel by Gwendolyn Chabrier titled *Behind the Barbed Wire*. It was published in French, English, Italian, and Russian. More recently, the United States Holocaust Memorial Museum presented me the Elie Wiesel Award.

ACKNOWLEDGMENT

I thank Dr. Wendy Lower of the United States Holocaust Memorial Museum in Washington, D.C., for her comments. The memoir is by far the better because of her suggestions.

Further, having written almost exclusively for an academic audience and publishers, I did not completely appreciate the aims of and differences in writing for a more general audience. I was fortunate to have had two outstanding professional copy editors to whom I will forever be indebted for having helped me bridge the two worlds: the late Edwina McMahon and Carole Campbell.

Chapter I
A CHARMED CHILDHOOD—THE 1930s

War talk was in the air. Some argued that the Baltic States were safe because Stalin's Russia and Hitler's Germany were militarily weak and Latvia, Lithuania, and Estonia served as buffer states between the two giants. Another argument advanced was that war talk was only talk, because no one had been able to forget the enormity of the human casualties suffered during the Great War and none would be willing to subject themselves to that experience again. Besides, Hitler, despite the bombastic anti-Soviet speeches he delivered in a laughably shrill voice, was surely acquainted with Napoleon's fate at Moscow. The conclusion: because neither side was able and willing to wage war, we Jews in beautiful Latvia, where life was considered paradise on earth, did not think of leaving—despite occasional anti-Semitic outbursts here and there. But that doesn't mean we were totally unaware.

The bell rang and housekeeper Stefa opened the door, admitting Aunt Rita (née Jacobson) mother's oldest sister. I had met her before in Riga (which was known as "Little Paris"), after she had relocated to Latvia from Vienna, where she had lived for many years, immediately following Hitler's annexation of Austria in early 1938. In our large and sumptuously appointed apartment in one of Libau's (Liepaja in the Latvian and Libava in the Russian) most exclusive apartment buildings—on Korn Street 27 (Graudu iela in the Latvian)—I was gazing into our dour-looking dining room, which had ebony furniture and leather chairs, listening to her and father argue in raised voices about the Nazis' treatment of Jews in Vienna. Aunt Rita related how on the day of Austria's annexation in March 1938, Jewish women in Vienna were ordered to take off their fur coats and use them to scrub and shine the cars of Nazis while Austrian bystanders jubilantly showed how much they were enjoying the sight. My father, Arkady Jacob Aron, a pre–World War I Dorpat- and Berlin-educated gastroenterologist, who was the first in Latvia to introduce insulin in the treatment of diabetes, characterized her story as a fairy tale. "German culture," something he often talked about, "does not tolerate such behavior," he insisted. He reminded Aunt Rita how gentlemanly German soldiers and officers had behaved during the German occupation of czarist Latvia in World War I. That she had witnessed these events in Austria did not change his mind. To me, all this was irrelevant. Uppermost in my mind was moving from dull Libau with some 65,000 inhabitants to exciting Riga with a population of close to half a million—a number hard to imagine—or, perhaps, even to New York—with all its skyscrapers and fast-moving cars that I used to watch in movies. Not having experienced war nor much prejudice as a Jew, I did not sense the seriousness of it all. Still my ears were wide open because I was a busybody.

According to mother and others, I lived in my own world and made the best of my early childhood, especially in the summer months before and after returning from holidays in Riga and the Riga beaches (known in Latvian as Jurmala). During the short and often hot and dry summer months, I had no school, no piano lessons with Mrs. Ettelka Winkler, except practicing boring piano scales for half an hour or so a day, and, regrettably, no English lessons. In good weather during the week, my loving but stern and strict mother, Klara (née Jacobson), my older brother by nearly ten years, Bernhard Boris, Bubi for short, who adored me but was also a big tease, and I spent time at the Jewish tennis club where I played on the junior court, watched mother play (not very well) but especially watched Bubi, whose serve was magnificent. He was a star performer who walked away with many trophies. There was even talk about Bubi competing at Wimbledon. He was my role-model tennis player. When mother happened not to be at the club and my strict German Baltic governess, Miss Brik, also was not present, I was placed under Bubi's supervision. At such times, I watched him play poker in the shack. When I was angry, I would tattle on him to our parents, despite the handsome bribe he had given me to keep my mouth shut. From the club, mother and I, and often also Bubi, proceeded to the nearby white sandy beach to meet friends. That's where I learned to swim. In no time, I was able to reach the second sandbar alone in the invigorating Baltic waters. Sometimes my permissive and warm-hearted papa surprised us after house calls. He quickly changed in the bathhouse, waded into the water, and swam near the shore.

Delicious snacks and drinks could be had at the snack bar or the adjoining café. For dinner at about 1:30 p.m., we often went to the nearby elegant Pavilion that had been specially erected so that one of the czars could enjoy the park setting near the beach while feasting and listening to the orchestra play his favorite music. On the terrace, I was captivated by the crawling lobsters in the fountain. From there, we either returned to the club or went home by trolley car or *drozhki* (horse-drawn cart).

In foul weather during the week we dined at home. Stefa usually prepared meals for me that I enjoyed: boiled frankfurters with English mustard and sauerkraut or hamburgers with mustard and mashed potatoes and a pickle on the side. My favorite dish and that of my parents and Bubi was veal roast with half-boiled potatoes roasted with the veal (the only dish mother knew how to prepare). I did not care for soup or fish—except anchovies. I enjoyed lettuce with tomatoes and vinegar. My favorite desserts were Italian chocolate ice cream from the Italian ice cream parlor downstairs in the building, home-baked cookies, cinnamon or cheese danishes, or cakes coupled with my favorite drink, hot cocoa. I had a sweet tooth.

In the dining room trouble not to my liking was afoot. While mother was engaged in conversation with father and often with our dinner guest bubbly cousin Manya (née Wainstein), Bubi drove me up the wall by making faces and bothering me with his long legs under the table. That not only deflected my attention, which I welcomed, from listening to father pontificating about German culture and dead and unknown authors such as Goethe and Schiller and to mother reciting her laundry list of Russian literary giants such as Tolstoy and Pushkin, but also, of critical importance to me, might make me miss some gossip about friends and events I could relate to.

Mother often teased me about my large ears growing even larger by listening to adult conversation not meant for children. Even worse, I loved to chatter and was told that I did so even in my sleep. For the sake of finding out what I wanted to know, I had to keep my mouth sealed, which I did with alacrity when gossip was enticing. For poor table manners I was often banished to my room under the strict supervision of my governess. How I missed my Russian nanny, whom I adored and loved above everyone else. With her I could never do anything wrong. Unfortunately, she was let go when I was about four and a half—despite my tears and protests at spending a long summer away from her in Riga and the Riga beach.

At times when I was unable to reach Bubi with my legs, I complained loudly and bitterly about his behavior and cried for sympathy. When attention was at last focused on me, I was often exonerated and Bubi was reprimanded by mamma who would say, "Bubinka [diminutive for Bubi], you are a big boy and Zockele [diminutive for George] is only a child." But more often than not, Bubi succeeded in playing ignorant or accused me of fomenting a ruckus, which at times I did but would not admit. After some rest, I was ready for afternoon and early evening activities that in the long Nordic summer days could go on and last as late as nine o'clock for me.

Depending on the weather, afternoons were taken up by rushing through some piano scales, walks in the parks with the governess, trolley car rides from one end of town to the other, playing with my best friend, Sascha Feiges, in his garden, teasing the rabbits in the cage, climbing to the top of a brick or stone wall, shooting spitballs at kids playing in the adjoining garden, and sneaking into the *Kammerlicht*, a movie house that belonged to the Feiges family. There was not a Tarzan, Jackie Coogan, Bobby Breen, or Shirley Temple film I did not see at the *Kammerlicht* or in other movie houses. I was obsessively in love with Shirley Temple—and even told friends that she was my cousin. I was convinced of it, and they believed me.

Few things could trump my Wednesday afternoons with mamma. I was permitted to determine what we were to do and what she was to wear. Favorite cafes included Peters, Petersburg, Bonitz, and Dürberg. Inhaling smoke, hopping from table to table, eating excellent cakes, and sipping cocoa were *de rigueur.* Savoring my cake and drink and pretending to draw, I usually acted as if I were totally absorbed in what I was doing, but actually I was listening hard for intriguing gossip and intimate adult conversation, not the drab putting on airs and pontificating of *Hochkultur.* How could I not be interested in the following complaint that led me to search for information that punctured my perception that babies were delivered to parents by storks.

One afternoon at Bonitz, I overheard a girlfriend of mamma's complain about her husband and the painful procedures she had to undergo to get rid of unwanted children. "Imagine Klärchen," she said, "how many children I would have had if I had failed to undergo these procedures." Mamma, on the other hand, said that she never had such troubles as papa was always very careful. I was dumbfounded, perplexed, and curious. My questions prompted me one day to sneak into papa's office, which was in the same apartment building we lived in, and lift from his bookcase several heavily illustrated medical books in German. Thumbing through one of the books, I stumbled on illustrations and photos depicting what looked to me to be the stomach of a woman into which was tucked a baby that was slowly entering the world helped along by hands of a human being. But where the opening was I could not tell. I ruled out the navel in favor of the rear end, but I was not even sure of that. Baffled, I pursued my quest. At an opportune moment when papa was on house calls, I sneaked into his office once more for another look, but instead, I saw his nurse, Marie, in his consulting room. After exchanging a few pleasantries, I said in a firm tone: "Marichen, please let me see what you have there," pointing to her crotch. She protested that this was something private and not for children. I would have none of that and ordered her to show me what she had between her legs. Reluctantly she spread her legs and moved her panties to one side, and I bowed to look and saw only a bush of light brown hair. The anus, I concluded, was the answer to the puzzle. In those days, human sexuality was not a topic discussed with children of any age, much less someone of my tender years.

Another story I heard at Café Bonitz came from father's cousin Minna Rabinovich. Her son Max, who was Feodor Chaliapin's accompanist, arrived from Hollywood in the U.S.A. begging her to move to Hollywood where he would build her a villa with a Hollywood kitchen in which she could even eat. She was utterly dismayed and said: "I should move to Hollywood and eat in the kitchen. Shocking" (*unerhört*). Mother expressed surprise and I could not imagine anybody eating in the kitchen. But living in Hollywood was more than exciting for me. I imagined being friends with my favorite movie stars, especially with my "cousin" Shirley Temple.

On one of the Wednesday outings, mamma suggested that she, Bubi, and I go to a five o'clock tea dance at Hotel Petersburg. Not having been to one in the past, I immediately agreed and was all excited. I instructed mother to wear what I considered to be a stunning dark blue dress, and I was attired in one of the latest creations of the seamstress, Fanny, who worked in our apartment to produce my wardrobe for two weeks in the spring and two weeks in the fall. As usual, within the first ten minutes, I succeeded in getting a stain on my clothes and mamma was upset. "Boy, oh, boy. For God's sake, where on earth do you always rummage?" I protested, saying innocently that I did not know how my garb had gotten dirty as I had not done a thing, and I had no idea how my hands had become dirty. I was quickly changed and off we went.

The three of us were seated at a table near the dance floor not very far from the orchestra. After several dances with Bubi, mamma was invited to dance by a gentleman. At first I found it amusing, but as soon as he drew her closer to him, I took matters into my own hands. I walked over to the crowded dance floor and inserted myself between the two. Mamma excused herself, and the two of us returned to the table. She thanked me for the intervention. With my mission accomplished, I thoroughly enjoyed my cake and cocoa.

I was protective of my mamma, even misreading a situation that posed no problem to her. For instance, mother's sister, my loving, warm, and permissive Aunt Hermine Kinginthai Doshiang (née Jacobson), wife of Xavier Kinginthai Doshiang, the late envoy of China (known for short as Dr. King Li) to Germany—after moving back to Riga in 1938 via Rome, Vienna, and Prague—paid a surprise visit to Libau. One morning, she sat on mamma's side of the bed and related a story to papa that had him in a trance.

I overheard her account of how she was fined for smoking in a first-class nonsmoking compartment on the way to Rome (she had lived for a time in Rome after her husband's death in 1935 before Mussolini began to be seriously infected by Hitler's anti-Semitism in 1938). The fine was imposed despite her diplomatic passport that, she thought, would provide immunity from such nuisances. Her reasoning: she was moving with her belongings across borders in two diplomatically sealed freight cars that were attached to the train on which she was a passenger, convinced such diplomatic status would be extended to her in the train's passenger car. As this was not the case, she had to pay a hefty fine of twenty marks. Papa's stares and trances were too much for me. After having listened to the exciting story, I despondently ran to look for mammy and found her in the kitchen talking with Stefa and Fenia, our laundry help, and reported to her that papa was listening to Aunt Hermine's story and staring at her with loving eyes. Mammy took my hand, and we both walked to the bedroom and all was well.

Thinking about Café Petersburg, another funny story comes to mind. One late spring, for some unknown reason, I stopped eating, not entirely but enough to be worrisome to my parents. Aunt Rita happened to be visiting from Riga and counseled mamma and papa not to be concerned. She was certain she would be able to entice me with a host of Viennese finger sandwiches. They would be intriguing, something new. On a tray she carried into the dining room a variety of sandwiches. I looked, ate two, and said no more, thank you. I was unimpressed by what she had prepared: cut up white bread, with butter, and thinly sliced chicken on one side and thinly cut slices of cucumber on the other. I refused to taste the rest but enjoyed the cake and hot cocoa.

No amount of pleading with me to eat helped. Finally, I struck a deal: early evenings mammy had to take me to Café Petersburg. It so happened that from early childhood I had liked white bread finger-sandwiches with butter, a slice of tomato, a slice of a hard-boiled egg topped with a small anchovy. I would then dip it into a cup of hot cocoa and completely enjoyed the concoction that emerged. The way in which I chose to eat the special sandwich was viewed as terribly unappetizing and socially unacceptable. Dismayed café guests complained to the manager—who promptly invited mammy and me to have supper in a private dining room. Meeting mother by chance in Atlantic City after the Second World War, the former manager asked whether I was still committed to consuming my signature concoction.

Worth recounting is another story that could have had a serious repercussion and even ended my charmed early childhood in pre–World War II Latvia had it not been for my papa's swift intervention. On getting up one morning, I found the apartment to be unusually quiet. Everyone was apparently asleep. Stefa's absence was curious, for she was always up early preparing breakfast. Apparently a party late in the evening after I had fallen asleep lasted until the wee hours. I noticed that the dining room table was considerably enlarged and contained lots of unwashed porcelain dishes, silver utensils, and crystal liquor glasses—some of which were only half or quarter empty. I decided to taste the drinks and made my way around the table. Within minutes, I became terribly dizzy and nauseated and began to scream. Realizing that I had imbibed a mixture of alcohols, papa put his finger down my throat, which made me vomit. Then he gave me some kind of liquid to sip—not the much-disliked soupspoon of cod liver oil I was forced to swallow almost every morning—and a little solid food. Mammy brought me into my bedroom and tucked me in and I fell asleep. When I woke up, mammy was at my side and all was well again.

On weekends in early and late summer, when not spending time at the tennis club and beach, we were driven for the day by our part-time driver, a Mr. Gratulnieks, to hotels in Bernaten or Iljen or traveled by trolley car to the hotel near Libau's airport. While my parents played cards in smoke-filled rooms and enjoyed wonderful finger sandwiches and sweets, I usually filled my belly with cheese and cinnamon danishes before leaving for the garden to play with the other children. On some weekends, we dined *en famille* in the garden of Hotel Petersburg after which, at times, we visited the Kik, the Jewish yacht club, where I enjoyed watching sailboats leaving and arriving while my parents played cards. On other occasions, my warm and loving Aunt Yette Wainstein, papa's sister, fetched me for outings. The first stop was usually Café Stein where we indulged in eating cakes and drinking cocoa. From there, we strolled to the park and her home at am Schwanenteich (at

Swan's Pond). In the garden, I would pluck gooseberries and currants and drink cocoa. I also enjoyed her hamburgers and mashed potatoes, the only two dishes she knew how to prepare. At times I would also go for walks with her daughter Nuta and Nuta's husband, Dr. Elie Bruskin. In late summer, there was always great excitement over at the tennis tournaments. Mother and I spent time at the club watching Bubi and others compete. Papa joined us whenever he could get away from his patients and research.

Midsummer was spent in part with mamma and aunts and uncles in Riga and at the Riga's seashore. Every time I heard the name "Riga" my ears tingled. It was the city of my dreams, a lively city with hundreds of thousands of inhabitants with many trolley car lines to Libau's two; a number of bus lines to Libau's none; wide, asphalt-paved streets to Libau's none; hotels, cafés, some illuminated with neon lights similar to one so lit in Libau; handsome, tall buildings, many with elevators, whereas Libau had only three with lifts; dial telephones with many digits, whereas Libau still had an operator-assisted system with just three digits; a department store with an escalator going up to the first floor—something unheard of in Libau; a zoo; and so on. The hustle and bustle, the motion and commotion engendered by so many people were electrifying.

My observations were those of a child of seven, eight, and nine, of course. But see what the late Ambassador George F. Kennan had to say about Riga in the early 1930s. Posted there as a young man in the American Legation, he noted in his *Memoirs, 1925–1950* (Boston, 1967) that "Riga had [a] highly cosmopolitan cultural life: newspapers and theaters in the Lettish, German, Russian, and Yiddish tongues, and vigorous Lutheran, Roman Catholic, Russian Orthodox, and Jewish religious communities. . . . In addition to its more serious amenities, Riga had a vigorous night life, much in the Petersburg tradition: vodka, champagne, gypsies, sleighs or *drozhki* with hugely bundled coachmen waiting at the door. . . . Riga was in many respects a minor edition of Petersburg. . . . To live [there] was . . . in many [ways] to live in Tsarist Russia. . . ."(29–30)

Why we did not live in Riga was beyond my comprehension. Café Otto Schwarz was livelier than any other, and more cigarette smoke filled that café than all of the cafés put together in Libau. Mamma's girlfriend Betty Schalit often drove us around town in her sports car, usually ending up at Café Otto Schwarz or at the Pavilion along the narrow river in *Schützengarten* (Strelnieku in the Latvian) near Elisabetes and Vilandes streets. I found my Riga relatives far more interesting than mamma and papa. Aunts Hermine, Tanya Schifftan (née Jacobson), and Leni Jacobson, smoked, and my parents did not. On occasion, I saw papa smoke when he played cards. But I was embarrassed by the stilted way in which he held a cigarette between his thumb and middle finger. His artificial manner of exhaling was only surpassed by his inability to blow smoke rings. Slim Hermine and Tanya often wore pant outfits and low-heeled shoes. Mamma would have none of that way of dressing. My parents were just not with it, not cool or *forsch* as we used to say in German. They reminded me more of Aunt Leni who lived comfortably with her brother, my Uncle Isidor Jacobson, on 5 Vilandes Street—only a stone's throw from the park. He used to play boring music on his organ and was a strict disciplinarian. I did not care for him much. At least Aunt Leni smoked and was very nice to me.

Our apartment in Libau was large and beautiful, with furniture and chandeliers from czarist palaces (these had been sold by the new Bolshevik government immediately following the Revolution) and six large Persian carpets. I contrasted it to Aunt Hermine's Riga apartment on 11 Elizabetes Street at the corner of Vilandes in the exclusive part of town known in German as the *Diplomatenviertel* (the diplomatic district), where I loved to stay. Her apartment was different from anything I had ever seen. It was filled with Chinese antiques. Late Uncle Xavier's sword, with which he had dueled at the university he attended in Germany, hung on the wall in the library. Mostly very comfortable furniture, a gramophone, and the thirteen large, very large, and extra large Persian carpets—a display that was often mentioned in conversation in Libau—caught the eye. I was most intrigued by the antique Chinese carpet that hung in the entrance hall. It depicted a dragon spewing fire. Impressive, too, was Aunt Hermine's huge square dining room table that accommodated many more than twelve, our round one in Libau would seat no more than a dozen.

My Aunt Tanya lived in Riga, too. Before moving to a villa in Kaiserwald (Mežaparks in the Latvian), Riga's most exclusive suburb), Aunt Tanya had lived with her mother-in-law Marta Schifftan next door to Aunt Hermine. Her apartment was sumptuously appointed, but it was far less intriguing to me because it resembled more our apartment at home. In my view, neither could match Aunt Hermine's. Nevertheless, I was struck by a large carpet of the skin of a tiger or leopard that her late husband, Karl Schifftan, had shot while they were on safari in Africa.

I loved the Riga beaches but not the living quarters there. Every summer Aunt Gusti (née Jacobson) and her husband, Uncle Oskar Ackermann, rented a bungalow in Meluži, among other resort towns. They were not attractive, and the mattresses were stuffed with straw that pricked and made me itch. The justification for living like that was that children had to be toughened up in the summer because it was good for growth and health—the object was to avoid illnesses in the coming long and severe winter. Playing in the large garden with cousins Samjon (Joni for short) and Ljuba (Lully for short) was fun as was swimming in the Baltic Sea. The attractions of the resort villages, including the ice cream parlors, were excellent. But, on balance, I preferred the comforts of Riga and Libau.

One event made an extraordinary impression on me. Arriving one summer in Dzintari early in the afternoon with mamma and my governess on the way to a bungalow that was not yet ready to be occupied, I went with them to a pension with about ten tables in the garden—at every one, people were playing cards. Mamma soon joined friends at one of the tables. After a couple of hours, we left and went to the nearby pavilion called Lido. Well-dressed people everywhere, eating, drinking, smoking, and table-hopping. Then came the program. Suddenly a purple-haired actress in a Madame Pompadour hoopskirt made her appearance and began to sing songs in Russian and German accompanied by a wonderful orchestra. It was all very exciting, especially the hoopskirt and hair of the chanteuse. The modern light music that accompanied her was wonderful, too, and I told mamma that I liked it much more than the boring music that my strict piano teacher Mrs. Winkler made me play and the music mother practiced daily on her rare Schweitzer cello in preparation for her monthly trios, quartets, or quintets at home and in the homes of other musicians. I just did not understand how anybody could enjoy *Kammermusik* (chamber music). My kind of music was the Lambeth Walk, the tango, and the waltz. Mamma did not convince me that one had first to play classical music before playing modern compositions. In the meantime, I immensely enjoyed the setting of the club, the extraordinary performance, and, of course, cake and hot cocoa.

I always dreaded the end of summer because of the advent of the dreary, dark, and cold winters and boring Čakste elementary school. Although I was fluent in Latvian, I grew up speaking German, some Russian, and a smattering of English, a language I was studying with alacrity with Miss Friedlender—a well-known English teacher in Libau who had been trained in England. Mamma was brought up speaking French, whereas now the lingua franca was English. Speaking English was considered cool, being with it, and that is where I always wanted to be—in the center of things. At school I once even corrected my English teacher's English, pointing out that in English "yes" is pronounced "yes" and not "yas." She insisted I was wrong and I let it be. She obviously did not forget the brashness of her best student in English class and gave me a 4 instead of a 5 (a B instead of an A) for the semester, when I surely deserved the 5.

But that was not all. One day I informed my parents that I knew the alphabet and how to count to one hundred. As I knew everything there was to know, I had no intention of doing boring homework. Of course, at the end of the semester, I hardly received passing grades save for English. I thus joined my brother, who was a voracious reader but had to take the last two years of his gymnasium classes over, as he, too, found school boring. Interestingly, my parents did not chastise me except that mamma had already begun to look carefully at my report cards in which I tried to hide failing grades by covering them up with blotting paper. She easily caught on to my trick and simply implored me to do better. My parents were very upset with Bubi and took him to task. They had high hopes that he would study—of all things—chemistry at Oxford or Cambridge.

It was at the Čakste school where I for the first time encountered anti-Semitism. Because Latvian was not my mother tongue I assumed I had an accent. One day I was called on to read a Latvian poem. In the middle of it, the teacher began to laugh and embarrassed me in front of my classmates by saying that I read and sound like a "Jew boy." Even though I did not know what it meant specifically, I knew it was an insult, which was particularly painful because it was done in a class where I fancied Veltiņa, a beautiful long-legged Latvian brunette. I reported the incident to my parents, and papa immediately telephoned the director of the school, Mr. Ulrich, who happened to be a patient of his and who had originally implored papa and mamma to send me to his school. The headmaster came to see my parents, apologized, and promised that an incident of that sort would never happen again. Back in school, he called me into his office and blabbered about school discipline and my duty to obey teachers. He made it sound as if what had happened was my fault.

Chapter II
END OF THE IDYLL—SOVIET OCCUPATION

Back from the Riga beach in late summer 1939 where I happily stayed with Aunt Hermine and followed the usual routine: Café Otto Schwarz, changing of the guards at the Freedom Monument, Uncle Oskar's appliance store on Elizabetes Street where I played with interesting gadgets, strolls on streets lined with Art Noveau buildings, and the zoo in Kaiserwald where a lion, after staring at the onlookers, turned around, raised his tail, and sprayed us with urine. What an exciting story to tell when I return to Libau.

To reach the zoo we either went by trolley car or bus. Going to the zoo was usually preceded and followed by visits to Aunt Tanya and Grandaunt Marta Schifftan in their upper-floor apartment in a handsome villa near the zoo. I immensely enjoyed listening to Grandaunt Marta's stories about trips with her late husband aboard luxury liners to New York, where she saw people who were black. As amazing to me as stories I heard from my parents, aunts, and uncles about trains running underground in Berlin, Paris, and London, it was simply beyond me to conceive of people being black. However much I enjoyed her stories and the handsome furniture, I, by and large, did not relish being there for long. Unlike Aunt Hermine, who adored me and devoted much time to me, Aunt Tanya was stiff and formal and paid little attention to me. Moreover, in her company everybody addressed everybody else by the formal *Sie*. With Aunt Hermine, we were more informal—I always had fun and I loved her dearly.

Toward the end of August there was tremendous excitement in Riga. The only subject of conversation among members of the family and friends at homes and cafés was that Stalin and Hitler had reached an agreement, according to which the Soviet Union and Nazi Germany would not go to war against each other. That development reaffirmed arguments I had previously heard in Libau that the Baltic countries were immune from conflict and life in paradise would continue. On September 1, Hitler invaded Poland; two days later, Great Britain and France declared war on Germany. But the storm that engulfed parts of Europe bypassed the Baltic States. Why? What no one knew at the time was that the so-called Ribbentrop-Molotov Non-aggression Pact apparently contained a secret protocol according to which Stalin obtained the right to acquire a sphere of influence to include the Baltic States in return for Hitler's getting free rein to settle matters with Poland over the issue of Danzig and the Polish Corridor.

As soon as we all heard of the signing of the non-aggression pact, mother came to fetch me and we immediately returned home to Libau. Following the outbreak of the war, friends came to visit and huddled around our shortwave radio to listen to Polish radio exhorting the people of Warsaw to hurry to shelters to protect themselves from approaching German warplanes. *Uvaga, uvaga,* (attention, attention) still rings in my ears, as do screaming air raid sirens and explosions. The German invasion was swift and effective, with the Nazi victory being helped by the Soviet invasion of the eastern part of Poland—part of the secret deal as we later learned. For the moment at least, the optimists were vindicated in their belief that Nazi-Soviet cooperation was further proof that the Baltic countries were safe from a German or Soviet attack.

Exciting to me were the events that followed one after the other. Shortly after the collapse of Poland, Soviet troops appeared on Latvian soil. Because of Libau's naval base and waters that never froze as well as the airfields nearby, the city became a vital strategic base for the Soviet armed forces. The Latvian government prohibited civilians from fraternizing with the strange-looking "guests in uniform" who, rumor had it (soon to be confirmed during the Soviet occupation of the country), rarely washed but amply sprayed their bodies with incredibly sweet-smelling cologne. We all applauded the heroic resistance of the Finns to the unprovoked Soviet invasion of their country, but expressed profound concern about Germany's successful U-boat warfare in the Atlantic—with all that that implied, especially as we had heard that Great Britain was not receiving enough war materiel. We all were exhilarated by the sinking of the German battleship *Admiral Graf Spee* near a very musical-sounding city, Montevideo in Uruguay, a city and country I had never heard of. After some months of relative quiet, difficult news again began to be broadcast on the radio, including the German occupation of Denmark and the Nazi invasion of Norway. The invasion of Holland, Belgium, and France followed not long thereafter.

The gathering clouds in the late summer of 1939 notwithstanding, my usual fall/winter/spring routine began: school, piano lessons with Mrs. Winkler at her home, English lessons, fun and games. I strung up yarn "webs" in my bedroom to simulate the overhead trolley car wires so I could play the role of a Riga trolley car conductor making sure that the poles of trolley cars did not disconnect from the maze of electric wiring above the place where trolley lines intersected. Also, based on chatter about the heavily fortified French and German frontiers, the supposedly impregnable Maginot and Siegfried lines, I constructed them in my room, manning both sides with tin soldiers and equipping the opposing armies with tanks, planes, and artillery pieces I made out of clay. Obviously I was the general in command of the Maginot Line and victorious over the Germans. But my luck soon ran out. With a cousin by marriage, James (Jimmy) Lau, who had recently moved with his parents from Riga to Libau where his father was the head of the Swedish-owned cork factory, we played war games in his huge living room and, in late spring, in his family's large garden, imagining that he was the general in charge of the Siegfried Line. Being considerably older than I and not giving me any quarter, he consistently outmaneuvered me, and the fate of my Maginot Line eventually began to reflect the situation that was developing on the Western Front.

That winter was both boring and fun. School, as usual, was monotonous as were piano lessons. My birthday party in November was exciting with playmates attending: Sascha Feiges, his cousin, Zina Jevelson, and Natascha Babst, among others. We enjoyed playing games in the living room and devouring the traditional birthday cake (Kringel in German) and, of course, drinking cocoa. I much looked forward to a trip to Riga during the Christmas recess. The mere idea of traveling to our exciting capital overshadowed everything else, including Libau's café life. There I attended a children's performance at the opera—something the Libau opera did not offer—and went several times to Café Schwarz with mother and Aunt Hermine. We also visited Aunt Leni and Uncle Isidor, who lived around the corner from Aunt Hermine, my relatives in Kaiserwald, for games with cousins Joni and Ljuba in town and, of course, to Uncle Oskar's store where I could help myself to all kinds of gadgets. At Passover time in Libau, I devoured baked matzoh with cottage cheese to which I added cinnamon and sugar.

In the meantime, I had to endure a few embarrassing situations that were of my making. A play for children was going to be performed in town and many classmates would attend, including Veltiņa. For the occasion, I insisted that I be properly dressed. This included black patent leather shoes. Mother demurred but I insisted. We went to the Plotkin shoe store on the Rosenplatz (Rožu Laukums in the Latvian) who custom-made shoes for my family's sensitive feet. Not to get my shiny shoes wet, I was dropped off by car and took my seat next to some of my classmates who began to laugh at me for wearing sissy shoes.

My work habits in school continued to be a problem, reflected in my grades, which continued to decline and were a source of embarrassment because I was being laughed at by some of my classmates. I felt I needed protection from my "enemies" so I formed a commando unit—nothing unusual—paying my troops each about 20 centimes a month. Not that it helped much. Feeling lost, not really knowing what to do, I simply began skipping school and walked the streets of Libau. But that did not work because I could not produce the following morning a note explaining my absence. Over time, I perfected a technique that worked. I began to feign coughs, convincing papa that I had to stay home. On the following morning, he wrote a note to the teacher signed Dr. Schwab in a manner that was totally unreadable. Hence, on top of all my troubles it now turned out that I had the burden of living with an illiterate father who was called by everyone *Herr Doktor* (Mr. Doctor)—even though he was unable to write. I, of course, made my outrage felt at home only to be smiled at. And even more incredible was the reaction of my teachers—they understood his scribbles.

Not surprisingly I began to have troubles with my piano teacher as well. Whenever I was not fully prepared, she made me stand in a corner facing the wall. At home I had to practice almost every day, while mamma, a professional cellist who had studied at the celebrated Riga Conservatory, sat in an adjoining room monitoring me like a hawk. Whenever I was not spied upon by mamma or the governess, I would try to tear off the big brass emblem that protruded from the Bechstein piano built in St. Petersburg and appeared ready to poke out my eyes. What intrigued me more than practicing the piano was the large brass chandelier with more than twenty light bulbs. According to mamma, who told me after the war, the fixture, like our uncomfortable but elegant mahogany furniture inlaid with brass and upholstered with antique gold covers in the living room, came from a czarist palace. Grandfather David Schwab purchased them, among many other items, from Soviet authorities right after the Bolshevik revolution when the new government sold off treasures for very little money to raise hard currency. Most of the purchases were given as gifts to his children. One large oil painting in particular captured my attention: father had purchased it in Russia while serving as a physician in the czarist army with the rank of colonel. It was the work of the Russian painter Ivan Aivazovski. It depicted desperate-looking men using oars to navigate over huge waves in a stormy sea. One of them was standing nearly upright in the rear—looking toward the horizon to see, I guess, if land was in sight.

For some reason, mamma took me to Riga earlier than usual in June 1940, and she returned to Libau after only a few days. Tension was in the air because of heightened Soviet troop activities in Libau. In Riga, I stayed with

Aunt Hermine and was scheduled to go to the Riga beach with Aunt Gusti, Uncle Oskar, and cousins Joni and Ljuba. That did not come to pass.

Not too many days after my arrival, we heard a commotion; in the distance, I could see from Aunt Hermine's balcony an unending procession of Latvians with red flags and heard a certain Soviet official—apparently Andrei Vishinsky—shouting into a microphone in Russian announcing, according to Aunt Hermine, something to the effect that the Soviet Union had heeded Latvia's invitation to liberate the country from its bourgeois enemies.

My parents telephoned saying that mamma was coming to fetch me. That evening mamma and the rest of the Riga family gathered in Aunt Leni's apartment. The atmosphere was dour and everyone was speaking in hushed voices. From time to time, Uncle Isidor walked into an adjoining room where he sat at the organ playing awful-sounding classical music. On the following afternoon we left for Libau.

Papa was at the station and looked worried. In the *drozhki* heading home, my parents, to my annoyance, whispered in Russian to make sure that the coachman did not overhear or understand what was being said and to prevent me from knowing what was going on. Their whispering in a language not well-known to me was not unusual. Whenever they did not want me to know something, they switched from German to Russian. But over the years I had picked up enough of the language to speak it a little, and, to their surprise, understand much more. (Bubi did not have this problem as both his nanny and governess were Russian.) The gist of the conversation revolved around the future, and papa assuring mamma that his medical specialty will see us through.

Changes in lifestyle were quick in coming. Although we continued to frequent the tennis club and the beach, café life was way down as was lunching at the Pavilion. Papa's private practice was drastically curtailed, and he was appointed to head a clinic in town where he earned 30 rubles a month in the new Soviet currency. Because money was never a subject of discussion—at least in front of me as we all seemed to have a certain disdain for it, as if it were something soiled—I was surprised to hear him mention his salary and laugh at the amount.

The city was soon overrun by Soviet soldiers and sailors, and the naval port was made off-limits to civilians. Blackouts were ordered; it was whispered that these were safety measure against German spy planes—which had flown over Libau almost at will shortly before the outbreak of hostilities—and bourgeois Great Britain was officially vilified for having started the war. Despite blackouts, social life continued on a considerably smaller scale. Cards still were played behind dark curtains, and mamma prepared and served finger sandwiches, home-baked sweets, tea, and coffee. For me this year was the worst in school. I failed every subject save English and was scheduled to take the year over again.

Papa had to end the employment of his nurse Marie. Live-in help was prohibited. Mamma could not replace Stefa who had been with us for 17 years and had recently married. From time to time, Fenya helped mamma. In the fall we were notified that we had to accommodate a Soviet soldier who was given my bedroom and I was moved to the living room. He was a very nice young man whom we rarely saw and to whom mamma presented a Western *eau de toilette* that had a very enduring scent. It was not long thereafter that we were ordered to vacate the apartment—because the building was to be converted into the headquarters of the Communist Party of Libau. To mamma's chagrin, the apartment we were able to secure on Peter Street (Kuršu iela in the Latvian) near the hay market was considerably smaller, only 6½ tiny rooms with no central heating. Mamma converted the windowless maid's room into a storage facility for papa's x-ray and other fancy medical machinery as well as part of his medical library. One room near the entrance was set aside for papa's consulting room, where he was still permitted to see patients. To reach the bathroom, my parents had to go through the children's room. One morning, for some reason, we woke up late and mamma hurried to prepare breakfast. To save time and ensure that I would not be late for school, she said that I would take my breakfast in the kitchen, which I refused—telling her that "I am not a servant." Food, especially meat, became scarce. I remember being sent to the main market to stand in line for one pound of veal, the maximum allowed to a shopper a day.

We, of course, had no choice but to adjust to the new way of life that, among other things, entailed subscribing to the Communist Party line. In other words, no one felt at ease speaking freely about politics in general and critiquing the system under which we were forced to live specifically. Despite my antipathy toward communism, which I had obviously acquired at home, my parents did not trust me for fear that I might repeat to my friends negative thoughts they entertained about the regime and that would then somehow find their way to the secret police with dire consequences for the family. "Spying" on my parents about what was going on was not easy. When discussing sensitive issues when I was nearby, they spoke in Russian. But once I overheard them say in German that at times even husbands and wives did not trust each other—something incomprehensible to me. I resented their distrust of me; I was one of the very few students in my class who refused to join the Soviet Communist youth movement—the Pioneers.

There were things, however, I immensely enjoyed. Following in the footsteps of my brother, I began to collect stamps and was especially impressed by the very colorful Soviet stamps. Of the films that made an indelible mark on me was one depicting the Moscow circus and also *Peter the Great* and *Potemkin*. I was also taken by striking photos and films depicting farmers happily singing Russian songs while working in the fields in the Caucasus and elsewhere in the Soviet Union. Films about the might of the Soviet armed forces were impressive and exciting, even though on numerous occasions I saw soldiers unable to start dated-looking army trucks and noticed that those that did work often spewed unusually foul-smelling fumes.

At school, teachers barraged students with the greatness of Lenin and Stalin, and, to my amazement, most students appeared to have been seduced by this propaganda, a word I learned from the whispers of my parents. Although Nazi Germany had signed the non-aggression pact with the Soviet Union, there was little evidence of schoolteachers' stressing the Soviet Union's close friendship with Nazi Germany. On balance, until mid-June 1941, we had the sense that we were safe, that is, the family was intact. For as long as we could at least appear to be good citizens, there was a chance that all would be well. Those who argued that the Baltic countries were buffer states whose territorial integrity would not be violated by the Soviet Union and Nazi Germany would soon be in for another shock—notwithstanding the fact that Hitler had vowed never to wage a two-front war and Great Britain was still in the war. On balance, the feeling was that Soviet domination was preferable to a Nazi one.

Exactly one week before the Nazi invasion of the Soviet Union on June 22, 1941, a mass deportation of civilians to deep Russia took place. Our phone began to ring early in the morning. Callers carefully informed papa that friends of the family and patients had been awakened and that soldiers had ordered them to pack personal belongings quickly and to be ready for a long trip. Papa, in turn, called influential friends, trying to intercede on their behalf. We were fearful that we would be next. As we soon found out, Communist agents had lists of alleged enemies of the state that included former members of the bourgeoisie or, broadly speaking, owners of the means of production and property owners in general. Within a short time we learned that the victims were hauled off in trucks to one of the town's railroad stations, I believe to the one near the bridge dividing the old town from new Libau.

My parents were obviously nervous about the fate of the family. Papa was "optimistic" that we would not be touched because of his specialty and the number of high-ranking Soviet officers who were his patients. On several occasions a highly cultured Soviet admiral of the old school even came to our home for supper. Nevertheless, it was widely known before 1940 that the Schwab family was not poor, in part because of papa's thriving medical practice and inheritance from his parents. His father had been a highly respected and prosperous grain merchant who owned a modern elevator-equipped red brick warehouse at the new Libau side of the civilian harbor. Whenever the governor of St. Petersburg visited Libau, he was a regular visitor at my grandparents' home. Grandfather Schwab had been the governor's bridge partner.

As the hours passed, we began to breathe more easily. I remember Aunt Yette coming up to report that she and her son Israel (Ljolja) were safe;

from mother's family in Riga we heard the same good news. But during the commotion Bubi slipped out of the house and with a few friends bicycled to the railroad tracks from where the victims were deported. Returning home after several hours, he reported seeing friends of the family and acquaintances who had been condemned by the regime and were now being deported. My parents were furious at his irresponsible and risky venture that could have endangered him and the family. I felt sorry for Bubi and burst into tears.

June 14 was a turning point in the Soviet occupation of Latvia. However much we had had to curtail our lifestyle, we had adjusted ourselves to the new realities without much fear for our lives. That relative complacency was shattered on that June day, and hatred for the Soviet regime increased enormously.

Chapter III
WAR

War! At last! How exciting, I thought. Only hours after guests had left the apartment following the usual evening of card playing, we were awakened by swastika-emblazoned planes early Sunday morning, June 22, 1941. They were diving out of the sky with a whistling and shrilling sound and dropping bombs all over town. Soviet anti-aircraft batteries targeted them, leaving black patches in the air as they missed their targets. Some of the planes flew so low that we could clearly see pilots waving at us as we watched from the balcony. I waved back.

The noise nearly drowned out the ringing telephone calling papa to hurry to the hospital where the wounded and dying were piling up. Relatives, friends, and patients also called and came over unannounced, seeking advice and consolation because no one knew officially until much later in the day that the Soviet Union was at war with Nazi Germany. And, it did not take me long to realize that war was not the game I used to play with Jimmy.

Between answering calls and rushing to get ready to leave for the hospital, I heard papinka (diminutive for papa) say it couldn't be war. Did not Hitler vow never to wage a two-front war? Great Britain was still far from finished. However unbelievable it might be, perhaps the Soviet Union had attacked Germany. Some who telephoned or came over after papinka had left had heard allegedly trustworthy stories that Soviet armies were at the gates of Königsberg and that Soviet bombers were over Berlin. When the news of the war was finally broadcast at midday, it was clear that the Soviet Union was officially at war and that Germany was the aggressor, despite the friendship treaty between the two countries.

Because of its strategic significance, Libau was heavily contested for one week and was in chaos. As soon as enemy planes approached and air raid sirens began to howl in the first few days and nights of air attacks, we took shelter in the building's basement. Bubinka, a deep sleeper, did not want to get out of bed at night and pleaded to be left alone, convinced that nothing would happen. I cried because I did not want to leave him behind. In any event, my parents refused to accept his pleas. Papa had originally thought that civilian targets would be spared, which did not happen. Even Aunt Yette's building in the exclusive residential Swan's Pond section of town was bombed. With air and naval attacks mounting, papa made us gather our belongings and we left the apartment to take shelter in the basement of the city's clinic in the center of town at the Hauptwachtplatz (Fireman's Square). As the air and naval attacks continued to increase, papinka made us once more gather our belongings and walk to the city's main hospital that was in the woods close to the Baltic Sea, quite a distance from the town's center. There we remained in the cellar until the Germans marched into Libau.

One or two days before their arrival, when it became evident that Soviet troops were being routed, there was some talk of us joining the exodus. That was not to be, for papa was told in no uncertain terms that if he were to leave his station and the city, it would be considered treason with all that that implied. Early one morning a German army command car drew up and papa, because of his fluency in German and his medical specialty, was asked to be part of the welcoming committee. On asking the German officer about policies toward Jews, papa was assured that they had nothing to worry about: all attention would be focused on defeating Bolshevism, and Jews would have to play a part in that endeavor. Satisfied with the answer, we once more gathered our belongings and walked home, hoping that the building in which we had lived still stood.

On our way the Germans did not molest us. I was struck by the large number of German horse-drawn columns and wondered about the absence of tanks and other motorized vehicles that we had heard so much about during the Polish and French campaigns. Our home was intact. Across the street was a large plot of land that had been empty until the Germans appropriated it and turned it into a parking lot for their horse-drawn carts with their German crews.

From the moment we entered the apartment, the phone began to ring and a string of visitors followed for days. As before, relatives, friends, and patients inquired about us. They relayed particularly alarming reports about Jews in small towns and villages being molested and killed and their living quarters being robbed by fellow Latvians. At first papinka thought that the reports were exaggerated, but as they mounted the rumors could no longer be ignored. I heard papa finally say that before the war, he would not have believed that fellow Latvians could stoop to the level of animals.

The assurances papinka received from the German officer soon evaporated and the unbelievable began to unfold.

Jews were prohibited from walking on sidewalks, frequenting non-Jewish stores, and mingling with non-Jews. Jews were ordered to wear yellow patches and deliver to a centrally located place valuables, including radios and bicycles. Within days, papinka was called on to identify the body of Aunt Yette's son Israel (Ljolja) Wainstein who had just been murdered, allegedly denounced by the lover of the beautiful Latvian girl he had recently married and who carried Israel's child. Papinka returned home white as a sheet. The beginning of the end had thus started for us as a family and as Jews. Papa ceased swooning over the greatness of German culture and instead reiterated that Germans and their Latvian collaborators would one day pay a hefty price for their base criminality.

In the days, weeks, and months that followed, the apartment was searched for valuables and plundered by a stream of Germans from the *Sicherheitsdienst* (SD; Security Service), *Schutzpolizei* (Schupo; Security Police), and *Kriegsmarine* (Navy)—now headquartered in the building in which we had lived before we were evicted by the Soviets. The Navy thieves arrived in a command car bearing a naval captain (also known as an inspector) whose name, I believe, was Ulmann. He was always accompanied by Latvian crews who hauled down three flights of stairs and loaded onto the waiting truck much of what we had failed to hide, including antique furniture, Persian carpets, works of art, chandeliers, old Russian silver, papa's medical library, x-ray and diathermia machines and equipment, and medical instruments.

Vivid in my memory is an episode that occurred toward the end of July, just before papinka was arrested. I observed him from the dining room. He stood in the living room, a hand resting against the piano and answered the tall and lean German *Schutzpolizei* officer who had visited the apartment before and now insisted that he be shown where additional valuables were hidden. With tears in his eyes, my papinka answered that he was only a physician and what the officer saw was all that was left of a lifetime of hard work in the healing arts. The *Schutzpolizei* officer looked around once more and left. Because the Latvian currency and the Soviet ruble were considered soft currencies, people with some means hoarded gold coins and rings, diamonds, brooches, pearls, gold watches, and dollar and pound bills. Papa and mammy succeeded in hiding valuables by burying some in the barn in our backyard, in a wall safe in the apartment of a Jewish patient, and elsewhere, including the Abelits—the banker and his wife who were patients of papa.

Papinka, wearing his Red Cross armband, and Bubinka left early one morning in late July for Fireman's Square where Jewish adults were ordered to assemble for work assignments. Some distance from the square, papinka noticed the approach of the notorious green SD trucks, the vehicles that transported Jewish cargo to its destiny via the women's prison and from there to the killing grounds near the lighthouse. Motioning to the Jews to scatter, papinka was caught, horribly beaten, kicked, one eye knocked out, and thrown down the stairs into the prison's basement. We first heard of this from a Latvian patient who rushed to tell mammy. Whereas the patient claimed to have seen this happen at the prison, as did one survivor after the war who gave me her account, others claim that this beating took place openly on Fireman's Square. Whatever the venue, eyewitnesses agree that papa was in excruciating pain. He searched for his eye and pleaded to be put to death. That was not to be, at least not then. Those who claimed that the heinous crime happened on Fireman's Square saw his semi-dead body thrown onto one of the SD trucks and hauled off to prison.

The terrible news caused hysterical outbursts by mammy, something I had never seen as she was always composed and understated. I was truly alarmed and wished that Bubi was not at work. In shock and in tears, mamma, in the coming days, left no stone unturned to obtain papa's release. For the next couple of days, she pleaded for help from his Latvian colleagues, patients, and even the SD. It was the SD murderer Erich Handke who committed the heinous crime. At last came a glimmer of hope. The criminal sadist Handke assured mammy during one of her visits that papa would be released once his injuries had healed. That did not happen: my papinka was shot dead in the vicinity of the lighthouse. (That abominable crime was a topic at the Hanover trial of Nazi war criminals in 1970.)

Incomprehensible to me was that I would never again see my papinka. Although fully aware of and frightfully concerned by what was going on, I tried to escape from it all by immersing myself in acting out war games with some of the war toys that Jimmy Lau and I used to play with. Also, using pencils and crayons, I filled sheets of paper with war planes, warships, and tanks. I also watched the German soldiers across the street attending to their horse-drawn wagons.

Lucky for us that level-headed Bubinka was around. He, so to speak, assumed the role of *pater familias*. After the horror of papinka's murder, mammuly was assigned to work as a laundress for the *Luftwaffe* (Air Force) at the naval base where Bubi also worked as an auto mechanic. Neither had any experience with either job. From time to time, mammuly managed to take me along to her workstation where I helped her fold the ironed laundry.

One day after returning from work, mammy recounted an incredible encounter that had occurred there. At her workstation, she was approached by an army *Unteroffizier* (corporal). Because of mammy's Aryan complexion and profile, he told her he could arrange for her to leave for Germany where she would be absorbed into the mainstream of German society. Mammy agreed provided that she could take her sons along. That was denied and that was the end of this curious proposal.

After the initial mass murders committed by Germans with their Latvian henchmen in the summer months, a semblance of stability returned despite *chapinkes* (snatchings) here and there. Handke, *Scharführer* Karl Emil Strott—also of the SD—and a Latvian in uniform who had only nine fingers visited the apartment from time to time to look around for what was left to steal. To bribe Handke and save Bubi and me, mammy presented him with a German Leica. Strott, who was a stamp collector, helped himself to Bubi's renowned collection—something that was acclaimed at an international exhibition of known pre–Second World War Jewish collectors in Philadelphia in the early 1960s. The Latvian received a Russian Leica.

Soon mammy was transferred from her workstation to the home of Mrs. Kronberg, the Latvian mistress of the head of the SD, Wolfgang Kügler. Mammy knew her from before the war when both had frequented the same beauty parlor. Mammy became her housekeeper, which provided advantages, including receiving extra food that she was able to slip clandestinely to other Jews at great risk to herself. Most important, when imminent danger loomed, Mrs. Kronberg suggested that mammy take me to her upstairs apartment in the two-family house, where I was well-fed and able to spend the day in relative security watching mammy clean. Over a period of time, mammy bribed Mrs. Kronberg with all sorts of things, including a Persian runner and some silver that my parents had hidden at the Abelit home. With familiar objects surrounding me, I felt quite comfortable in the elegantly appointed apartment. I had no idea how close I was to death.

At that time we moved to a rear flat in the former Kessel villa, which was across the street from the future location of the ghetto only a few minutes from the center of town. We lived in one room, and Mrs. Kessel with her two daughters, Rosa and Mia, lived in the other room. (Mr. Kessel had been murdered.) Before long Bubi and Mia fell in love and were married by the head of the Jewish community, Mr. Zalman Israelit, and his deputy, the attorney Mr. Menash (Monia) Kaganski, at the small Jewish Community Office that was also located on the Kessel property, which had belonged to the Kessel family before the war.

December 1941 was yet another horror-filled month. At the beginning of the month we started to hear of a serious Soviet counteroffensive in the region of Moscow. That report was followed by Hitler's declaration of war on the United States as a result of Japan's attack on Pearl Harbor. We were elated. The consensus among Jews was that there was no way now that Hitler could even dream of victory. But the slaughter of Jews continued. In the middle of the month, Jews were ordered not to leave their premises for two days. The meaning of this was clear: a major *Aktion* (killing) was scheduled to take place. A scramble for *Sicherheitsscheine* (security documents), officially stamped letters stating that the holder and family not be touched because of the vital work they were performing for the war effort, ensued. Mamminka secured for herself, for us, and the Kessels an awesome-looking letter with a green SD stamp and a swastika in the middle. Following the announcement, mammy immediately went to see Aunt Yette who lived in the part of the building at Swan's Pond that was still intact and worked for the Germans cleaning up the city's rubble. Mammy begged her to move in with us, which she refused to do because she did not want to leave the apartment unattended. On the days we were sequestered, a member of the SD who mammy knew came with several Latvians, inspected mammy's document, and left. Aunt Yette became one of the thousands of Libau's Jewish victims who were rounded up, herded into the women's prison, and transported to Skede where they were forced to strip in the coldest winter on record and shot dead by Germans in the company of their Latvian accomplices. Thanks to mammy's job, we were left physically unharmed.

Following the mass slaughter, a semblance of order gradually returned, that is, working, hiding, and clandestinely receiving news from the BBC. During that dismally freezing winter, news was more than heartening, it gave us some window to the outside world. The news about the Moscow front was embellished by *ME Agentur* (short in Yiddish for *Men Sogt Agentur*—"It is said Agency") that exaggerated or invented stories relayed orally and aimed at reinforcing the already good tidings that we would soon be liberated. But, at times *ME Agentur* spread stories to the contrary, including that we would be shot before the Soviets arrived. Strange, we now looked to be liberated by the once-hated communists.

Although much had already been stolen and hidden, we continued to be relatively warmly dressed in the bitter cold winter. Nevertheless, I developed frostbite on my little and index fingers and toes, which resulted in discoloration, swelling, and terrible itching. I, who had just turned ten, was consumed with thinking much about my war experiences and the unpleasant and repressive Soviet occupation that I would have gladly exchanged for the horrors I was now subjected to and the anxiety of not knowing what the next hour or day would have in store for me and my family.

What I could not fathom was papinka's supposed wrongdoings that led to his being murdered and why mamminka, Bubinka, and I were being punished, and I asked what everyone else did: Why does God not help us? After all, we are His people, something I failed to understand and did not think too much about. Stranger thoughts swirled in my mind. Once walking in the bitter cold on the cobblestone street near the central marketplace, I thought that maybe a Nazi victory should be welcomed for that might somehow dissolve the terrible fate that had befallen us. There would no longer be war, and everyone would live in peace once more but I would be without papinka to whom I had been very much attached. But those and similar abnormal thoughts soon perished in the face of realities on the ground. On the same day, as I continued to walk a little farther toward our apartment, I noticed in the distance walking toward me on the sidewalk the girl Veltiņa I once fancied in school. I suddenly felt embarrassed about not being permitted to walk on the sidewalk, forced to wear yellow patches, and prohibited from talking to non-Jews. As our eyes met, we both turned our faces in opposite directions. For the first time in my young life and I believe for the last time, I experienced the feeling of shame for being Jewish.

In early 1942, we were forced to move again. This time to a four-room apartment and kitchen in a small house near the *Anlagen* (park) on Alejas Street, a stone's throw from my school—for which I had no warm feelings. Mammy had a room to herself; Bubi, Mia, and I shared a room that adjoined hers; Mrs. Anna Bub had a room to herself; and Lea Beutler and Bella

Blumberg the other. Of the seven, four survived the war: mammy Mia, Bella, and I.

During the day I was left at home alone while the others went to their workstations after assembling at Fireman's Square. Things were relatively quiet: no German and Latvian thieves came to the flat, perhaps realizing that most of the valuables had been stolen or hidden. While I was alone all day, I passed the time making drawings of tanks, airplanes, and warships. I hid this activity in case of a sudden intrusion. Though food was rationed, we did not starve. The barter system worked well with fellow Jews and clandestinely with Latvians and even some Germans. As previously mentioned, thanks to her work for Mrs. Kronberg, mamminka contributed extra food to the larder.

In early summer of 1942, the remnants of the Jewish community, numbering a little more than 800 from the pre-war community of about 8,000, were ordered to move into a ghetto located near the center of town. It was sealed by a barbed wire fence that was patrolled by Latvian guards in black uniform. We were assigned to one room of a two-room and kitchen basement apartment on Waisenhaus (Bāriņu in the Latvian) Street in a building that once belonged to the Ludzin family and that faced the Kessel villa across the street on the other side of the fence. The apartment lacked a toilet, which was located at the rear entrance of the building on the main floor, a new experience for me. Mammy determined that I, straddling the border between being a child and an adult in those abnormal circumstances, should be considered a worker and arranged for me to work in the ghetto's vegetable garden whose supervisor was Mrs. Sophie Sacks. We planted seeds and grew potatoes, tomatoes, cucumbers, cabbage, and so on. Watering the seeds and watching them sprout was a wonderful endeavor that I enjoyed immensely. It also helped me for moments not to think of the dismal troubles, which included mamminka, Bubinka, and Mia falling prey to the terror and, of course, me being killed.

Although those returning from work were usually searched for smuggled food or other items, the searches were not thorough thanks to the well-bribed ghetto commandant, Franz Kerscher, who, though German, happened to be a relatively mild human being—as was his short Latvian counterpart, an elderly, white-haired man in a Latvian captain's uniform who had been assigned to the ghetto but was largely ignored by the commandant as I was soon to observe first-hand. Because of mammy's work for Kügler's mistress, she was more gently treated at the gate.

My work soon changed. Kerscher was looking for a messenger boy fluent in German. The Jewish head of the ghetto, Mr. Israelit, suggested to mammy that I accept the job and I was reassigned. My work most mornings at the commandant's headquarters situated at the ghetto's main gate included handing out tags with numbers. Every inmate had to have one when leaving the ghetto in the morning and returning it in the evening. By looking at the board on which the numbers were recorded, the commandant had an instant view of who was in and out of the ghetto. In addition, I was often ordered to fetch from and deliver to the SD and the home of the head of the SS, Dr. Fritz Dietrich, watches that were repaired in the ghetto workshop and suits and uniforms that were made to order or had to be repaired and other objects.

Before and after occasional SD raids, arrests, and the theft of merchandise from the ghetto's grocery store by two inmates (they were arrested and executed), life was tolerable. At one of the raids, I was ordered to accompany the SD men who quizzed me about hidden valuables and simultaneously praised mammy for the excellent work she was doing for Mrs. Kronberg. I pleaded ignorance, which they seemed to accept, although I was vaguely aware that valuables were hidden in the ghetto but did not know where. On one occasion, I remember Mr. Israelit and Mr. Kaganski coming to see mammy for a gold coin in order to secure the release of someone who had recently been arrested but had been promised release for a fee.

During less-tense weeks and months, classes were organized by Push Weinreich, wife of one of the ghetto physicians, Dr. Weinreich, whose specialty was ear, nose, and throat. Because of my disdain for school and the work for Kerscher, I rarely attended. I tried to play with some of the kids, but was often laughed at because I did not speak Yiddish and was called *Jaecke* (a derogatory term for German Jews). With tears in my eyes, I ran to mammy to complain and was comforted when she said that she, too, did not speak Yiddish nor had papinka. They considered Yiddish a jargon, not a language. Nevertheless, I began to acquire a smattering of the spoken tongue and gradually I became acceptable to the other kids. Volleyball games were arranged as well as songfests at which recently composed morale-boosting songs and poems were sung and recited in Yiddish mocking the German hordes and their cohorts. A regular visitor to our basement continued to be Chaim Feigelman; he brought us the latest news as he had a hidden short-wave radio and was able to listen to the BBC.

Hell broke loose in September 1943. Inmates were told that the ghetto would be dissolved and the prisoners transported to a concentration camp near Riga in Kaiserwald. *ME Agentur* buzzed with a million rumors. Because of her position as Mrs. Kronberg's housekeeper, mammy was perceived to be privy to inside information. She was not but that did not deter inmates from pouring into our basement quarters, anxious to have a word with her. The consensus that emerged was that we would be transported to Riga but not to be slaughtered, which could be accomplished more efficiently in nearby Skede. The BBC news in the recent past had reported additional dramatic German reverses at Stalingrad and Kursk and the bombing of German cities by American and British planes and Mussolini's Italy at bay, which inspired us and led us to believe that because of increasing German manpower shortages, Jews would be spared and gainfully used in the war effort.

On this optimistic note, we readied ourselves for the trip. Clothing was repaired, cleaned, and ironed, and gold coins and diamonds were ingeniously sewn into coats, jackets, brassieres, and corsets. Off we marched with suitcases and hand luggage containing food and other necessities to the Libau rail cargo (*Güterbahnhof*) station where, in the afternoon only hours before the beginning of Yom Kippur in October 1943, we were chased onto cattle cars. Never having been in one, I was shocked by the lack of sanitary facilities; in the overcrowded space we set aside a corner to attend to our biological needs in a bucket that was not emptied during the trip. The stench in the poorly ventilated cattle car was beyond description.

To minimize the smell and the terrible discomfort of being squeezed like sardines in a tin, I consoled myself with the fact that I was safe with mammuly, Bubinka, and Mia nearby, and I soon began to daydream of my fabulous days in Riga: the trolley cars and buses, the zoo, the smoke-filled Café Otto Schwarz, Aunt Hermine's and Aunt Tanya's stunningly appointed apartments, the drives with Betty Schalit, the Lido at the Riga beach, and playing with wild cousin Joni.

I awakened from a brief nap just before the train stopped and the doors were opened in the early morning. We were welcomed by barking German shepherds, SS men with rifles, and others in strange-looking zebra-like uniforms shouting "Out!" "Out!" "Pigs!" "Miserable Jewish creatures!" This must be a mistake, I thought. As we were shoved out of the cattle cars, we were beaten with truncheons, whips, and the butts of rifles and were forced to run with our luggage toward a nearby huge and strange-looking square with curious looking constructs called "barracks" that I had not seen before. The entire complex was surrounded by barbed wire, similar to the Libau ghetto. We were ordered to throw all our belongings onto a large pile of suitcases and hand luggage and were told that we could retrieve our belongings shortly. Mammy, Bubi, and Mia were reluctant to do so, but I urged them to comply because of the promise made. There was no further discussion as the decision was made for us by the assaults carried out by the Germans in the company of their zebra-dressed cohorts, non-Jews who were incarcerated, as I soon found out, for criminal and other kinds of activities.

Relieved of our luggage, we were herded like animals into a large barrack. The men were soon separated from the women and led to showers where we were ordered to undress, leave our clothing and shoes neatly behind in a pile, which, we were told, we could retrieve after the shower. This was not to be. Instead, we were issued used garments and clogs that did not fit, making most of us look like clowns. We even managed to laugh at one another. Bubi and I were assigned to one of the barracks that easily had a hundred bunk beds with straw mattresses and straw pillows that pricked the body and thin, dark-gray blankets. The barrack had no bathtubs or showers. Several long sinks with cold water pipes and numerous handles situated diagonally across from our barrack served as the men's washroom. The toilet in the rear of our barrack consisted of an open cesspool surrounded by wooden planks. No water. No paper. Plenty of chlorine. Indescribably filthy, smelly, and very, very cold, especially at night. That the pampered me did not fall into the pit and drown is one of the miracles of the war. It was also in Kaiserwald where for the first time I became acquainted with the eggs of lice and the hatched offspring. The lice roamed all over the body, especially in the hairy parts to which I did not yet have a claim except on my head, and in the seams of clothing. Delousing consisted of catching the crawling lice, which was not difficult, and crunching them to death between the fingernails of our thumbs. The eggs met the same fate.

However difficult the conditions were, no matter where we were incarcerated, the religious among us usually managed to find a corner in our quarters where they prayed to and pleaded with God for relief. But to no avail. Not having been brought up in a religious home, I neither understood the Hebrew language nor the meaning of the prayers. Nevertheless, I shared with everyone the intense hope that He would soon respond to our pleas.

Appell, or roll call, too, was something new. Mornings and evenings we had to line up in front of our barrack for head counts. We were now known by numbers and no longer by first and last names. To appear as tall as possible and thus hopefully not be selected for being useless and shipped off to the killing grounds, I tried to avoid the front row and built with my clogs a sandbar on which I stood on my toes as the SS man approached—usually accompanied by one of the sadistic non-Jewish inmates known as *Kapos*. Those mostly criminal inmates ranked above the Jewish prisoners and were treated more mildly by the SS. More often than not, they were considerably more sadistic than their SS masters. One German criminal in particular stood out. Tall and strikingly handsome, he was known in the camp as "Mr. X." His good looks were only surpassed by his brutality.

The women's camp adjoined ours and was separated by a barbed wire fence. Oral contact was easy, and over my protestation mammy threw across the fence a part of her ration of the usually foul, stale, and moldy bread. In addition, our morning and evening rations consisted of a little substitute jam, sometimes accompanied by a little brown sugar or margarine and watery coffee and watery soup with sandy turnips or cabbage at midday. To make sure that I got a little of the more solid soup that was at the bottom of the pot, I tried to place myself as often as possible toward the end of the line. As noted, in the evening, the morning menu reappeared. The inedible food was a prescription for diarrhea, which was widespread.

Only a few days after our arrival at Kaiserwald, Bubi was alleged to have been selected and taken to a *Kasernierung* (work camp) in the city run by the German *Reichsbahn* (Germany's railroad system). Fearful to leave me in the camp alone during the day, mammy somehow arranged that I be assigned to her work battalion, called *Tanklager*; she worked in an oil depot terminal in Riga. We left on foot early in the morning and returned in the evening. On the marches to and from work, we were often ordered to sing. The Yiddish songs we sang spoofed the German murderers and their local accomplices. The songs were morale boosters that reflected our conviction that Nazi Germany and its allies were about to lose the war. The question was how best to maneuver in the interim in order to survive so that we could be witnesses, take revenge, and tell the world of the true meaning of German *Kultur*.

At the oil depot, mammy and I, among many others, were assigned to shovel sand onto wheelbarrows and push them to their destination. Doing so in our starved and emaciated state in the bitter cold was frightfully difficult. From time to time, we were permitted to go to a nearby shack where the slave laborers were able to slice a potato that prisoners managed to *organize* (the code word for appropriate) and fry against the stove to quell hunger pangs, help stop the chronic diarrhea, and keep our bodies warm for ten minutes.

From early childhood, I had suffered from inflammation of my tonsils and appendicitis. Although my tonsils had been removed by Dr. Mintz in Riga shortly before the Soviet occupation, the slated operation to remove my appendix was made impossible by the German occupation. While slaving at the oil depot, I had an attack and Dr. Max Sick, a surgeon from Libau (nicknamed Homen), who had become a camp physician, admitted me to a so-called camp infirmary that was in the rear of my barrack; I was able to rest there for several days. On hearing of a forthcoming inspection, he asked me to vanish from the infirmary, which I did, and was able to rejoin the oil depot work battalion.

News reached the camp that the *Reichsbahn* satellite camp was tolerable and that the camp's commandant, a German railway functionary, possessed human qualities. From time to time, a *Reichsbahn* truck arrived at the camp with requests for specific inmates, and mammy received news from Bubi and a request that she do everything possible to enable us to join him. A gift for the commandant would facilitate matters, he suggested. Mammy was able to sneak out a note to Bubi who managed to get it to Mr. Abelit in Libau. He honored mammy's request that one of her fur coats be sent to the commandant for his wife. To make sure that I would get to Bubi, I was left behind in the camp and had to wait about a week for the truck to arrive. Mammy, unfortunately, was unable to join me and was at the oil terminal when I left Kaiserwald with the help of a patient of papa's—Hinda Foss, who was well-regarded by the SS establishment in Libau and Kaiserwald. She pushed me into the truck.

For the days I remained waiting in Kaiserwald, I was assigned to shovel snow in front of the commandant's headquarters. One day the commandant, SS *Sturmbahnführer* Albert Sauer, came out and walked toward me and said that he did not like the way I was performing my duty. He slapped my face so hard that I fell in the snow and almost lost consciousness. Fellow prisoners managed to bring me to the camp's infirmary where Dr. Sick attended to me and released me the same day.

Indeed, the *Reichsbahn* work camp was considerably better than Kaiserwald. The food and sanitary conditions were better. That translated into a lukewarm shower in a common shower quarter once a week, fewer eggs of lice and their offspring, beatings less frequent, bunk beds, and warmer barracks.

I slept peacefully across from Bubi. We had news that mammy had succeeded in getting out of Kaiserwald and was now in a work camp called SS *Gaertnerei* (SS Nursery Garden). Mia, too, was in a work camp. The news from the world that continued to seep in was most encouraging: German and Axis armies continued to be repulsed on all fronts, and German cities were being mercilessly bombed by the British and Americans. All in all, morale was high. Were I to be killed, I thought, at least I would die convinced that

Germany's demise was assured. But the imminence of Germany's projected defeat intensified my desire to survive, and the all-consuming issue was how best to maneuver to stay alive. If only we could hold out, we would welcome to Riga the once-detested Soviet armies with open arms.

Like Bubi, I declared my specialty to be electricity, and, as an electrician I was assigned to his workstation in one of the huge railroad hangars where battery-powered railroad cars were being overhauled. Bubi's expertise, in my view, was awesome, and I usually assisted him by charging batteries, changing fuses and light bulbs, and checking and often replacing worn-out wiring, among other such chores. Whenever a German SS man would appear, we were alerted by an inmate shouting "*schischo*," which stood for six, I believe, and resonated well in the acoustically solid hangar.

At the *Reichsbahn*, I had another appendix attack and was taken to the camp's so-called infirmary. The doctor, a Lithuanian Jew who claimed to have known papa, treated me gently and applied warm compresses to the painful area and confined me to the infirmary for several days in June 1944 until the pains were gone.

In July–early August 1944, not long after the unsuccessful attempt to kill Hitler failed, there was a commotion. Shortly after returning from work, all hell broke loose. Out! Out! (*Appell! Appell!*) Chased into a barrack outside the camp by unfamiliar SS guards who had just arrived, men were separated from women and ordered to undress, line up, and one by one pass inspection by *Reichsbahn* Commandant Köhler, the SS physician of Kaiserwald, Dr. Eduard Krebsbach, and his medical aide, SS *Oberscharführer* Heinz Günther Wisner. While the three were talking, joking, and laughing, Wisner mainly ordered inmates to go right or left. As we approached the troika, Bubi and I were certain that Köhler would see to it that no harm came to us in anticipation of receiving additional bribes. That was not to be: Bubi and I were separated. I was ordered to the right and Bubi to the left. Back at the barrack in camp, I tried to convince myself that Bubi would soon follow even though deep down I felt it was over. (In the 1980s, I was called twice to testify against Wisner in Düsseldorf. Despite damning testimonies by survivors, including Professor Gertrude

Schneider, he received a light prison sentence of five years.) Unable to fall asleep and despondent when Bubi did not return after calling out for him in the barrack, I finally accepted the fact that it was his end: Bubinka's time to be killed had arrived. I was now at a complete loss, not knowing how to manage all alone, and once more blamed my parents for having abandoned me. Quietly crying for Bubinka who had watched over me and who even insisted on giving me half of his meager ration so that I not be hungry and grow, I gradually fell asleep, reconciling myself to the fact that I was not the only one in this predicament.

Sensing my despair, Jule Goldberg, who in Libau labored in the SD with mammy, approached me and said that he would look after me as much as possible, even going so far as to say that for as long as he lived I, too, would live. He was known for his good looks, powerful muscles, and excellence as a yachtsman. He was married to the beautiful Eugenia, also a *Reichsbahn* slave laborer.

At the beginning of August, we were told that the *Reichsbahn's* satellite work camp would be liquidated and the camp inmates would be transported to Germany where we would continue to work for the *Reichsbahn*. Although elated at the proximity of Soviet troops, the inmates did not say much about what was felt to be inevitable, namely, our slaughter and the vow to take German and Latvian murderers with us into the graves.

Soon we were forced to march to the Riga harbor where an imposing looking ship, the *Bremerhafen*, awaited the human cargo of thousands of prisoners from Kaiserwald and satellite camps. Chased aboard and down a stairway to a barrack-like space with bunk beds and bare floors, I secured one for myself next to Jule and other *Reichsbahn* inmates.

Now the rumor mill sprang into action. Some speculated that we would be drowned in the Baltic Sea, whereas others thought that the Germans would not want to sink the ship that appeared to us to be a troop carrier. While arguments flared back and forth, others on board were certain that we would be thrown overboard. Few believed that we would reach a port in Germany. Some were sure that Soviet planes would not attack the ship because they would see on deck many inmates wearing the easily recognizable zebra-like uniforms that we had recently been ordered to don. I don't remember anyone mentioning the possibility of a submarine attack.

Curious about the ship, I was eager to reach the upper deck. I looked up the staircase to see if SS guards were watching. A woman whose hair was cropped stared down at me and, not recognizing her, I paid no attention. Suddenly I heard a familiar voice calling "Zockele, Zockele." I looked at her once more and discovered my hairless mammy. As we slowly sailed in the Bay of Riga in perfect Baltic summer weather, mammy and I watched several artillery shells explode nearby on land. That meant that the Soviets were truly not far away. For the next few days, we managed to spend time together on deck.

In the course of our meetings, mammy related to me that those who were selected from the *Reichsbahn* reached Kaiserwald on the way to be slaughtered. She had spoken with Bubi several times across the barbed wire fence separating the men from the women. By promising bribes to some of the higher-ups, mammy thought she might be able to save Bubinka, but finally he refused to go to the fence. The last time mammy saw him, he promised her that he and his buddies would make sure to take some of the German and Latvian killers with them. (To the best of our knowledge, the killings took place either at Rumbula or Bikerniek forests.) With papinka and Bubinka gone, we both spilled bitter tears.

During the time we were able to spend on deck, we reminisced about our wonderful and warm past, commiserated over our deep hurts, and vowed never to give in and never to return to cursed Latvia. Based on the answers of former Riga inmates, mammy had the feeling that her entire Riga family had been wiped out. One glimmer of hope was Aunt Hermine. Perhaps her Chinese diplomatic passport was helpful; perhaps she had fled to Russia. Who knew?

Once more, mammy reminded me of papa's brother Robert, in London, and my first cousins in the United States. She also talked about papa's sister, Fanny, and her husband, Leiba Galgut, a first cousin, living in Johannesburg, South Africa. Mammy also profusely thanked Jule for looking after me. In turn, he reminded her of how helpful she had been in providing food and news while working for Kügler's mistress. Mammy insisted on sharing her ration with me, claiming, as at Kaiserwald, that she was not hungry.

Surprisingly, the disembarkation went quite smoothly without much mistreatment from the German SS guards. It was thought that they acted that way because on German soil they did not want to shock the local population with their bestiality. But the euphoric sense that we would be treated more humanely was dispelled once we reached Stutthof, an extermination camp, near Danzig. The reception was reminiscent of our arrival at Kaiserwald. Beatings, kickings, and chasings by SS guards with rifles. Some had at their sides fierce-looking and wildly barking German police dogs. It seemed like homecoming to Kaiserwald. The only hope was that the *Reichsbahn* satellite camp would materialize somewhere in Germany.

As at Kaiserwald, the men were separated from the women. Otherwise, there were few similarities between the two concentration camps, Kaiserwald and Stutthof. The latter was huge, and the double-row, barbed wire fence surrounding the camp was electrified. The camp also had watchtowers manned by SS guards with machine guns. We learned two new words: *gas chamber* and *crematorium* as a result of finding out that those designated to be murdered were first gassed in a shower-like construct, with their bodies subsequently cremated. As was the practice at Kaiserwald, we continued to be known by our assigned numbers and not by name. *Appell*, food rations, and sanitary facilities varied little from Kaiserwald. Hunger, lice, and diarrhea were steady companions. (I leave to the reader's imagination what our underwear looked like and how awful we smelled.) In the barrack, I now slept on the floor atop a straw mattress, with a straw pillow and under a thin blanket. I felt that my work was physically harder—perhaps because I was weaker.

Following *Appell* in the very early morning and after the morning ration similar to that at Kaiserwald's, I was assigned to shovel sand onto wheelbarrows—just as I had done at the oil terminal—for constructing what we were told were stoves with tall chimneys, that is, crematoriums. The midday meal consisted of very watery turnip or cabbage soup full of sand, much worse than provided at Kaiserwald. It was accompanied by the usual stale and moldy slice of bread. The ration break was momentary; we were quickly chased back to work. Constantly under the watch of sadistic SS guards and like-minded *Kapos*, we were unable to snatch a moment of rest unless given permission to visit the latrine.

Following *Appell*, the evening's routine began. It was a replay of the morning's activities: the ration was acquired and consumed; then came latrine visits; delousing (often futile); and washing oneself as best one could in totally inadequate facilities. As at Kaiserwald, religious Jews huddled in the rear of the barrack where they offered prayers to God. Five or six hours of sleep interrupted by numerous latrine visits lay ahead. Camp inmates were so isolated from the outside world that, with few exceptions, even the rumor mills ceased to function. Our sole consolation was the certitude that the Germans and their allies were on the run.

Not long after arriving at Stutthof, the *Reichsbahn* contingent with a few exceptions was told that we were to be sent to a satellite camp where the work that we had done in Riga would be continued. One difference was Dr. Gaspari, a very well-known Austrian-Jewish surgeon who was acquainted with papa's work; he was assigned to our group, replacing the doctor who had accompanied us from Riga.

Knowing that the word of a German is not worth a farthing or, as mammy used to say in German, *Ein Mann ein Wort, kein Mann kein Wort*. Nevertheless, a good number of us believed that we would be transported somewhere to work for the German war machine. The pessimists were convinced, however, that the trip would be our last and would terminate in a killing ground. To our great surprise, the *Reichsbahn* contingent was given new clogs, clean underwear, and zebra clothing, towels, some soap, and about twice the usual morning and evening ration. Perhaps a greater surprise came when we were ordered to board a normal passenger train that was set aside for us instead of the usual cattle cars. The trip in beautiful weather was pleasant even though the train was overcrowded. The countryside was handsomely manicured and peaceful, unharmed by war. After years of deprivation, I used a proper toilet and even managed to scrub with rough toilet paper and cold water the lower part of my body in privacy behind closed doors.

On our arrival in the town of Stolp in the province of Pomerania, we were forced to walk a short distance to our new quarters. The women were separated from the men. To reach our habitat, the men had to pass through a gate and a yard that was enclosed by a non-electric barbed wire fence on one side and by a huge stone brick wall on the other side. There we were shown what appeared to have been a large railroad hangar or workshop turned into barrack-like quarters with multi-tiered bunk beds equipped with the usual straw mattresses, straw pillows, and thin dark-gray blankets. Despite sanitary facilities that were better than at Stutthof and at Kaiserwald, lice continued to keep us company.

The new place was administered by a low-ranking SS man with the assistance of a few SS guards and *Reichsbahn* overseers. The chief *Reichsbahn* official assigned to us and who appeared to wield considerable power was a tall, slim man whose name I believe was spelled Schiebe. The satellite camp's daily routine was akin to what we had experienced at Kaiserwald and Stutthof: early-morning and evening roll call in the yard and morning, noon, and evening inadequate rations. Because we lived close to the Stolp railroad station and next to railroad tracks, we were able to watch with the greatest of satisfaction the never-ending stream of trains passing by filled with heavily bandaged wounded German soldiers and officers.

My work assignment in the nearby railroad workshop, a part of which housed the women prisoners and a small infirmary, was of a kind I had not seen or done, namely, carpentry. I certainly could not admit my ignorance, and in no time I learned how to smooth surface planks with a plane and sandpaper, for what purpose I had no idea. However difficult the work was for the emaciated me, it was at least indoors and not as difficult as shoveling sand into wheelbarrows. Supervision was less harsh than that at the *Reichsbahn* in Riga, as was physical abuse by the Germans. The two German Jewish capos, Grünwald and Kurt Kendziorek who hailed from Lübeck, made up with their sadism for the "leniency" of the Germans. For any infringement, including in the extreme case of stealing food from fellow prisoners, Kendziorek did not spare his truncheon and whip from the weak, emaciated, and often sick prisoners.

Two events deserve particular mention: my birthday in November 1944 and the hanging of five male prisoners. Both occurred as Germany, thankfully, was reeling on all fronts. The SS woman in charge of the female prisoners, jointly with her counterpart on the male side, agreed that Jule and I would be allowed into the women's habitat to celebrate my birthday, perhaps it even was my bar mitzvah, as I had only a vague knowledge of what that meant. For the occasion, Eugenia somehow managed to bake a potato cake, the most delicious thing I had tasted in years. In the presence of the SS woman, Jule, Eugenia, and the women slave laborers sang songs, including one of my favorites, "The Lambeth Walk," with lyrics in English. Everyone, including the SS woman, seemed to have a good time participating in this unprecedented event.

The euphoria that followed the celebration was soon shattered. A rumor made the rounds that potatoes, cabbage, and turnips, among other vegetables, had fallen off an open railroad freight car and five of our boys who worked nearby were alleged to have "organized" (ill-gotten in ghetto language) some of the loot. It was also rumored that they would soon be severely punished, despite their pleas of innocence. Rumor also had it that the five had been framed to cover up the identity of the true culprits, a few Germans. Soon it became official that the five would be hanged in our presence.

For me this was to be a novel experience. Although acquainted by now with dead bodies, I could not imagine how human beings could be hanged. I had not the faintest idea what fellow inmates were talking about, the mechanics of hanging, the gallows, the noose, the rope. One day we were forced to assemble in the yard and witness the horrendous crime that was being perpetrated. Even worse, one of the victims was only half-dead; he was hanging on the rope and jerking involuntarily. He was finally shot in the head. And we were warned that death would be the fate of anyone found stealing.

However exhausted I was from the near day-long spectacle, I could not fall asleep and once more blamed my parents for their failure to protect me. Despite Jule's presence, I felt basically abandoned by my parents, who were responsible for my well-being. I was thinking of my impending death despite the crumbling German war machine. Finally, I looked around and, as usual, noted that I was not alone in this predicament. Reconciled to my fate, though feeling sorry for myself, I fell asleep, crying for mammy, papinka, and Bubinka.

Early in the New Year, in February 1945, the *Reichsbahn's* satellite camp was dissolved and the inmates were transported in cattle cars to Danzig. According to rumors, we were to be sent from there to Stutthof. The trip to Danzig, which should have taken no more than a couple of hours, took several days under horrendous sanitary conditions and totally inadequate food rations. On arriving in bitter cold Danzig, we were chased out of the cattle cars, beaten, and forced to march for hours to one of Stutthof's satellite camps called Burggraben. Skeletons too weak to walk on the death march were shot dead by the SS guards. However weak and cold I was, I persisted with Jule next to me.

At Burggraben, we were greeted by a new reality: no guards that I can remember, hardly any rations, walking with clogs in mud, sleeping on cold floors, and no work, which enabled me to catch up on much-needed sleep, at least something positive. Soviet forces were nearby. We basically existed in no-man's-land, experiencing something really new—the exchange of artillery fire over our heads with hardly a shell falling on the camp.

Suddenly, I was alerted that a Lithuanian relative from papa's side of the family was looking for me. He was a sick young man lying in bed in a kind of infirmary. Initially, I was reluctant to visit him as I was afraid that he would ask me for bread of which I had very little left. When he saw me he smiled, said he was glad to meet me, asked about my parents and brother, and expressed the wish to see me again. That was not to be. Only about a week or so after our arrival, SS guards arrived in trucks and evacuated us to Stutthof.

The Stutthof of March/April 1945 was markedly different from the camp in 1944. Then, inmates were free from typhoid; now the disease was rampant—in large measure because of the filthy lice infestation, awful sanitary conditions, and undernourishment. Luckily, I was spared this dreadful disease because papa had immunized the family from the plague and other horrifying illnesses at the very beginning of the Nazi occupation. During our short stay in Stutthof, Jule was terribly bitten by one of the SS guard's bulldogs and his leg became very swollen.

The location of our barrack was elsewhere from where we had first been located—close to the gas chamber and crematorium, the chimney of the latter was clearly visible, with the ovens spewing smoke into the sky. In contrast to Burggraben, we heard artillery exchanges far away. The camp was on occasion attacked by Soviet fighter planes, and, in one instance, as I lay on the ground, face in the sand, and hands covering my head, a piece of shrapnel landed only inches from me.

Sometime in the fourth week of April, we were told that we would be evacuated to Danzig but not told our final destination. One day we received our usual ration of inedible bread, margarine, and some substitute jelly and off we marched a short distance and were then chased onto open, narrow-gauge railroad cars. The Danzig I remembered from our death march to Burggraben I did not recognize now. Perhaps this was not even Danzig. At the destination, the walking skeletons were ordered to board barges—a venture marked by the usual ration of beatings.

The accommodations were a horror. Because there was no ladder or stairs to the lower deck, the less fortunate were helped by those who had the strength to descend by way of a human ladder. They helped us to slide down. The compartment was filthy, smelled of manure, and was overcrowded. There was no room for everyone to sit, not to speak of stretching out. Squeezed like sardines, we took turns sitting. As prisoners died of starvation or disease, their bodies were thrown overboard and the compartment became progressively less crowded and more comfortable.

A corner was set aside for our biological needs and a bucket full of urine and excrement was continually lifted up to the deck and emptied into the Baltic Sea. Those of us who reached the deck with the help of inmates were able to urinate and defecate into the sea by squatting and holding on to the railing. That option proved dangerous as some lost their balance and fell into the sea, while others were kicked into the water by SS guards and drowned. On one occasion as I was relieving myself, I recognized a Jewish

Latvian woman from Libau treading water and looking helplessly at me, but I did not know her name. On another occasion while squatting and holding on to the railing and defecating, shortly after some inmates had overheard SS guards speaking of Hitler having been killed fighting the Soviets in Berlin, an SS guard approached me and I was convinced that this was to be my end as well. He looked at me, and I, full of fright, looked at him, and he passed me by.

Suddenly one morning we noticed land and were told by the SS guards that we were docking in Hamburg for food and drinking water. Just as abruptly, after some food and drinking water had been brought aboard the barge, we were told by the SS guards that we would have to leave in a hurry as American troops were in the center of the city. In the course of the following night, we learned that our SS guards and tugboats had abandoned us on the high seas, allegedly on or near a minefield. Luckily, one of the compartments was occupied by Norwegian prisoners of war who were better fed than we. To reach land, they collected our blankets that they turned into sails and by early morning we saw land. The plan was to disembark with the help of the Norwegians and begin to walk toward the Americans in the direction of Lübeck and Hamburg.

By now I was utterly exhausted and weak and begged Jule to leave me aboard the barge. He would have none of it and, despite his swollen leg and general weakness, he helped me to get up to the deck and the Norwegians helped us down into a rowboat that they had found on shore; we were only about 50 meters from land. We reached the shore relatively dry in the cold morning.

There was no sign of a German in uniform or even German civilians peeking at us from nearby small houses. As prisoners continued to disembark—some even waded to shore—and as we prepared to start our march, I once more pleaded with Jule to leave me behind as I had no strength left in my body. Stubborn as always, he would not let go of me. Even so, the march to freedom came to naught.

On the morning of May 3, 1945, German naval units appeared and began shooting dead those unable to stand and walk and prisoners in rowboats or wading from the barges. They even mounted the barges and shot those still aboard. The remnants were ordered to line up and forced to march. Soon we crossed a bridge into Neustadt in Holstein, a small town, and shortly thereafter we reached an enormous U-boat school with many well-constructed buildings and barracks and a huge soccer field that was crowded with thousands of Jewish and non-Jewish prisoners and many SS guards. We were told that we soon would board the ship *Athen* that would take us to another ship, the *Cap Arcona*, once a well-known German luxury liner that was waiting for its human cargo not far from shore. As I gradually made my way to the point of embarkation in full view of the *Cap Arcona*, British fighter planes attacked the ship. The *Cap Arcona* capsized with thousands of prisoners aboard as we later learned. Unfortunately, very few survived that catastrophe.

In the chaos that followed, I lost Jule; I was not in a hurry to board and placed myself toward the very end of the line. Nearby I noticed a huge pile of weapons and what I thought was food being watched over by a German soldier. Painfully hungry and thirsty I, with my last ounce of strength, dragged myself over and asked the unarmed guard for a slice of bread. In my delirious state, I tried to bite into what I discovered was a bar of soap, which I mistook for bread. He told me to walk over to the nearby British tank that had placed itself between the pile and *Athen*. I once more looked at the soap and the pistol almost next to it. The thought occurred to me to pick it up and shoot the guard only to realize that I would not know how to handle the gun and then there was my dread of seeing blood. I slowly dragged my weak and tired feet toward the tank and saw soldiers in uniforms I did not recognize. I approached the tank and heard soldiers speak English. I begged one of the soldiers for a slice of bread. Instead, he gave me several biscuits. Excruciatingly starved, dazed but free at last. But what now?

Chapter IV

STREET BOY

Emaciated and limping Jews, non-Jews, British soldiers, military vehicles, and army ambulances with Red Cross banners swarmed all over the huge U-boat base, where many of us survivors huddled on the soccer field. The dreaded German SS men in their unmistakable green uniforms, army soldiers, and sailors were nowhere to be seen. I recognized Jewish survivors barely able to drag their feet breaking into naval canteens and helping themselves to whatever was on the shelves and on the floor. I followed suit and barely managed to drag by the handle a familiar looking can filled with substitute marmalade. I dragged it aimlessly, for I had no idea where to go and what to do. Suddenly Jule appeared as if I had willed his return and told me that he with two former *Reichsbahn* inmates had quartered themselves in a clean room in one of the barracks on the base. There I found a clean bunk bed for myself. I sat down and enjoyed the treat created from their bread and margarine and my marmalade. Although afflicted by hunger, I was able to consume only small portions, for my stomach apparently had shrunk considerably. Jule had a much larger appetite but did not stuff himself. Many who did died.

After a short while we heard knocks at the door. Several former Polish inmates, probably capos, entered the room, looked around, liked what they saw, and ordered us to vacate the premises. Despite his dog bites and physical weakness, Jule and the two other roommates read the intruders the riot act and the Poles vanished.

After nearly a week of resting, sleeping, obtaining some food from the British, and meeting former camp buddies with whom we daydreamed about the future, which had appeared bleak, I suddenly collapsed on May 8—the day of the official end of the Second World War in Europe. A British military ambulance rushed me to the town's hospital, where I remained for over a week recovering from general bodily weakness.

I was raving madly from hunger as I was only given small amounts of warm porridge and water several times a day and was told that this was the best cure for my condition. Jule, also hospitalized and suffering terribly from the dog bites, came to visit me. On one occasion when I was delirious, craving food, I remember screaming at him. He just stared at me for some time and left.

After gradually regaining strength, I was returned by a British military ambulance to the base that, in the meantime, had been converted into a huge displaced persons camp. Just before leaving the hospital, I ran into the former Jewish capo, the sadist Kurt Kendziorek, who informed me that he, too, would be released from the hospital later in the day and that I should convey his greetings to our mutual friends. On my return to a large barrack that had been turned into a rehabilitation quarter, I was reunited with a number of former camp inmates whom I immediately informed of the cruel Kendziorek's imminent arrival. As expected, they rapidly organized a welcoming party at which he was clobbered with fists and chairs. Bleeding profusely, Kendziorek was returned to the hospital. That was my last encounter with that walking horror.

Because I was still weak and emaciated, I rested a lot and watched older former inmates play poker and blackjack with German currency. The money, I was told, came from selling cigarettes on the black market in town— cigarettes obtained from British soldiers. I borrowed some money and began to play as well and had beginner's luck.

With loot in my pockets, I, too, began to make my way to town—passing the railroad station that was packed with unarmed, unshaven, filthy-looking German soldiers in unkempt uniforms. What a wonderful sight it was to observe these so-called *Übermenschen* begging us survivors for bread and cigarette butts. In town, I struck up an acquaintance with a German-Jewish gentleman who was married to a German woman. In the foyer of their small apartment, they had a huge dog that allegedly once belonged to Heinrich Himmler. She was very protective of her puppies and did not like me to come close to her and her offspring. On one of my visits, the gentleman sat me down in his living room and asked me questions about my background and wartime experiences, which he recorded on pads of paper.

Those few weeks came to an abrupt end when I once more collapsed in the barrack and was immediately returned to the hospital. The diagnosis was identical to the one rendered before, general bodily weakness. In the course of my recovery, which took more than a week, I was visited by Soviet officers accompanied by their British counterparts. I was urged by the Soviets to return to my homeland, Latvia, where I would be reunited with family and friends. The British urged me to accept the invitation, but I categorically refused, remembering mamma's directive never to return to Latvia but to move west—to England or America. As I later learned, many of those who accepted the offer were sent to deep Russia. Those who did not die there succeeded in returning to Latvia in the 1960s and 1970s.

For reasons unknown to me, the British military ambulance did not return me to the displaced persons camp. Instead, I was driven some five kilometers from Neustadt to a Latvian children's home in a suburb-like setting called Haffkrug. I was well-received as a son of Latvia. Everyone spoke Latvian, sang Latvian songs, danced Latvian folk dances, and talked much about returning to the homeland. Some of the Latvian staff claimed to have known papa and to have been patients of his. The head of the home was a woman who often traveled to Lübeck where, among others, she met with General Dankers, a name that did not mean a thing to me. According to the head of the children's home, the general wanted to meet me, which, fortunately, did not come to pass. (I subsequently learned that he was a notorious anti-Semite.) Yet, despite the warmth with which I was received, I did not truly feel that I belonged in that milieu where the focus was on returning to Latvia. On a day when the head of the children's home was visiting Lübeck, I made my way back on foot to the DP camp in Neustadt; I never returned to the children's home.

Once more I was assigned to the rehabilitation barrack where some new faces greeted me. Jule, in the meantime, had left for Kiel where his wife, Eugenia, had been liberated. As before, the former Jewish prison inmates were busy playing cards and were engaged in black marketeering. With some money left over from my previous success, I resumed playing cards and my luck held.

Some of my older camp buddies talked me into traveling to nearby Lübeck. There, I was told, they would "beat off their troubles" (in the Yiddish: *obschlogen die tsores)*. Not yet fourteen, still weak, and not fully physically mature, I did not yet understand the meaning of getting rid of one's troubles. I thought it meant going to movies and cabarets. Not daring to reveal my ignorance, I did not ask questions and agreed to go with them to Lübeck.

The trip was nothing like what I had expected. A short walk from the railroad station led to a street by the name Clemens, I believe, which had twelve numbered buildings—six on each side of the street. In the doorways and windows of buildings I and IA, stood or sat very attractive young girls inviting us in. My three buddies soon disappeared, and I was left alone to fend for myself. Not really knowing what to do and politely refusing invitations, I walked back and forth on the street, just looking around and trying to quiet my pounding heart. I was struck by the contrast of the women standing in the doorways and sitting in the windows of houses XI and XII with those in I and IA. The former appeared to be in their forties or fifties and terribly overweight. On the return trip to Neustadt, my buddies compared notes and cruelly snickered at me for not having joined them.

I was hiding my shame that I was a sissy. In addition to not being fully grown, I did not yet have pubic hair to speak of. Nevertheless, I agreed to join them on their next outing, even though I was sure that I would not go back. After considerable prodding and teasing, I went along on their next trip. I paid some twenty marks to a young attractive brunette. Showing understanding of my innocence and fright, she patiently and lovingly introduced me to a phenomenally enjoyable experience. Finally, I understood the meaning of *obschlogen die tsores*.

I entered the bordello a child and left feeling a man ready to conquer the world. On the train trip back to Neustadt, I joined my buddies in laughter and in comparing notes. Merriment notwithstanding, deep down I was despondent—wondering whether my mother had survived and where she might be and what I should do without her and papa and Bubi. I sensed that she was alive, but had no clue how to find her in war-torn Germany. Mail service to the United States and England had not yet been restored. With pockets full of money, and even some hidden under my bed in the barrack, I had the urge to strike out and see the world—remembering stories my parents, relatives, and friends had told about their travels.

My frame of reference was, of course, stories I had heard from Aunt Hermine—her stories overshadowed those of my other relatives, including my parents, even though they shared some of the excitement when they were in Berlin frequenting *Kabaret der Komiker*, dinner parties with diplomats, dancing in Paris nightclubs. President Hindenburg insisting that Aunt Hermine, whom he called *meine Garbo* (my Garbo), be seated next to him, and so on. One unforgettable story was of a dinner party with diplomats at the residence of Aunt Hermine and Uncle Xavier, which papa and mamma had attended. The gossip about fellow diplomats was scathing—so much so that nobody dared get up to use the facilities for fear of becoming the target of gossip. Another story I never forgot and mamma told it over and over again related when she, papa, uncles, and aunts were on a trip to Paris from Berlin with some relatives joining from Vienna—they were dazzled by the food at Maxim's. Mamma asked to be shown the kitchen and was horrified to see cats on the counter. I also remembered the brand names of cigarettes aunts Hermine and Tanya smoked—Went Patent and Diplomat. What had also impressed me was Aunt Rita's luggage: on arriving in Libau for a visit, she brought her suitcase that I marveled at because of the beautiful labels of hotels she stayed at in Rome, Venice, Zurich, and elsewhere—places I was sure to visit. Aunt Tanya, who also lived with her husband, Karl, in Berlin noted that Berlin was only a village in comparison with Paris and Paris a village in comparison with London.

Remembering also relatives in Riga chatting about famous distant, musical relatives by the name of Mendelssohn, some of whom lived in Hamburg, it occurred to me to take a train to that city on the pretext of looking for them and seeing the city to broaden my horizons. I arrived at Hamburg's heavily damaged but bustling main railroad station (*Hauptbahnhof*) in late September or early October with a small suitcase. Wandering in and around the station, I was shocked to see the destruction all around me—which reminded me of the destruction of Libau but even worse. I was at a total loss about where to go, what to eat, in short, what to do. Apparently noticing my dilemma at the station, the police approached me and asked for identification papers; I presented those I had obtained in Neustadt's DP camp. After consultations with higher-ups at a police station, I was informed that no such family lived now in Hamburg and was driven to a Jewish children's home in the Hamburg suburb of Blankenese, the city's equivalent of Greenwich, Connecticut. A few child survivors were already there and more were scheduled to arrive. Fellow survivors from Libau Hirsh Dorbian and Joske Genton arrived somewhat later, and I made new friends with the half-Jewish Rolf Redlich who hailed from Berlin, Wolfgang Teichtahl who originally came from Vienna, and Szlamek Bresler from Poland.

On the large estate overlooking the Elbe River stood three solidly constructed buildings and a gatehouse where the estate's caretaker lived with his wife and dog that had belonged to the Warburgs. The owner of the estate, I learned was a banker by the name of Max Warburg, whose family had been dispossessed of the estate by the Nazis; he regained it immediately after the war. Not living there, the family made it available to some Jewish organizations—the American Joint Distribution Committee and British Relief Unit—for the purpose of sheltering a small number of child survivors.

What a relief life on this tranquil and scenic estate was. Originally I was placed in the guesthouse, which was on a small hill, and then was moved to the White House—the main building. The three-story structure even had an elevator. The children's home was administered by the American Joint Distribution Committee. I remember Selma Bendrehmer who hailed from the Bronx proudly wearing a handsome American military uniform, as did Charlotte Rosenbaum, even though she was from Metz, France. Other staff included Egon Fink from the U.S. and Hilda of the British Relief Unit who wore a British military uniform. From time to time, we were visited by an imposingly tall and heavy high Joint official in American military uniform by the name of Rothman.

In the rear of the White House was a barrack where, after morning calisthenics and breakfast, we studied the Hebrew language, Jewish history, the Jewish-Arab struggle over the Holy Land, the geography of the region, and the Jewish-British struggle over Jews being permitted to enter Palestine. Instructors were members of the Jewish Brigade, including Zvi Teier and Ben Yehudah, both in clearly identifiable British uniforms. We were heavily indoctrinated with Zionist ideology and for the need for us to prepare to enter the Holy Land. To reach it, Jews had to evade the British blockade for which we were being prepared mentally and physically by keeping our bodies in shape. This illegal immigration was known as *alijah bet* in contrast to the very small number of legal immigrants who received British certificates—I believe 1,500 a month. To me, who had been brought up in an assimilated home, welcoming the Sabbath was very meaningful. Following the festive meal, we folk danced and sang Hebrew songs, which I enjoyed immensely. Some of the dances called for boys to invite girls and vice versa. I was particularly attracted to Rosi from Czechoslovakia who later left for a kibbutz in Palestine.

The war years coupled with the Jewish education I was now receiving continued to sensitize me to Jewishness. Without becoming religious, including not adhering to dietary laws, I was beginning to be impressed by the richness of Jewish history and my cultural heritage. In short, I was on the way of becoming a proud Jew prepared to fight for the liberation of the biblical Jewish homeland of Palestine.

Even though the material covered in the classes I attended in the barrack near the White House was interesting and influenced my evolving mindset, I, as in Libau, continued to have difficulties warming up to school routine. Unlike most of the kids who listened to the teachers, some of us— out of boredom—shot spitballs at them. Obviously aware of our wartime experiences, they did not get too upset and counseled us on the value of education in general and what it would mean for building a Jewish state.

In Blankenese, I was finally able to scribble some words to relatives in England and the United States telling them that I was alive. My "announcements" were sent by military mail. Addressing my uncle in London, I simply wrote on the envelope Mr. Robert Schwab, London, England, neglecting to indicate that it be sent to Shell Oil where he was one of the directors. Obviously he did not receive any of my semiliterate epistles. Nor did my scribbles reach my cousin Nuta and her husband, Dr. Elie Bruskin, in Hartford, Connecticut. Addressing letters to the husband of my cousin Manya, David Alder, in Salt Lake City, Utah, I ascribed to him the title director of Shell Oil. On receiving several of my announcements, the manager of the Shell gasoline station in Salt Lake City looked up the name David Alder in the phone book. There he was listed as the owner of an insurance agency. On telephoning David Alder, the Shell manager asked whether the name George Schwab meant anything to him. David confirmed that I was his wife's cousin. Thus contact with some of my relatives was established by way of Salt Lake City.

In the meantime mamma, who had been liberated by the Soviets in March 1945 in the small town of Chinov, not far from Stolp and Lauenburg, heard that there were many Jews in Lodz, Poland, and decided to travel there in the summer of 1945 in the hope of obtaining information about my fate. On leaving a trolley car in Lodz, she was recognized by a woman who called out *Frau* (Mrs.) Dr. Schwab. That lady from Libau, Mrs. Dorbian, informed her that I was alive and living in the British zone. Overwhelmed by the news, mother neglected to ask where in the British zone. Back in Lauenburg, where she was working as a nurse in a Soviet hospital, mamma packed her few belongings and with some money in her pockets she made her way to Berlin, a city she knew from visits in the late 1920s and early 1930s. There she rented a room in Schöneberg and visited the American Joint Distribution Committee. Because she was a fair-skinned, blue-eyed blonde unable to speak Yiddish, the Joint assumed she was a German, and on her numerous visits refused her pleas for help to locate her son who had survived four years of hell.

At last one lady at the Joint said that she believed mamma's story and would help her locate her son. On mamma's behalf she sent letters by military mail to our relatives in England and the United States, which they received; this lady of the Joint also succeeded in establishing telephone contact between my mother in Berlin and me in Hamburg. We both cried and promised to look for ways to reunite.

Once a week we were able to speak by way of a military telephone. In the meantime, our U.S. relatives especially began to bombard us with packages containing clothing, cigarettes, chocolate, canned meats, coffee, and so on. In addition, every letter I received by military mail contained a five or ten dollar bill. My cousins wrote that the cigarettes and coffee were not meant for me but to be used by me to exchange for things I needed.

Discipline at the school was not strict. Under the pretext of looking for relatives and seeing the city, I soon made my way to Hamburg's *Reeperbahn*—the amusement part of town also known as the red light district. Bribing a bouncer with two cigarettes, I was admitted to a dance parlor whose name I believe was Alhambra or Alcatraz. There I had a beer or two and, like a man of the world I imagined myself to be, smoked a few American Camel cigarettes that scratched my throat. I could hardly stand smoking, but as a man I felt compelled to do so. To be "with it" was the name of the game. The immersion into a world of pleasure helped me at least temporarily overcome memories of my painful past and sad present. Beneath my happy-go-lucky facade, I was emotionally unsettled. Despite my emaciated looks, which had been aggravated by a recent appendectomy in a hospital in the Altona district of Hamburg, older women invited me to dance—I hardly knew how—and asked me for cigarettes and chocolate, which I dispensed with alacrity. At the time, I was convinced that this dive, where I was always warmly welcomed, was the height of elegance in cosmopolitan, bombed-out Hamburg.

I also hired a driver who claimed that his family owned a factory that produced parts for machines and employed 200 people in Hamburg-Harburg. The owners offered to sell it to me for 10 lbs. of coffee and 40,000 cigarettes. There was no way I could muster the quantities asked for. Nor did I know anything about owning a factory or, for that matter, any kind of business. I was just eager to have a good time, enjoying being a man of the world on the verge of turning fourteen.

At about the same time, Jule reappeared on the scene. He was now the driver for Norbert Wollheim, a German-Jewish gentleman who headed the Jewish community of the British zone. He lived with his wife in Lübeck. On their way to Bergen-Belsen's DP camp, Norbert and Jule would, at times, pick me up in Blankenese and together we would drive to the camp. There I was introduced to, among others, Yosele Rosensaft, head of the large Jewish part of the DP camp. The huge camp also had a Polish district, where it was dangerous for Jews to be seen—especially after dark when some were beaten for no other reason than being Jewish. I was told that Jews were even shot at. As Poles were widely known for their rabid anti-Semitism, that section of the camp was, of course, avoided by Jews during the day as well.

Norbert spoke Yiddish with a German accent that I was able to follow. It was akin to the Yiddish spoken in my part of Latvia, which, as already noted, I had picked up during the war. It was different with Yosele's Yiddish, which I had difficulty following. Both Jule and Norbert understood him and translated his questions about Blankenese, which I answered in a yiddishized German. On one of the return trips, Norbert invited me to stay overnight at his home in Lübeck where I was told I would meet his wife. She was very attractive and they lived in a lovely section of town. On another occasion, Jule brought me to Kiel where he lived with Eugenia in the nearby DP camp at Eckernförde. Our reunion was warm and wonderful.

One day at Blankenese I received an invitation to appear at the Joint's suite on the second floor of the White House. Apparently some staff members were suspicious of my Jewish heritage and thought that I was perhaps a German in disguise. I was asked about my background, wartime whereabouts, and eyewitnesses at Blankenese who could identify me as a survivor, something I was immediately able to provide.

On several occasions during my weekly conversations with mamma, she mentioned that after we were reunited, in the not-too-distant future, she hoped that we would join our relatives in the United States who expected us. On learning that my plan was to go to Palestine, she assured me that, once reunited, we would jointly decide what would be best for us. One day I was informed by Selma and Charlotte that I would shortly be reunited with mother, but because U.S. military vehicles had to obtain permission from Soviet authorities to travel in the Soviet zone of occupation, the reunion could not take place immediately. The month of my departure was finally set for May 1946, and it was Selma in U.S. military uniform who accompanied me in a military vehicle with an American military driver.

In the course of that drive, which took many hours, I began to wonder whether reunification would spell the end of my independence. As a man of the world, I would refuse to live the way I lived back in Latvia—be under control of a strict governess and a relatively strict mother, both of whom would supervise all my activities, especially piano lessons, and, above all, make me to go to school. It suddenly occurred to me that living with mamma might not be such a good idea after all.

At last we arrived at Naumann Street in Schöneberg, a very nice working-class district in the center of Berlin; it was in the American sector and not bombed out. Selma and I walked up the stairs—mamma was waiting at the door. In the hallway, mamma and I exchanged kisses. To introduce the new me, I asked an unexpected first question: What is the nightclub situation like in Berlin? Apparently not startled by the question, mamma replied: It is an interesting question. As a woman alone in Berlin, I could not investigate it. Now that you are here, we will be able to explore it together. Disarmed by mamma, I was satisfied with the answer.

In the coming weeks, mother showed me around the Berlin she knew. I was eager to see where aunts Tanya and Hermine lived in the Charlottenburg district of the city—respectively on Oliver Square and Bleibtreu Street immediately off the Kurfürstendamm, the city residence of Aunt Hermine and Uncle Xavier. The official residence of the embassy was in Krumme Lanke, a suburb. Grandaunt Marta had lived for a while in Grunewald, also a suburb.

Although parts of Berlin were bombed out, sections on the Kurfüstendamm near the zoo were relatively intact. There we went to cafés and movies, sometimes two or three a day. We also visited the Chancellery, which was heavily damaged, and even went into Hitler's office. In the same area near Potsdammer Square and the Brandenburg Gate, we viewed the semi-destroyed ministries of Propaganda and Air Force. Seeing Berlin, especially in the context of a largely destroyed evil capital and a former brilliant city where the devil revealed himself to be a coward and took his own life, was a dream come true. As survivors, mamma and I walked with our heads high and joyfully watched the so-called German *Übermenschen* in rags, begging for food and cigarettes and scrounging in search of cigarette butts. Although we could not bring back those we loved, at least we could see the Germans get what they deserved for their passionate support of Hitler and his fellow criminals.

Between May 1946 and February 1947, the month we left for the United States, mamma convinced me to accompany her to a performance of *Pagliacci* with a world-renowned tenor from Italy whose name, I believe, was Beniamino Gigli. To my great surprise, I immensely enjoyed the performance. The story of the clown, the music, and the singing captivated me. Nearby on the Friedrich Street in the Soviet sector was a well-known café where, according to mamma, a famous gypsy violinist by the name of George Boulanger played Roma music, which, she thought, I would enjoy as well, and she was right. I began to reevaluate mamma and gradually came to the conclusion that she was much more "with it" than I had given her credit for in Latvia.

To help me forget the horrors of the war, including the nightmares that haunted me for years, mamma did not mind accommodating me and my newly awakened passion for exploring what Berlin still had to offer. On the constructive side, she suggested that we visit the DP camp in the Berlin suburb of Schlachtensee. There she had a few friends she wanted me to meet. Among others, we met Max Kaufmann of Riga whom I remembered from Libau and the Riga concentration camp. He was writing a book on the Jewish catastrophe in Latvia and extensively interviewed mother and me about our wartime experiences. It was published in Germany in 1947 under the title *Churbn Lettland: Die Vernichtung der Juden Lettlands* (*Churbn Lettland: The Destruction of the Jews of Latvia.*[1]). On visiting the DP camp's school, I saw a good number of boys and girls of all ages with whom I thought

I could be friends and did not mind to apply. Thus, I was surprised that the head of the school placed me in the highest grade, despite the fact that I was the youngest and still quite illiterate. Nevertheless, I was looking forward to this new experience—learning, of course, was not uppermost in my mind.

Daily during the week I commuted to Schlachtensee. More subjects were taught, and, even though we learned Hebrew, the students were not excessively exposed to preparing for illegal immigration to Palestine. That is not to say, however, that Palestine as a destination for us Jews was removed from consideration. *Aliyah* (Ascent) to Israel was much talked about, followed by talk of leaving for the United States. Mamma, remembering how impressed I was by American movies before the war, reinforced this by not talking about the United States excessively, but inviting me to accompany her to American movies, which I loved, especially those depicting the skyscrapers and other wonders of New York. I also admired the tempo of the people.

To my astonishment, students took school seriously. When once I lobbed a spitball at the teacher, I was reprimanded by him as well as by my peers. Because I was eager to get back to town to continue exploring Berlin with mammy and visit friends who lived in town, especially the Kahns who resided with their young daughter Edith on Friedrich Street in the Soviet sector, I rarely participated in the variety of cultural activities offered at the camp.

Nevertheless, I enjoyed my classmates, especially the three well-dressed older Polish girlfriends who appeared very sophisticated and spoke mostly Polish with one another: Renia Laks, Rachelka Feigenbaum, and Tunia Rybak. Like me, they enjoyed what Berlin had to offer. Considering myself a man of the world, I saw no reason why we should not combine forces and enjoy things together. On several occasions I asked to join them on their exploits in town. I remember Renia, probably seventeen at the time, snickering at this nearly fifteen-year-old jerk, as she called me, with whom she and the other two would have nothing to do socially. Others I became friendly with included Feliks Freidenreich, Roma Lichtenthal, Itzke Lewin, Arnold Kerr, and the Zycer brothers.

School was tolerable. Most enjoyable were class outings to *Sansoucci* in Potstdam, the castle of Frederick the Great, the Berlin zoo in the center of town, visits to museums, and the theater where we saw Schiller's *The Robbers* and Brecht's *Threepenny Opera*. I was overwhelmed by the music.

Although still thinking of going to Palestine, I began to waver under the influence of American movies, my cousins in the U.S. telling us that they had applied for visas and paid the Joint Distribution Committee for second-class tickets for us to cross the Atlantic aboard one of the Queens. In the meantime, parcels of food, clothing, and letters with dollar bills continued to reach us. On several occasions, mamma said that there was no future for us in Europe or in Palestine, where we had no relatives. Repeating from time to time the proverb that "a man without an education [*Bildung* in the German embraces education and culture] is no man," she told me that in the United States I would receive a proper education under normal circumstances. At the same time, mamma promised that once I reached twenty-one, I would be able to decide whether to immigrate to Palestine or not.

Although I was conflicted, New York did exert a strong pull. I also felt responsible for my mamma who, I knew, had suffered enormously during the war. We all had been brought up to always smile "no matter how deep the hurt may be."

Unknown to me, mamma had registered us with the Joint to leave for New York. Late in the year, they notified mamma that we were scheduled to leave early in 1947. We assumed that we would board one of the Queens either in France or in England. The news of embarking from either country was exciting, and my passion for leaving for Palestine receded. I informed my classmates of the latest developments and learned that Renia Laks, her sister Chris Lerman, and brother-in-law Miles Lerman (future chairman of the U.S. Holocaust Memorial Museum in Washington, D.C.) had received identical notices.

As it turned out, the Joint did not honor the tickets purchased for us to sail on one of the superliners. As we later found out, the difference in cost between sailing on a luxury liner and troop transport was considerable, the Joint, in an effort to aid as many refugees as possible in reaching the shores of the United States, lumped us in with the rest. Thus, in late January, together with the Lermans and Renia, we boarded a passenger train for Bremen.

There we were placed in a transit camp only to learn that our trip had been postponed because of a coal miners' strike in the United States. Using this opportunity to visit friends in the Bergen-Belsen DP camp, Mr. and Mrs. Lerman set off, leaving Renia with us. A few days later the news reached us that we were about to embark. Mother, in the absence of the Lermans, took it upon herself to persuade the authorities that Renia had been left in mother's custody and had to sail with us no matter what. After permission was granted, the Lermans returned, breathless, just in time before we all sailed together for New York.

Aboard the troop carrier S.S. *Marine Perch*, Miles and I bunked together, as did mamma and Chris. Renia was placed with a younger group of girls. The stormy weather on the Atlantic caused the ship to roll right and left and the front to descend between the waves that smashed onto the deck—we all were seasick. In tranquil moments, we met on deck. The night before our arrival in New York in February, I was determined to stay on deck all night as rumor had it that the lights of New York were visible for tens of miles out to sea. That was not the case, and so it turned out to be my first disappointment. When we finally docked in the afternoon at a Hudson River pier in the West 40s, I was disappointed once more: the West Side Highway was poorly lit, the street under it looked dilapidated and had hardly any lights, no skyscrapers in sight, and the terminal was cold and not very clean. We parted with the Lermans, vowing to stay in touch, and disembarked.

To our great surprise, we were warmly welcomed by Aunt Ida Schoenberger (née Firkser), whose first husband Bernhard Schwab, had fallen victim to the influenza epidemic that followed the Great War. Her second husband, an American citizen, died while they were on a luxury cruise from the United States to Europe. Also at the pier were Raya (née Taub and a relation by marriage) and Gustav Smith, a German Jew who had come to Libau after Hitler's accession to power and married Raya in Libau. The couple had immigrated to the United States shortly before the outbreak of the Second World War.

The taxi trip on the West Side Highway to Brooklyn was a disappointment as well. I missed seeing skyscrapers and the reputed lights of New York.

The bridge to Brooklyn was spectacular though. But the trip to Brooklyn's Borough Park section was unbelievably dull: no tall buildings, nondescript small houses, and poorly lit streets. Arriving at Aunt Ida's three-story townhouse, we were heartily greeted by Aunt Ida's third husband, a lovely and warm rabbi. His world, as mother told me, was different from mother's and mine as well as from that of Aunt Ida's in Libau and those of her two worldly husbands. We were also welcomed by Aunt Ida's daughter Ellen Licht (née Schwab) from her first marriage, her husband, Barney, and son Bernard. They occupied the second floor of the townhouse. For the next six weeks, the large living room on the main floor did double duty: a living room during the day and our bedroom at night.

That same evening we were visited by Aunt Ida's half-sister Marcia Schwartz, originally from Libau, whom mother knew well, and her husband, Bernie, who was in the clothing business and presented me with an Eisenhower jacket that I proudly wore for years. Aunt Ida's son, Harry Schwab, came over, as did Rabbi Schoenberger's daughter Gerri Samuelson and her husband, Leo, also a businessman. They planned to introduce us to a Manhattan restaurant we would surely enjoy. We also had welcoming letters with enclosures from cousins Manya and Nuta. I soon forgot my disappointments, welcomed the warmth with which we were received, and looked forward to exploring New York.

Note

1. It was reprinted in Germany in 1999, and an authoritative English translation appeared with a foreword by me, and introduction in 2010. An enlarged edition in English appeared in Riga in 2019.

Chapter V
STREET BOY TAMED

The disappointments vanished quickly. New York soon lived up to my expectations—grandiose and exciting and, above all, liberating. Walking up and down Brooklyn's 13ᵗʰ Avenue in the late 1940s was an experience: the enclosed food market was almost the size of Libau's large outdoor and indoor market combined—almost anything could be purchased, including my favorite fruit, bananas. For extra pennies, items still rationed, like sugar, could be had. A bakery on the avenue displayed in the window the most imaginative and delicious-looking tarts with plenty of whipped cream, which reminded me of my boyhood days in Libau and Riga. Another store displayed handsome jackets, suits, and shirts for boys and men. Overall, I was reminded of prewar Libau and Riga, but the scale, of course, was not comparable. It was a world of plenty—anything money could buy. Money, way back in Latvia, had rarely been mentioned. Talking about money was considered bad manners. In New York, on the other hand, I was struck by how much people talked about the greenback. Another experience that overwhelmed me was that I, a lad of fifteen, was listened to by adults and could even engage with them in serious conversation. In Europe, children could be seen but not heard.

The days and weeks following our arrival were socially active. Gerri and Leo Samuelson drove us and Aunt Ida around in their Pontiac showing us Manhattan, which was followed by us going to the Russian Tea Room on

West 57th Street. The authentic Russian cuisine was good. Prior to going to the restaurant, Aunt Ida warned us not to be surprised by the table manners of many Americans, especially the way they held forks and knives. "They stab steaks with the fork and then butcher it with the knife." By 1947, mother and I were no longer starved survivors—but we could not get used to the gargantuan portions that were served in restaurants. Gerri and Leo also invited us to accompany them to Radio City Music Hall in mid-Manhattan, where mother and I were overwhelmed by the Rockettes, the film (*The Boy with Green Hair*, I believe), and the architecture of the cinema. On some weekends we were picked up for the day by Bernie and Marcia who drove us to their home in Laurelton, Long Island. There we met their children, Peter and Marjorie (Cookie). In late spring I would ride Peter's bicycle as much as I wanted. Soon after our arrival in New York, cousin Nuta came to visit us from West Hartford. We had a wonderful and warm reunion— we had not seen her since 1939. When we saw her in New York she was expecting a child; when he arrived, they named him Sam. We talked a lot about the family, wartime experiences, and life in the United States. Not long thereafter we began to take the train from Grand Central Station in New York—an architectural gem—to Hartford. We were met there by Nuta and her husband, Elie, whom we also had not seen since prewar days. In their wonderful and warm home in West Hartford, we met their daughter Eve, and, in due time, baby Sam. Assuming that we were still starved, she introduced us to steaks that were delicious but also enormous. Neither mother nor I were able to finish even half of what was served. Remembering that in mid-winter I had always enjoyed goose in Libau, Nuta promised that we would have it in December.

Back in New York, Gerri and Leo invited us and Aunt Ida to accompany them to the Roxy movie house in mid-Manhattan, which was also an architectural gem. In fact, all the movie houses we visited in Manhattan and Brooklyn were, unlike those in Europe, architecturally most impressive.

Not long after our arrival, we were notified that a group of Latvian Jews residing in the New York region wished to meet us. The gathering was a social event and took place at the Roxy. We had hardly entered when mother was recognized by Selig and Sonia Rosovsky, old family friends who embraced her—we shed many tears. The reunion was moving as was the evening—at which mother met other friends and acquaintances from before the war, including Sonia's brother Boris (born a Rosovsky) and eventually Fira and, in due time, their daughter Olga. At the home of Selig and Sonia on West End Avenue, whom we visited frequently, we met their sons Henry, a future dean of Harvard, and Alex. Henry introduced me to the sights of New York—driving me in his father's Hudson, whose front right seat could recline almost into a bed. Wonders never ceased to pop up in America. Often the Rosovskys also invited us to share the high holidays at their home.

Boris and Fira loved to play gin rummy, which mother quickly learned; for the rest of their lives they played cards with friends almost as often as they used to play *kunken* in Libau and Riga—usually three to four times a week.

In the social whirlwind that followed our arrival, nothing was further from my mind than school. But Rabbi Schoenberger informed me on several occasions that going to school was mandatory. According to the Borough Park school district, I had to be enrolled at New Utrecht High School in the Bensonhurst section of Brooklyn. One day at the end of February or the beginning of March, Rabbi Schoenberger and I took the West End Express to New Utrecht High. Waiting to be interviewed by a school official, I was taken aback.

Unlike my women teachers in Latvia, I was startled to see what I thought were teachers—young and beautiful women with nail polish, lipstick, and fashionable hairdos. At last, I thought, school would be fun and I looked forward eagerly to attending classes—the sooner the better. Upon learning, to my surprise, that they were not teachers but mostly Italian and Jewish schoolgirls, I was even more eager—my raging hormones on the verge of exploding. In European schools, girls were forbidden to use lipstick or nail polish and usually had to wear uniforms or nondescript dresses. Teachers, usually older women, wore drab dresses.

With my disdain for formal learning, the semi-illiterate "know it all" that I was could never have achieved in Europe what I did in the States, namely, finish high school in two years. In the course of my studies, I had several memorable teachers, including Dr. Mintz, whose passion for Shakespeare electrified the English class. He made us memorize soliloquies from *Macbeth*, *Hamlet*, and *Romeo and Juliet* and made us recite them in class. He failed in his endeavors to recruit me for the Communist Party, despite efforts to convince me that my repressive experiences under communism in Latvia were attributable to erroneous interpretation and application by Latvians of the true communist ideals as practiced in the Soviet Union proper. I gradually discovered that this politically naïve academic—who had no clue what he was talking about—was not unique among academics and non-academics in the United States. I immensely enjoyed Miss Finkelstein's history class. She sparked my interest in studying the consequences of the Great War, especially the Treaty of Versailles and how this led to the rise of Hitler and National Socialism and the outbreak of the Second World War. Until then, I had looked at the Second World War through the lens of my experiences and how the Germans were soundly defeated at the battles of Moscow, Stalingrad, Kursk, and El Alamein. In Hebrew class with Mr. Snow (who, every day, entered the classroom in a different suit), I continued to learn the language as my new-found buddies in school were committed Zionists of the Zev Jabotinsky's Revisionist persuasion (as was I) and were deeply immersed in the study of Hebrew and the history of the Jewish people, with an emphasis on the recent past.

The first summer in New York was exciting. For one who grew up along the shores of the Baltic Sea, the ocean's water at Brooklyn's Coney Island and Brighton Beach was almost as warm as a bath. Many of my friends from New Utrecht frequented Bay 15. We had a lot of fun fooling around in the water and on the beach, eating Nathan's frankfurters on the boardwalk and taking advantage of the many exciting rides for which Coney Island was famous. In August I spent close to a month in a summer camp in the beautiful Catskill Mountains—arranged for me by an Association for New Americans, an affiliate of the Joint Distribution Committee.

At Camp Paradise in Fleischmanns, New York, I was particularly shocked by the color war at the end of the summer. Campers and councillors were divided into two opposing teams that in "warlike" fashion competed in games aimed at conquering the opponent's territory. This involved devising tactics for conquest. Perhaps because of my wartime experiences, I could not get over one particular incident: councillors of opposing teams sitting under a tree joking and laughing. I was certain that they discussed the tactics of their respective teams with one another—to me this was treason.

New Utrecht was a hotbed of Zionist activities. I was willingly drawn into joining the Borough Park chapter of the Revisionist Party's youth movement Betar (Brit Trumpeldor). The party and the youth movement had been founded in Riga in the early 1920s; the youth movement subsequently became a feeder for the underground military organization Irgun Zvai Leumi of Israel. Part of the agenda was not new to me: the need to break the British blockade, rid Palestine of the British occupation, and move Jews en masse to Palestine. Toward that end, Betar's task in the United States was to help members strategize on how to achieve the ultimate goal. The Jewish Brigade teachers in Blankenese introduced us to the work of the semi-legal Palmach movement, which was under Haganah's leadership (whose aims were almost identical). I first heard of the underground Irgun movement in Berlin in the context of it having blown up the King David Hotel in Jerusalem in the summer of 1946.

At Betar in Brooklyn, I first heard of the more radical underground movement—the Stern Gang (Fighters for the Freedom of Israel). The goal was basically the same but tactics differed. Palmach did not largely believe in violence—Irgun and Stern did. However, they differed on the use of violence. Irgun adhered to the principle of aiming at military targets and in so doing it forewarned the enemy of what to expect in the hope that they would evacuate civilians. The more radical Stern Gang considered all Brits foes deserving of no quarter—thus ruling out forewarning the foe. Given my past, I inclined toward the Stern Gang. Further, all revisionists, including Irgun and Stern, were committed to a sovereign Palestine to include the territory west and east of the Jordan River. As is well-known, the British separated the eastern part from the western part for administrative reasons and called the eastern part of Transjordan.

Under peer pressure from my new buddies—mostly religious and very religious boys and some girls—I joined the Borough Park chapter of Betar.

Under their influence, I began to frequent synagogues on the Sabbath and on high holidays. On these days I stopped carrying money in my pockets, ceased performing work, including writing, and traveling. But what I had no idea about was the meaning of a kosher household—except for the fact that meat and dairy products could not be mixed. At home or in public, I never adhered to these strictures.

Because I was still at an age at which I felt compelled to teach mother the difference between right and wrong, I reprimanded her for, among other things, not being religious, carrying a pocketbook with money on the Sabbath and on high holidays, shopping, and traveling on the Sabbath. At one point, she gently told me: "Georginka, what you know now I have forgotten long ago." This remark made an impression on me, and I gradually ceased my critiques, Later in life, I always had to smile when my three sons tried to teach my wife, Eleonora, and me what is and is not acceptable.

Early in the new semester, a schism occurred in the Brooklyn chapter of Betar. The controversy centered on whether or not to forewarn the British that an attack was imminent. I sided with those who argued that no quarter be given to the Brits and joined those of my buddies who opted for the Stern Gang. The Stern Gang was known for having assassinated, among others, Lord Moyne, the notorious anti-Semitic British minister resident in Egypt, in 1944, and Count Folke Bernadotte of Sweden in September 1948 for favoring a truncated Israel

At a ceremony in Brooklyn, somewhere in Crown Heights I believe, a neighborhood I was not acquainted with, we swore allegiance by placing the right hand on a German Mauser, a handgun, that was on top of a Hebrew Bible and committed to fighting the British occupation to the very end of it and to fight for the creation of a sovereign Jewish state on both sides of the Jordan River. It was made clear to us that we belonged to an elite movement and that a good number of our activities would be conducted in strict secrecy.

In the course of the year and a half I belonged to the movement, we were indoctrinated by Palestinian Sternists wanted by the British, one in particular who had a hefty price on his head—I believe £5,000.00. In addition to attending indoctrination sessions, chores for beginners included collecting money in *pushkes* (charity boxes) for the liberation of Palestine—even going so far as to extort money from parents (in my case, I was instructed to secure greenbacks from my mother's savings account, I refused)—attending to general chores at our Manhattan headquarters on Second Avenue, and learning how to handle small arms.

An emotionally very disagreeable event took place in the course of my membership in the movement. Near our headquarters on Second Avenue was a small Jewish prayer and study room called a *shtibl*. One day I went to say Kaddish for my father. The rabbi asked me to put on my arm *tefillin* (phylacteries), small cubic leather boxes containing scripture passages. I told him that I did not know how because I was not brought up in a religious home and spent the war years in a ghetto and concentration camps and was, therefore, unable to be prepared for my bar mitzvah. He listened and told me in no uncertain terms that in view of my secular upbringing, my family and I deserved what we had suffered during the war. I walked out of the *shtibl* and for years I refused to enter a synagogue. Nevertheless, I continued to consider myself a proud Jew committed to the realization of a Jewish homeland in all of Palestine.

During this period, another episode occurred that deserves to be recounted. On one occasion a buddy of mine and I were cleaning small arms behind closed doors in my bedroom. Mother, hearing clicks, knocked at the door and asked to speak with me. She asked what we were doing, and, on telling her of our activity, she did not appear shocked and instructed us to immediately close the window so that neighbors not grow suspicious and call the police.

The declaration of the Jewish state's independence in May 1948 notwithstanding, the Stern Gang did not disband. That summer, the noted Wall Street attorney Murray Josephson (brother of the author of the *The Robber Barons*) and his wife made their large summer estate in Lakewood, New Jersey, available to us. There we pitched tents, received some military training in assassination tactics and how to survive in the desert by, among other means, eating snake meat we found on the property (I refused). I was also asked to Hebraize my name from George David Schwab to David Ben

Aron (David [named after my grandfather]) son of Aron (father's name), which I refused as well.

After returning from Lakewood at the end of the summer, we heard that the FBI together with Scotland Yard were on our trail—looking for the military hardware we had acquired and stored somewhere on Manhattan's Lower East Side ready to be smuggled into Israel for use in its struggle against the Arab aggressors. I had no knowledge of how we acquired this matériel nor of the existence of a storage facility until I was ordered to appear there to fetch a carton that I had to unobtrusively dump into the East River. While some of my buddies were caught and arrested—Mr. Josephson managed to arrange their rapid release—I succeeded in evading our pursuers. Some talk was also heard about the need to assassinate Sir Gladwyn Jebb, a British official at UNO in Lake Success, Long Island, because he represented a government inimical to the true interests of Israel as understood by the Stern Gang. I received hints that I, among others, would be ordered to shadow him daily.

In the fall of 1948, about half a year after the creation of the state of Israel, I gradually began to question the new course of the Stern Gang. Now that we had at least one part of Palestine as a sovereign Jewish state, I failed to understand why we did not disband. An argument advanced for its continuation was the uneasiness over the leadership of the new state—especially their lack of interest in acquiring territory that had traditionally belonged to Palestine that, eventually, had become the occupied Jordanian part of Palestine. As noted earlier, abandoning the goal of the two sides of the Jordan River belonging to Palestine—now Israel—was tantamount to treason. Hence, it was concluded, that some of the leaders of the new state of Israel deserved to be assassinated.

To me the mere idea of killing fellow Jews, especially after the millions we had just lost, was abominable. Further, a new element had entered our ideological indoctrination: in addition to the traditional nationalism to which we had been sensitized, our leaders were also beginning to talk about the merits of Marxist-Leninist ideology. As one who not long since had to endure Soviet rule in Latvia—despite the fact that during the war we celebrated Soviet victories and considered the Soviets as liberators—I would have nothing to do with that as well and decided to leave the movement.

Severing ties turned out to be no easy matter. A "court" was convened in a basement of an apartment building on 13th Avenue between 51st and 52nd Streets in Brooklyn. In the presence of my buddies and Israeli leaders still in exile in New York, I was permitted to air my objections. Because I persisted in my decision to leave the movement, the punishment was clearly stipulated: were I ever to divulge secrets of the movement's activities, compromise on the goal of an Israel on both sides of the Jordan River, and approach or even try to associate with former buddies or cellmates, my life would be in jeopardy. This threat did not cause me to lose much sleep.

But, after having devoted all my free time to the movement and becoming intimate with fellow gang members, including falling in love with a cellmate who was in love with another cellmate, separation was a very difficult pill to swallow. It took me more than half a year to recover from the deep hurt engendered by the separation.

Although I did not relate to mother details of my travails, she, I believe, sensed my state of mind and tried to fill it at least in part by encouraging me to accompany her to American movies I had enjoyed so much in Berlin, visiting the Schoenbergers in Brooklyn, Gerri and Leo Samuelson and their son Arthur, also in Brooklyn, the Schwartzes in Laurelton, the Bruskins in West Hartford, and the Rosovskys in Manhattan. To my surprise, I enjoyed the visits because of the fascinating stories they exchanged of prewar life in Latvia and in czarist Russia.

One story I heard on numerous occasions was mother talking with Marcia Schwartz, Aunt Ida Schoenberger's half-sister, about Aunt Ida. It was so horrendous and amusing that it deserves to be related. On one of their transatlantic crossings, Aunt Ida's second husband, a well-to-do American from Milwaukee, developed a blood clot and died aboard ship. Rather than returning the body in a coffin to the States for proper burial, Aunt Ida had him stored on ice in Paris and continued on by train to visit the family in Latvia. Unannounced, she appeared one day at our apartment elegantly attired with a huge hat and a big smile. On being asked about her husband, she related to mother what had happened.

This bizarre story reminded me of another I heard for the first time in New York told by eyewitnesses to Uncle Xavier's funeral in Berlin. Related by Dr. Ernst Neustadt and his wife Tekla (née Remigolski of Riga), his coffin was draped in Chinese and Nazi swastika flags. In the presence of Jewish mourners and members of the diplomatic corps, leading Nazi foreign office officials kissed Aunt Hermine's hand, expressing their deep sympathy on her tragic loss and assuring her that if she were to remain in Germany, all diplomatic courtesies would be accorded to her. She thanked the officials, blew hand-kisses, and said that she will be out of Germany within 48 hours.

The emotional hurt engendered by my separation from my buddies notwithstanding, I performed relatively well at school and graduated from New Utrecht High in 1949. The question of higher education was in the air for some time and I was strongly urged by Rabbi Schoenberger, among others, to attend New York's City College. There was some talk of my going to Brandeis on a scholarship. But, while still a member of the Stern Gang, I had heard that those about to enter college should strongly consider City College, because a Jewish refugee professor, Hans Kohn, taught there. He was considered to be the world's leading authority on nationalism. Although hardly understanding the implications of a quality education, almost everyone I talked to had the highest praise for City College. I took the exceedingly difficult entrance examination and was admitted as a non-matriculated student. To matriculate, I had to earn 30 credits and maintain a B average or 60 credits, maintaining a C average—which I did.

Not until I entered City College did I believe that I would ever become a voracious reader of serious literature in the social sciences and humanities. Although some teachers at New Utrecht High had sparked my interest in Shakespeare and in modern European history, especially Germany's recent past, I did not follow through on these subjects until entering City College.

I immensely enjoyed the art and music appreciation courses taught by renowned art historian Professor Walter Pach and concert pianist Fritz Jahoda. They opened my eyes and ears to the wonders and beauties of Western art and, lo and behold, to classical music (which mother had not succeeded in doing, perhaps because I was forced for many years to play the piano)—especially works in the Romantic tradition. But mainly I focused on ancient, medieval, and modern European history, political philosophy, and political theory.

The two-semester ancient history course taught by Professor Edward Rosen, a world-renowned scholar in the history of science, was an experience. The voluminous readings assigned had to be studied very carefully as students were mercilessly subjected to the Socratic method, according to which precise questions demanded exact answers. Unannounced quizzes were routine. The love I developed for ancient history was further cemented by Professor Haley's class on ancient political theory and Professor K. D. Irani's class on the history of philosophy. Professor Irani's intriguing personality no doubt played a role: a born teacher and a classroom actor, he would persuasively argue, without notes, in beautiful Oxford English one position on an issue and then turn around and argue just as convincingly the exact opposite—leaving students utterly baffled about where he stood. He was probably the most provocative professor I had at City College. Professors Aaron Noland, Oscar Janowsky, and Louis Snyder (whose credentials as a scholar were mixed) furthered my interest in modern European history, contemporary European history, and the history of European imperialism. I never had a course with Hans Kohn. While he was on leave, I took his course with a visiting professor from Columbia University, Professor Wuorinen.

Had I not gone to City College, I don't know whether I would have followed a lifelong path of intellectual adventure. On mentioning my attendance at City College to some fellow survivors, they questioned its relevance and even dismissed such education with the comment that they had acquired diplomas of life. I must admit that there were moments when I was inclined to follow in their footsteps, but mother was always in the background repeating a mantra that, in her view, "a man without an education is not a man." That and thinking about my papa and how proud he would have been made me lean in the direction of pursuing intellectual adventures.

While at City College, Israel continued to loom in my mind, and I became involved with a centrist general Zionist youth movement *Hanoar Hatzioni* (Youth of Zion). Members met in a building on East Broadway on the Lower East Side, where, in addition to learning more of the history of the Jewish people, we socialized, sang Israeli songs, folk danced, and discussed the miracles that were shaping modern Israel. Suddenly, some members were offered a free trip to Israel to attend a leadership training program in Jerusalem that would last about half a year and would also include time to work on a kibbutz and become acquainted with the country through excursions. With mother's consent, I accepted the offer with alacrity and took a leave of absence from City College.

The two weeks aboard the Homeric Line's S.S. *Atlantic* with brief land excursions along the European side of the of the Mediterranean Sea was a lot of fun, as were the evening activities on the high seas: games, social dancing, cabarets, and more. What I found curious and also intriguing was older women flirting with me, but I could not imagine me partnering even for one night with someone of about 40, close to mother's age.

On landing in Haifa, the group was taken by bus to Katamon, a suburb of Jerusalem. There we were ensconced in a villa only yards from a barbed wire fence that separated Jewish Jerusalem from the occupied Jordanian part of the city. The villa, which once belonged to an Arab family, had a toilet that I was convinced was a work in progress only. I complained to our Israeli leader, who smiled and instructed me on how to use an Arab toilet. It was an uncomfortable experience.

The curriculum was standard, and, because much of it was in Hebrew, my skills in the language improved materially. Some of us audited courses at Hebrew University. As one of my interests was British literature, I, from time to time, attended a course taught by a Brooklyn College professor in a barrack next door to the King David Hotel. Sightseeing in Jerusalem and environs was historically instructive. Evenings were usually devoted to social activities, including folk dancing and singing Hebrew songs.

Friday evenings I was usually invited to welcome the Sabbath at the home of Dr. and Mrs. Anushka Eiges and their two children, Gideon and Irit; Mrs. Eiges had been a close friend of mother's in Libau. On these occasions, I was also invited to take a bath in a regular bathtub, which was most welcome. Occasionally on Saturdays I was picked up by Nathan Berkman, son of Oka and Dunia (née Rosovsky), who drove me around Jerusalem and Tel Aviv in his parents' car, pointing out historical sites. On one Saturday, as we were leaving Katamon, an Orthodox Jewish neighborhood, some youngsters began throwing stones at the car. I shouted from the window in Hebrew: "It is forbidden to desecrate the Sabbath"—upon which the stone-throwing increased. Nathan stepped hard on the gas and we were glad to be out of Katamon.

When in Tel Aviv, I stayed overnight with the Berkmans in the north of the city. Dunia loved café life and we frequented Café Roval not far from the Berkman apartment. Because the country was in the midst of austerity, the selection of sweets was wanting. But on one celebratory occasion, Oka and Dunia invited me to accompany them to a restaurant where food was ample, tasty, and, I assume, very expensive. I was told that this is an exception. But when visiting my parents' good friends Owsej and Maschinka Mizroch (owners of Wolfschmidt Vodka and considered to have been the wealthiest Jewish family in Latvia) in their sumptuously appointed villa on top of Mount Carmel in Haifa, I was astonished at the lifestyle. Arriving in typical kibbutz attire, including boots, to be greeted by elegantly dressed people playing cards at different tables and being served a variety of delicious finger sandwiches, cakes, coffee, and tea reminiscent of prewar Libau and Riga. I assume that because of my attire and my half-starved behavior—devouring the goodies as if I had not eaten in years—the hosts invited me to visit their daughter who lived downstairs.

When not studying in Jerusalem, I also visited Jule and Eugenia Goldberg in Tel Litvinski, where I met their son Michael, born in Germany after the war, for the first time. The reunion was wonderful and warm and I stayed with them for several days. Jule had been among the first to come to visit me in Jerusalem. With the group, we undertook numerous sightseeing trips; with a fellow student, we hitchhiked to Eilat from Beersheba on a seltzer truck. We were stuck there for a number of days until we were able to hitchhike back to Beersheba. Having run out of funds on our return trip, I begged for money in Beersheba until we had enough to take a bus to Tel Aviv. Finally, the group was assigned to spend time working on two kibbutzim: Tel Yitzhak, roughly between Tel Aviv and Natanyia, and Hasolelim in the north not far from Nazareth. I could not adjust to kibbutz life.

Assigned to milk cows at Tel Yitzhak but unable to coordinate the motions, I obtained very little milk. The few liters I managed to squeeze out from time to time, I lost most of it to cows kicking the bucket. I was reassigned to the chicken coop. The smell was so incredibly foul that I vomited on more than one occasion. Hence, my job was changed once more and I was sent to the vegetable garden. I rather liked it and was reminded of my experience in the Libau ghetto's garden.

Halfway through our stay, I came to the conclusion that moving to Israel was out of the question for me. What influenced my decision included the prejudices I encountered on the part of Ashkenazi Jews toward North African Jews and, to an extent, also Yemenite Jews. They called them *kushim*, blacks, with all that that implied. To me, the survivor, this was unacceptable. Although not yet twenty and only at the beginning of my intellectual adventures, I, with my sophomoric arrogance of knowing it all, found the intellectual climate in Israel wanting. I also did not want to leave mother behind. She loved the United States.

My decision notwithstanding, I was not going to abandon supporting liberal democratic Israel, a country that was surrounded by foes intent on eliminating it and throwing the Israelis into the Mediterranean Sea. Sovereign Israel had the right to defend itself and needed to marshal its limited resources to survive—and I applauded the United States and American Jews for their support.

I was relieved, though, to embark with the group on the two-week voyage home. The return trip was a lot of fun. A day-long stop in Piraeus enabled us to take the subway into Athens and visit the Acropolis and the university. The ship stopped for several days in Naples, enabling us to visit this beautiful city and nearby Pompeii. From Naples, we took the train to Rome and spent three days visiting historic sites, including the Vatican. We finally hopped on an overnight train for Genoa where we were just in time to catch the liner for New York. Aboard ship, I enjoyed myself immensely—meeting people, attending cabaret evenings, and dancing until the wee hours.

Mother welcomed me at the pier in New York as did my City College friend Adam Kanarek—who was in the company of a most attractive girl. He assured me that there was nothing between them and that the field was open to me. I began to pursue her and found myself in love once more. A daughter of a prominent rabbi, Miriam was extraordinarily bright and was much liked by mother. We hit it off very well until I learned that I was not her only beau. The disappointment affected me greatly and also affected my studies. Nevertheless, I graduated from City College with honors and received a one-year scholarship to continue my studies at Columbia University.

To distract me from my romantic woes, mother, who was staying with a cousin (Rosa Jacobson, née Vovsi, originally from Dvinsk) in Miami, suggested that I visit her and I did. There I was shocked when one day I took a bus and sat down in a seat in the rear of the bus. I had, unknowingly, "desegregated" the bus as the seats in the back were for African-Americans— the seats in the front were for whites. The driver reprimanded me and told in no uncertain terms to move. This was even worse than what I had encountered in Israel and reminded me of when I was prohibited from walking on the sidewalk during the Nazi occupation of Libau.

While still at City College, I immensely enjoyed swimming and not only obtained there my instructor's badge but was also invited by the swimming instructor to assist him in teaching undergraduate students to swim. This enabled me to obtain summer employment as a councillor at Camp Alpine on Cape Cod in Massachusetts, where I met Robert Mundheim, later dean of the law school at the University of Pennsylvania; as a swimming instructor at Camp With A Wind in the Poconos in Pennsylvania, where I directed the girls' side of the waterfront and met a lifelong friend, the camp's physician Vladimir (Wlado) Nenoff. I also worked at camp Berkshire Pines in the Berkshires, where I met another lifelong friend, Sanford (Sandy) Saideman and acquired a new girlfriend, Judy—also a rabbi's daughter.

On returning home one summer, the heat was so unbearable that I decided to become a lifeguard; I qualified after taking a test and was assigned to Bay 15 and 16 in Coney Island. Bay 16 was known as the toughest bay, where muscular Italian boys tried to impress their girlfriends by showing how they could "drown" lifeguards. When one of them feigned distress that appeared legitimate, I quickly swam out to him. The routine was usually the same: as I approached the supposedly drowning man, he would jump on me and try to pull me under. As I had been trained to work under water, I would begin by getting a solid grip around his neck and then his chest and, partially under water, pull him back to shore—where he was greeted by a police officer who led him away. I was subsequently transferred to Brighton Beach's Bay 9—a civilized workstation.

The difference between the bays notwithstanding, lifeguards were considered heroes by girls and women. It was not beyond our noble occupation to take advantage of our lofty status.

Tea in Libau before World War I. From top left: Yette Schwab, Fanny Schwab, Leo Schwab, Lionel (Leiba) Galgut, Amalia Galgut Schwab, David Hirsch Israel Schwab, Henoch Galgut, Sima Romm, Fanny Galgut Romm, Herman Romm, and Dr. Arkady Jacob Aron Schwab

Grandfather David and Grandmother Amalia Schwab

My father, Dr. Arkady Schwab,
served in the Imperial Russian
Army as a physician with the rank
of colonel during World War I

Uncle Robert Schwab with his wife Nellie, London, 1936

Uncle Leo Schwab with his wife, Erna Taub Schwab, Kovno, 1936

Grandfather Jacob Jacobson with grandmother Slova Gerschkewitsch Jacobson

My mother, Klara Jacobson Schwab, with my father, Libau, late 1920s

Mother, father, and brother, Bernhard Boris (Bubi), Libau, early 1930s

Aunt Hermine Jacobson Kinginthai Doshiang. President Hindenburg of Weimar, Germany, considered her "to be his Garbo and had to be seated next to him" at diplomatic dinners, Berlin, early 1930s

George David Schwab is flanked by his mother and Bubi, Libau, mid-1930s

With flowers—George saying farewell to cousin Manya Wainstein who departed for the United States in 1936. Cousin Nuta Wainstein (extreme right) followed her in the late 1930s. To my right: Ette Bojarski

Family dinner at the home of Oskar and Gusti Jacobson Ackermann, Riga, late 1930s. From left: Oskar Ackermann, Aunts Leni and Rita Jacobson, my father, Grandaunt Marta Schifftan, behind her is my Uncle Isidor Jacobson, cousin Ljuba Ackermann, my mother, Aunts Hermine and Gusti

Cousin Samjon (Joni) with his mother, Gusti, Riga, 1937

Bubi with cousin Ljuba at the the Riga beach (Jurmala) in 1938

New Year's party at the home of Roza Schulman in Libau in the late 1930s. My father is the first person on the left in the top row; to his left are: Mr. Hirschman, Mr. Salja Grinberg, Mrs. Esja Mau, Mr. David Mau, my mother, unidentified lady, Mrs. Roza Schulman, Mr. Helman, Mrs Zirinski, Mrs. Taubchen Taub Grinberg, two unidentified gentlemen. In the second row, far right, Mrs. Anuschka Helman, third from right, Mrs. Ettelka Winkler, sixth from right, Mrs. Asja Feiges, eight from right, Mrs. Latter, far left, Mrs. Hirschman. Front row, left: Mr. Jascha Rabinovich

*George, summer 1945, in Neustadt/
Holstein, Germany*

Mother with me and Edith Kahn following a visit to the Berlin Zoo in 1946

On our way to New York aboard the troop carrier S.S. Marine Perch. *From left:*
Mr. & Mrs. Miles Lerman and mother; kneeling: Renia Laks (Chris Lerman's sister) and I

George graduates from New Utrecht High School, Brooklyn, 1949

With mother and Aunt Ida Schoenberger, New York, 1950

George begging in Beersheba, Israel, 1951

George serves as a lifeguard at Coney Island and Brighton Beach, Brooklyn, 1952

George receiving his MA from Columbia University in 1955. Attendees, from left: Helen Usiskin, mother, Maya Yardney, and Marcia Schwartz

Farewell to my studies in Paris in 1958. From left: Dr. Hans-Joachim Arndt, Denise Rendu, George, and Pamela Moore

Mother and I in a gondola in Venice in 1959

Mother and I attending a Latvian Jewish Memorial Service organized by Max Kaufmann in New York in 1960

In 1962, I attended an exhibition of noted Jewish stamp collectors who had perished during the war. I am standing in front of a photo of Bubi, reading about him as a collector

Eleonora Storch, my wife-to-be

Engagement party in Stockholm in 1965. From left: Hilel (Gilel) Storch (Eleonora's father), Mrs. Ragnar Martinsson, Anya Storch (Eleonora's mother), George, Eleonora Storch, Ruth Storch Molander (Eleonora's sister), and Marcus Storch (Eleonora's brother)

Eleonora on Marcus's lap, Ruth, George, Jan Molander (Ruth's husband)

For the unorthodox ways that Gilel Storch used to save Jews in the last months of
World War II, he earned from the British foreign policy establishment the epithets
"stateless," "arrogant," "lunatic"

With Rabbi Joachim Prinz—who had just married us—at his home in New Jersey in 1965

Wedding celebration at the home of Rabbi Prinz. From left: Lydia and Dr. Vladimir Nenoff, Sanford Saideman, Esq., Nuta Bruskin, Edythe and !sac Meilach, Dr. Elie Bruskin, groom George breaking the glass, Eleonora and Rabbi Prinz

The Schwab triple treat: Claude, Solan, Clarence, New York, 1969

From left: Clarence, Solan, and Claude at the wedding of cousin Jessica Reichman to Howard Deutsch in Johannesburg, South Africa, 1973

Grandfather Gilel, whom the children adored and vice versa, Stockholm, 1973

From left: Solan, Claude, and Clarence at the Lycée Française de New York in 1974

Visiting cousins James (Jimmy) and Dr. Barbara Lau in Ambach, Germany, in 1978. From left: Solan, Claude, Clarence

Barbara Lau, second from right, visiting us in Megève, France, 1980.
Photo by Jimmy Lau

Bar Mitzvah boys: Clarence, Claude, and Solan, New York, 1982

Clarence with degrees from Columbia and Harvard

Claude with degrees from the University of Pennsylvania and Columbia

Solan with degrees from the University of Chicago and Georgetown Law

Claude announcing "time to party"

Party

From left: Dr. Harold Proshansky, president of CUNY's Graduate Center, and Elie Wiesel

From left: Cousins Lenore Gladstone Levin, Gerry and Myra Sutin, and Aaron Levin, all are doctors

Marriage of SoIan to Lisa Davis, Las Vegas, 1999

Marriage of Clarence to Pamela Haas, New York, 2000

Claude, marriage to Diana Han, Beverly Hills, 2017

Family portrait with my sons, daughter-in-law, and grandchildren. From top left: Clarence, George, Claude, Zachary, Pamela, Eleonora (Ellie), Solan, Michael, and Jonah, New York, 2011

Noah at 2½ in our dining room, New York, 2019

June 28, 2020 Noah aged 3 welcomes sister Ava Eleana aged 2 days

Professor Hans J. Morgenthau, founder and first chairman of the National Committee on American Foreign Policy (NCAFP)

George Schwab with President Richard Nixon at his home in New Jersey

*In 1987, George Schwab presented the NCAFP's inaugural "Humanitarian and Peace Award"
to Prof. Elie Wiesel. NCAFP president Ambassador Francis L. Kellogg is looking on*

NOW ONLY

$1.00

DAILY ◉ NEWS

00   http://www.mostnewyork.com   NEW YORK'S HOMETOWN NEWSPAPER   Sunday, A

EXCL

NORTHERN IRELAND ACCORD

BEHIND THE DEAL

A small group, including CUNY history professor George Schwab (c.), smuggled Sinn Fein leader Gerry Adams (r.) into New York in 1994 under the alias Schlomo Brezhnitz. Together with John Hume (l.) a member of a moderate Catholic politicall party, they negotiated at the Waldorf-Astoria.

Jim Dwye reveals how the seeds of peace were planted i New York

George Schwab is flanked by John Hume and Gerry Adams, New York, 1994

132

From left: William J. Flynn, Gerry Adams, George Schwab, and Thomas J. Moran, New York, 1994

From left: Ambassador Angier Biddle Duke, Rev. Ian Paisley, Dr. Frances Degen Horowitz (president of CUNY's Graduate Center), and George Schwab at a meeting about the Northern Irish peace process, New York, 1994

Eleonora Schwab and David Rockefeller

With Ambassador George F. Kennan and Dr. Henry A. Kissinger

With His Majesty King Hussein of Jordan, New York, 1995

H.E. Jiang Zemin, President of the People's Republic of China, welcoming George Schwab, head of the NCAFP delegation, Beijing, 1996

With Ambassador Abba Eban

With Secretary of State Colin L. Powell at the Department of State in 2003

From left: William J. Flynn, Sheila Johnson Robbins, Edith and William M. Rudolf, George Schwab, and Kenneth Bialkin, Esq.

From left: George Schwab, Jo Carole Lauder, Happy Rockefeller, General David Petraeus, and Sheila Johnson Robbins, New York, 2009

With Sheila Johnson Robbins at a Nobel festivity dinner in Stockholm in 2009

At a reception at my home: From left: Mikhail Baryshnikov, President Vaira Vike-Freiberga of Latvia, and George Schwab

With President Martti Ahtisaari of Finland

H.E. Ma Ying-Jeou, President of the Republic of China, welcoming George Schwab, head of the NCAFP delegation, Taipei, 2013

With President Bill Clinton

With Jo Carole Lauder on the occasion her receiving the NCAFP's inaugural "Award for Excellence in Cultural Diplomacy and International Engagement," New York, 2016

To George,
Movements for real and lasting change are sustained by the relationships we build with one another.
Thank you for your support.

Michelle Obama

Greetings from Michelle Obama

With Vice President Joseph R. Biden, Jr. on the occasion of his receiving the NCAFP's Hans J. Morgenthau Award, New York, 2017

At the Jewish Community Center in Riga on the occasion of the first reunion of Latvian Jews in 1993. From left: Sanford Saideman, Joan Peters, Mona Schlachter, George and Eleonora Schwab

The Hon. Per Ahlmark addressing the Jewish community of Riga in 1993; Dr. Gregory Krupnikov served as translator

George speaking to survivors, descendants, and friends at Libau's Lighthouse Memorial where Libau's Jews, including my father, were murdered in July 1941

At the Walk of the Righteous, which leads to the mass graves of Skede near Libau

The menorah at Skede commemorates the murder of most of Libau's Jews in December 1941

Addressing survivors, descendants, and friends at the Skede Memorial

With President Vike-Freiberga on the occasion of her dedicating the Eleonora Schwab Library, Riga, 2001

Lunch at the Sergejs Zaharjins estate in Libau. From left: Barbara Lau, Lola Garvin, Jelena Zaharjina, Sergejs Zaharjins, me, Sheila Robbins, Selwyn Haas, and Ilana Ivanova

Sheila Robbins' immediate family. From left: Page Sargisson Robbins, Tobey, Sheila, Harvest, and Peter Robbins

Family photo taken in Libau in 2011. From left: Dr. Peter Schwartz, Bari, Marjorie, and Lori Rosenstreich, Barbara Lau, I am standing behind her, to my left are Gunilla Storch, Arlene Schwartz, Sheila Robbins, Jimmy Lau (kneeling)

At the Zaharjins' estate in Libau. From left: Svetlana Zaharjina, Sheila Robbins, Ilja Segals, me, Sergejs Zaharjins, Alex Zaharjins, Nikita Vorobjov (child), Valerijs Zaharjins, Irina Zaharjina, and Sergejs Binkovskis

Saying farewell to my Schwab grandparents at the Jewish cemetery in Libau

פ"נ
הורינו הוקרים
ישראל הזו הירש האשה מלשה חנ
בר אברהם בכר ד' ישראל
שוואב
נפטרן אב חר פא נפטרה הכא סלן ורדצר
תנצבה
Hier ruhe unsere unvergessliche Eltern
Malke Chin a u Israel David Hirsch
Schvab

Chapter VI
INTELLECTUAL & OTHER COLUMBIA ADVENTURES

What prompted me to accept a scholarship to study political science and history at Columbia University? I had heard Professor Franz Neumann speak about Nazi Germany at City College and had been deeply impressed. Upon entering Columbia in 1954, I learned that he had just died in an automobile accident in Switzerland. Nonetheless, I continued my intellectual adventure at this august institution.

Although City College had prepared me well for graduate studies, the two institutions were not alike. City College then was an undergraduate institution; Columbia was an undergraduate and graduate center of learning. Students at both institutions were highly motivated and competitive.

Intellectual discourse between and among City College students was more often than not boisterous and at times even raucous, whereas at Columbia discussions and arguments, though no less intense, were gentlemanly. At City College how students dressed often bordered on the garish, while at Columbia dress was, on balance, understated and quite conservative. The difference between the majority of City College and Columbia students can be described as the former coming largely from working- and lower-middle-class economic backgrounds, whereas the latter came from middle-, upper-middle, and upper-class economic backgrounds. Both institutions attracted a good number of European students who had

150

come to the United States immediately prior, during, and right after the Second World War. Unsurprisingly, the European students gravitated toward one another because of their more cosmopolitan backgrounds.

I preferred the general atmosphere at Columbia to that of City College. I made new friends, including Jeanine Parisier and her husband-to-be Roland Plottel; Hessy Levinsons, whose parents had been patients of my father in Latvia, and Hessy's husband-to-be Earl Taft; Klaus Pringsheim, nephew of Thomas Mann; Evelyn Hirsch; James (Jim) Barros; and Macha de Gunzburg, among others. A number of City College friends had also entered Columbia, including Alex Groth, Sam Backer, and Michael Rywkin. And, not to forget my old friends who did not attend Columbia but with whom I remained close, including Adam Kanarek, Renia and Victor Gelb and Olga Rosovsky. With the exception of Roland, Earl, Jim, and Victor, all were European-born.

With Neumann dead I was assigned to Herbert Deane—a student of Neumann's—as my political science adviser. His Ph.D. dissertation had dealt with the political ideas of Harold Laski; it won him the prestigious Clark F. Ansley Award for 1953.

To qualify for my master's degree, I had to select a topic for my M.A. essay. Because of my knowledge of German, Deane suggested that I research and write on a highly controversial German political and legal theorist and constitutional lawyer, Carl Schmitt—a name I was not acquainted with. According to Deane, Neumann had talked a lot about this seminal thinker in his lectures and seminars. Because no scholarly works had appeared about his ideas in the English-speaking world and no English translations of his works were available, little was known about him. Deane went so far as to suggest that such an essay could serve as the basis for my Ph.D. dissertation. My efforts, he said, would be pioneering.

Before committing myself to researching and writing about Schmitt, I began to read in the secondary English literature whatever I could find about him. The impression I obtained from Neumann, William Ebenstein, and others was negative—namely, that Schmitt was brilliant but void of character and that he had paved the way for the Nazi conquest and was a vitriolic anti-Semite. Despite some positive references to him by Hannah Arendt, Clinton Rossiter, and Frederick Watkins, I followed Neumann's and Ebenstein's assessment of Schmitt. They reinforced the negative sentiments I harbored about the German people for their enthusiastic embrace of Hitler.

Negative comments notwithstanding, and the considerable amount of reading I had already done on the Third Reich while at City College bolstered me—I felt reasonably confident that I could write about Schmitt's ideas. At that time, I did not understand the complexity of the issues that had led to the demise of the Weimar Republic. Stated succinctly, I totally missed the critical interplay of German history, political and legal theory, and constitutional law in working toward an understanding of the Weimar Republic.

Not comprehending a considerable amount of what I had read and eager to obtain my M.A. degree, I decided to focus on Schmitt's political theories. With this in mind, I went to see Deane and informed him accordingly. He agreed. While reading sections of my work, he encouraged me to go on and from time to time continued to mention that it is a good foundation for a Ph.D. dissertation. I simply nodded.

In the course of two semesters I completed 30 credits and wrote the master's essay that, in my opinion, was not worth reading. The Columbia graduation ceremony in 1955 was impressive. The ceremony was attended by my mother; my relative Marcia Schwartz; Helen Usiskin, a close family friend from Libau, flew in from London; she had left Latvia before the outbreak of the war to study in England; and my then-girlfriend Maya.

I finally agreed to continue with my studies. On informing my mother accordingly, she was overjoyed and said how proud papinka and Bubinka would have been of me. Papi would often say to mother that his university years were among the best of his life. Thus, more than halfway through with my coursework, I applied for and was accepted to Columbia's Ph.D. program in political science.

To proceed with my doctoral studies, I had to take an additional 30 credits. I felt this was surely worth it—in my two years at Columbia, I had learned much. My love for classical Greece had been deepened by Professor

Martin Ostwald's seminar on Plato and Aristotle. It did not take me long, however, to draw a parallel between the Greeks of the Classical period who made a distinction between Greeks and non-Greeks. Greeks of that time considered those from the east as human beings of a lesser breed, simply because they did not live the Greek way of life: within the confines of a polis or city-state with all that that implied—especially Greek males being able to govern themselves. This reminded me of the extent of the Nazi distinction between *Übermensch* and *Untermensch*. Having lived under two totalitarian systems, I now developed a deeper understanding of the political workings of such systems by studying Hannah Arendt's *Origins of Totalitarianism*, Franz Neumann's *Behemoth*, and Lenin's *"Left-Wing" Communism: An Infantile Disorder*, among other works. From Professor Michael Florinsky's lectures, I learned of the workings of command economies in totalitarian one-party states. Going beyond this topic, I immensely enjoyed the lectures on economics by Professor William Vickrey—who went on to receive a Nobel Prize in economics. Though I did not much understand the graphs he enjoyed drawing on the blackboard, he was a charismatic lecturer who enjoyed teaching and showing off his vast knowledge of economics. In short, he was an actor. I also learned much from Professor Lindsay Rogers about the British parliamentary system, which I began to admire. He also instilled in me an appreciation of the great debates that took place in the British Parliament, especially those between Disraeli and Gladstone in the nineteenth century. On my own I read and reread the six volumes of *The Second World War* by Winston Churchill. The political theories of Hobbes, Locke, and John Stuart Mill were well-taught by Professor Deane; these thinkers deepened my intellectual understanding and appreciation of liberalism.

Time was rapidly approaching for me to select a topic for my doctoral dissertation. To continue with Schmitt or not was my dilemma. Given my wartime experiences, the negative references to him, and still not fully understanding the history of the Weimar Republic, as well as often being puzzled by the discrepancies between what Schmitt wrote and what I read about his ideas were factors that militated against my committing to years of research and writing about Schmitt and his ideas. Stated succinctly, I was not even sure that I was intellectually equipped to handle the subject that involved so many disciplines.

But Deane persisted. We needed, he told me again, a scholarly work on Schmitt's ideas, and, because I had already invested so much time in Schmitt, I would make an important contribution to scholarship by introducing him to the English-speaking world. He even went so far as to suggest that I visit Schmitt in Germany and that Deane would write a letter of introduction. To me the idea of visiting a repulsive character was beyond the pale. I was even thinking that this Nazi devil could, with his cohorts, engineer my being murdered. I tried to put the whole issue out of my mind and continued to busy myself with my studies and social life.

By May 1956, I was finished with my coursework and began to seriously prepare for the Ph.D. oral examination. In addition to the usual amount of reading necessary for the orals, Deane kept prodding me to continue to read and reread Schmitt's works. Obviously sensitive to the question of anti-Semitism, I failed to encounter any indications of it prior to 1933. On the contrary, he had much praise for a good number of Jews, including Hugo Preuss, a father of the Weimar Constitution; and had dedicated his seminal work on constitutional theory to his Jewish friend Fritz Eisler who had been killed in the Great War. Because of the anti-Semitism that crept into his writings after 1933 (which bordered on the obscene by 1935 and 1936) and then his sudden softening of his anti-Jewishness for reasons I did not know at the time, I concluded that his anti-Semitism was opportunistic—an expression of ambition made to advance in the Third Reich. Deane persisted and I eventually acquiesced.

As I continued to read Schmitt, what also became clear to me was that paying him a visit might actually prove interesting and valuable. I loathed writing letters, but I finally did write to introduce myself. He immediately replied and invited me to pay him a visit. He inquired when I planned to arrive and about the thrust of my dissertation—which was the development of his political ideas between 1921 and 1936. Why 1936?

Among other questions I intended to answer in my thesis were why Schmitt's critique of the Weimar constitution was materially different from those of others who, unlike Schmitt, had not been demonized after the war?

Why did his anti-Semitic outbursts recede after 1936? Why did he, after 1936, with one major exception, begin to focus his attention on international relations and international law? Hence, I thought I had a compact period to deal with and would be able to answer some fundamental questions—and contribute to scholarship. Deane was pleased and gave me the green light to proceed.

I left for Europe on the French liner *Île de France* in the late spring of 1957. From the Hotel Lutetia on Paris's Left Bank, I was centrally located in relation to museums and other cultural institutions that I was eager to visit and, above all, to locate a relative of ours, Alexander Scher, who, with his wife Rosa (née Berlin, a cousin of Isaiah Berlin), lived before the war on *rue de la Faisanderie* on the Right Bank. The concierge informed me that they had been deported to Auschwitz and that their belongings had been confiscated by the Nazis. I was saddened, though not surprised, by the news.

From Paris I traveled to Berlin by way of the Soviet zone. There I visited the documentation center in Grunewald to study Schmitt's Nazi file. It contained next to nothing—the place and date of his birth and the date he joined the Nazi Party (May 1, 1933). Before departing for Plettenberg in Westphalia, I explored the rebuilt Berlin; evenings I spent time in one of the hot nightspots, the "in place," the Resi bar. Every numbered table was connected to a pneumatic mailing system via which one could send messages inviting a young lady at table 18, for example, to meet me on the dance floor and, if all went well, perhaps for a nightcap afterwards.

I then moved on to the industrial town of Plettenberg via Cologne and Hagen. There I registered at the small Hotel Ostermann and was assigned to the largest and best room—which, nevertheless, lacked a private toilet and a bathroom. My room overlooked a nearby railroad crossing with trains passing by almost non-stop day and night. The noise of the trains, the ringing of the railroad gates, and impatient German car drivers honking when gates did not open quickly after a train had passed were unbearable. I did not anticipate remaining in Plettenberg for very long, so I thought that I could take it. As soon as it became evident that I would have to remain longer, I moved to the Hotel Deutsches Haus.

It had previously been agreed that I would come to Schmitt's residence at 4:30 in the afternoon, which I did with my heart pounding. The door to the small villa was opened by Schmitt's housekeeper/secretary Anni Stand, who invited me into the warmly furnished living room, which also had a piano. Some minutes later the door opened and Professor Schmitt walked in. His appearance surprised me. About 5 feet 3 or 4 inches with a stern face and lips almost invisible when he was not speaking, he was dressed in a suit and tie. He reminded me more of a shrewd but laid-back Wall Street millionaire or a lawyer rather than a nervous, chain-smoking Paris Left Bank intellectual. After a few welcoming remarks in English, he switched to German and invited me to join him for coffee and cake.

Although I tried to pay close attention to what he was saying and the questions he was asking about the thrust of my dissertation, I could not help but think of him as a devil and me sitting at his feet. Following coffee and cake, Schmitt invited me to accompany him on his afternoon constitutional in the hilly terrain surrounding Plettenberg. Was this a trick? Am I about to be abducted? Will the Germans finally get me? I was not so much concerned about my fate, but leaving my mother behind with all that she had been forced to endure troubled me to no end.

As it turned out, the almost daily afternoon walks we took were harmless and unusually fruitful intellectually. In my nearly annual summer visits thereafter, I learned more from him about political and legal theory, German constitutional law, and international relations than from anybody else. Insights I obtained on ancient, medieval, and modern history were equally astonishing—as was his knowledge and understanding of the great minds of Western political thought, including Plato, Aristotle, Machiavelli, Hobbes, Locke, Rousseau, Hegel, Marx, and Lenin. He was also a lover of classical music, of German Expressionist art (he collected the works of the painter Werner Gilles), an admirer of Shakespeare, Melville, Schiller, and Goethe. If ever there was a Renaissance man, Schmitt was it in my opinion. Still, I could not comprehend how a man with his vast knowledge and high culture could stoop to the level to which he had regarding Jews after Hitler's accession to power.

In my mind, I battled on how best to rationalize my association with this man. The easy answer was that I was doing research for my Ph.D. dissertation and had followed my adviser's suggestion that I visit and interview Schmitt. I also rationalized that, despite his past, the learning and insights I gained were some very small compensation for what I had endured during and after the war. But once I became fully convinced from my studies that his anti-Semitism was not racial in the Nazi sense but derived from Catholic and Protestant teachings that afflicted much of the Christian world. I was also challenged and encouraged by the thought that I would be making a major contribution to scholarship

On the first series of walks, we discussed the scope of my dissertation. Schmitt tried to convince me to confine my research to the pre-Nazi period. Not only would I, according to him, learn much about the Weimar constitution and the Weimar state, which would shed new light on the period in general, I would also dispose of the widespread myth about him as a gravedigger of Weimar and reveal, instead, how he had hoped to thwart Hitler's rise to power. Treating the subject from this perspective, he assured me, would constitute a vital contribution to scholarship.

I opined that this would not be acceptable to Deane and reiterated that my research would have to include the Nazi years between 1933 and 1936. It was not yet entirely clear to me why, after 1936, he had suddenly ceased to deal with constitutional law, legal and political theory, and largely ignored the Jewish issue and turned his attention to international law and relations. I asked him why his attitude toward Jews had changed, insofar as his attacks had become less vitriolic after 1936. He said that all these issues would become clear if I were to confine myself to the pre-Hitler years. Schmitt warned me that the Nazi period is so controversial that I might become embroiled in arguments that could have negative consequences for the fate of my dissertation, for the future of my academic career, and, perhaps, even for me personally.

I politely dismissed his concerns. Not in my wildest dreams could I imagine that I would in any way be compromised by submitting a Ph.D. dissertation written in the scholarly tradition of Leopold von Ranke—a tradition in which I had been trained at City College and at Columbia. Unable to dissuade me, Schmitt finally looked at me seeming to think that this poor American Ph.D. candidate is truly naïve.

What soon became clear to me was that were I to wish to research and write a major scholarly work on Schmitt's ideas, I would have to change my travel plans. Because of my thirst to see much of Europe, my original plan had been to stay in Plettenberg for about four or five days followed by visits to Copenhagen, Munich, Salzburg, Vienna, and Venice before settling in Paris to study French for my second language examination—a requirement for the doctorate. I changed my travel plans by simply extending my stay in Plettenberg for several weeks and going to Paris about two weeks later than anticipated.

On rereading the works of Schmitt, I realized that to truly understand the framework within which he had operated, I must immerse myself in Weimar constitutional issues and legal theory—something I had studiously avoided for my master's essay.

To my surprise, a topic I was drawn to centered on the interplay between legal methods of acquiring political power and illegal methods, that is, by constitutionally prescribed means in contrast to capturing power by extra-legal means, including violence. In crushing the Weimar Republic, Hitler, after his release from prison, had employed both strategies simultaneously, just as Lenin had prescribed in *"Left-Wing" Communism: An Infantile Disorder*—in which he castigated so-called revolutionaries who were unwilling to combine both methods. The issue of legality and illegality with all that that implied—especially in relation to how the Weimar constitution could be amended or, perhaps, even abrogated and how to respond to material challenges—engendered heated controversies among Weimar constitutional experts, with Schmitt deeply immersed in these disputations.

While engrossed in conversation with Schmitt on our walks, I also took note of the stream of accomplished intellects who visited him and with whom I also became friendly, including, among others, Johannes Gross, Rüdiger Altmann, Hans-Joachim Arndt, Hans Barion, Ernst-Wolfgang Böckenförde, Joseph Kaiser, Roman Schnur, Helmut Quaritsch, Ernst Hüsmert, and the

German Expressionist painter Werner Gilles—some of whose works I have since acquired. All the fascinating intellectual discussions to which I was privy centered mostly on Germany's recent past and on the Bonn Republic—not a word about the Jewish tragedy. As Ernst Hüsmert explained to me at many of our breakfasts where he introduced me to drinking *Stainhaegers*, a sort of German vodka, Germans are a well-brought up and cultured people who would never kill millions of people as alleged. As I was quick to learn, Germany had not yet begun to face its Nazi past. Whenever I tried to draw Schmitt into a discussion of the millions of Jews who had been murdered, he did not believe this to be true, but were it so, he said, it would be nothing short of "criminal."

From my initial conversations with him on this topic what emerged was: with the exception of Leo Strauss, he spoke bitterly of his former friends and students who had fled Germany. According to Schmitt, without understanding what it means to live in a totalitarian one-party state, those like the noted Catholic intellectual of Jewish descent Walter Gurian, the Jewish left-wing Marxist litterateur Otto Kirchheimer (as Schmitt liked to call his former student), and Franz Neumann more so than his jealous colleagues at the University of Berlin and elsewhere in Germany gradually began to savagely attack him after he joined the Nazi Party on May 1, 1933. Hence, he felt, the door had closed to him and his family on the possibility of fleeing Germany. By exposing his pre-1933 past—including his association with Jews and Marxists, his opposition to the Nazis' gaining power, his understanding of race (which had nothing to do with the Nazi conception), and his deep involvement with Catholicism—Schmitt was convinced, he told me, that his life was in danger and, therefore, he had to show the Nazi leaders his commitment to the new Germany. Moreover, he was certain that these, among other charges, had led to the vehement attacks against him by the SS publication *Das Schwarze Korps* (The Black Corps) in December 1936—of which I knew nothing. The publication warned him in no uncertain terms to cease parading as a Nazi ideologue and accused him of opportunism—a conclusion I had already reached myself in New York, which was reinforced after speaking with him and reading *Das Schwarze Korps*.

The attacks, especially the warning that his life might be in jeopardy, prompted him to abandon addressing issues of legal and political theoretical and constitutional law in favor of addressing issues of international law and international relations. In regard to anti-Semitism, I learned from Ernst-Wolfgang Böckenförde that his Slavic wife was a notorious anti-Semite and that she may have infected him. This was confirmed to me by other of his friends.

On asking why Schmitt did not have himself denazified after the war, he had strong words for what he considered to be a sham. According to him, in exchange for a bribe, a clean bill of health could be obtained in regard to one's Nazi past. Many former prominent Nazis, including former university colleagues, were now running around in Germany waving *Persilscheine* certificates (so-called after a well-known German detergent) and occupying high positions in the government, universities, and businesses and laughingly denouncing Hitler's Third Reich. He also had harsh words for Chancellor Konrad Adenauer for having hired a former Nazi, Hans Globke, an author of the notorious Nuremberg Laws of 1935. Schmitt said to me that he did not want to have anything to do with this circus and was perfectly content to live on his pension in his ancestral home.

Our daily routine was suddenly disturbed when I learned from Schmitt that his only child, Anima, was about to marry a professor of political science and law at the University of Santiago de Compostella in Spain. Anima had also informed her father that she would shortly arrive for a visit as would her husband-to-be. Neither Schmitt nor Anni was enthusiastic about Anima marrying a man of an entirely different culture and living so far away in the north of Spain. Their antipathy was exacerbated by his looks—he was very short and extremely slim. People in Plettenberg I was given to understand by Anni and Ernst were asking: "Why not this American Schwab instead of the Spaniard?" Schmitt, too, hinted that this would be a desirable outcome. At that time he did not yet know that I was Jewish.

Simultaneously, I was courted by the corpulent owner of a kiosk that I often frequented for a wonderful tomato and chicken salad on a roll and a Coke. She was eager for me to become involved with her plump daughter. For female companionship I did not look to either daughter.

All in all, my situation in Plettenberg became so bizarre that I could not help but think of the great German philosopher Hegel who once noted that at times it is difficult to distinguish where tragedy ends and comedy begins. Hence, I decided to leave Plettenberg but promised to attend Anima's wedding in Heidelberg in December.

My Czech-born college friend Fred Jelinek, an engineering student, had traveled to Plettenberg via Paris; met Schmitt and Anni; and then the two of us left by train for Copenhagen and from there for the music festivals in Salzburg and sightseeing trips to Vienna and Venice. Everywhere we went we had a wonderful time: Tivoli in Copenhagen, swimming in Klampenborg, visiting Hamlet's castle, swimming in the Adriatic, and meeting Hillary—a strikingly attractive woman from London who was visiting Venice.

An amusing encounter in Vienna deserves mention. On leaving the Opera late one evening, Fred and I decided to take a stroll on Kärtner Street toward the Dom. We had hardly turned the corner when we were accosted quite aggressively by elegantly attired prostitutes in their twenties and early thirties trying to get us to purchase their services. As we expressed no interest, they even offered their services for love and not money. On asking one what she did during the war, she proudly answered me in wonderful and warm Viennese: *Ich habe mich zum Hradcin heraufgefickt* (I fucked my way up to the Hradcin)— the Prague Castle that was the headquarters of the SS during the Nazi occupation of Czechoslovakia.

Fred and I parted in Venice. He returned to the States and I proceeded to Paris. Of course, I went straight to the Latin Quarter and rented a room in a small hotel on *rue* Racine at the corner of Boulevard St. Michel in the fifth *arrondissement*. My dingy room faced the boulevard, had a comfortable bed, and a small desk with a weak light bulb but lacked a private toilet and bathing facilities. Electricity was scarce and at times we had none for hours. The central heating system, too, left much to be desired. To keep warm, I always had a bottle of wine nearby. Discomforts did not bother me, what mattered was living in the city of Sartre and Camus and Braque and Picasso. I quickly even got used to the smells in the Metro—a mixture of body odor and Channel #5—and, on occasion, a curtain falling in the middle of a performance at the Opera. My favorite café was Les Deux Magots and, next door on Boulevard Saint-Germain, Café de Flore. Chain-smoking intellectuals nervously engaged in what I assumed were deeply intellectual discussions and arguments in which mouth, hands, and fingers were orchestrated to score points as also was the case at one of my favorite restaurants: La Coupole on Boulevard Montparnasse. How different and exciting from the laid-back atmosphere at Columbia and even raucous City College. All this and more on usually less than $10 a day.

Despite the electrically charged intellectual atmosphere, I was surprised to gradually learn that I was better prepared than some French university students to discuss hotly debated issues. Arguing, for example, with French left-wing students about why Marxist-Leninist thought would not widely catch on in the free West, my French counterparts were well-equipped with quotations from Marx, Engels, Lenin, and Stalin but had, I soon began to suspect, not read their works in depth.

About a week after my arrival, I registered for classes at the Alliance Française and later for a course on French civilization taught by Maurice Duverger at the Sorbonne. Both places were swarming with foreign students inhaling the intellectual atmosphere and experiencing the cultural and, at times, the carnal riches that the city offered. With the university's identity card, you could for a dollar or so even enjoy some wine on weekday evenings at a good number of well-known nightspots.

Always on the lookout for female companionship, which I had no trouble finding, I, on Anima's suggestion, eventually, telephoned her friend Denise, and for much of the rest of my stay in Paris we enjoyed each other's company.

A lovely and attractive woman who, I believe, was somewhat older than I, Denise lived with her wonderful, warm, and hospitable parents on Avenue d'Iena in the 16th *arrondissement*. A graduate of the Sorbonne in Classics, she was a churchgoing Catholic, yet entertained liberal and libertine views. Together, we traveled to Anima's wedding in Heidelberg, making a leisurely return to Paris by way of Zurich, Lausanne, and Brussels. Even in our closest moments we addressed each other by the formal *vous,* reminding me of my late Aunt Tanya in Riga, where this kind of formality was *de rigueur*. I was told that people who frequented Schmitt's home while his wife was alive were amused by the same kind of formality between the two.

The idea of marrying Denise never seriously entered my mind, even though I was attracted to her, to her classical education, high culture, and French and Belgian pedigrees. The decisive event that put the idea of marriage out of my mind happened on a rainy and dreary afternoon as we were walking along the Quay d'Orsay toward my hotel. In a discussion of French policies toward Tunisia and Algeria, Denise, an ardent admirer of Prime Minister Pierre Mendes-France and of his enlightened approach regarding Muslims in those countries suddenly said: "Yet, when I look into his eyes, I see the Jew in him." Well, this was enough for me and, in a gentlemanly fashion, I gradually disengaged myself from this relationship—even though I still kept seeing her in Paris on occasion during my subsequent trips to the city.

Not long after my arrival in Paris, I received a phone call from Hans-Joachim Arndt who had just arrived from Germany with a grant to study under the legendary political scientist Raymond Aron at Science Po. To be closer to me, he changed hotels and moved into mine. As Schmitt was of great interest to him as well, we spent hours walking the streets of Paris discussing him and his works. At Arndt's insistence we dined at good restaurants, which at times annoyed me as I saw no reason why it was necessary to spend more than four or five dollars for deliciously prepared meals. After several weeks, I challenged his gastronomic excesses and suggested that we dine in exclusive restaurants, for example, Maxim's. Expecting that he could not for long afford to spend between ten and fifteen dollars or more for a meal, our prohibitive outings ceased shortly thereafter.

On Schmitt's suggestion, we contacted the right-wing conservative author Armin Mohler, Ernst Jünger's secretary and correspondent for Switzerland's *Die Tat* and Germany's *Die Zeit* who, although Swiss, had had some SS connections during the Second World War. I, with my background and intent on finding out as much as possible about Schmitt and company, felt at times like an investigative journalist. Another of Schmitt's contacts was Alexandre Kojève—he hailed from Russia and had Jewish roots. He was known for his legendary lectures on Hegel in Paris in the 1930s and had had an enormous impact on existentialist thinking.

Both Mohler and Kojève could not stop talking about Schmitt and, having recently come from Plettenberg, I was pumped for information on his private and intellectual activities. Both also urged me, as did Schmitt, to contact a Professor Jacob Taubes at The Jewish Theological Seminary in New York. A son of a Swiss rabbi, he was a disciple of the Kabbalah scholar Gershom Scholem. The three were particularly impressed with his work on eschatology and his open-mindedness toward Schmitt that, in part, he obtained from the late Walter Benjamin's debt to Schmitt's concept of sovereignty. With the exception of Scholem, the names were new to me, and it was fascinating to learn how they directly or indirectly interacted, irrespective of backgrounds. On more than one occasion, Schmitt would tell me that Jews understood his thoughts better than anybody else.

Sitting one day with Kojève at the Deux Magots café, he noted that there are not many around in the world who could come close Schmitt's intellect. In Germany, according to Kojève, he is the only one worth speaking with. He also confessed to me his disillusion with the low intellectual level of French university students and how he was satisfied to do his own work, sit in a café, and, from time to time, pay a visit to a woman.

In Paris I also met my friend Pamela Moore, the celebrity author of *Chocolates for Breakfast* and soon to be married to Adam Kanarek. She was into left-wing politics and, on occasion, convinced me to participate in the Paris protest marches against French colonial policies in North Africa.

In my numerous outings to museums, I was usually drawn to Cubist art. It inspired me to think of the essence and appearance of objects and of human beings, whereas Impressionist art I found to be sugary and little more than color photography. At one of my visits to the Museum of Modern Art on Avenue Wilson, I spotted a marine scene by an artist whose name—Georges Dayez—was not familiar to me but whose work spoke to me immediately. Seascapes of his reminded me of the morosely gray-green Libau waters in the fall. In due time I became a collector of his works, followed by a close personal friendship.

Toward the end of December, I decided to travel to London and visit my uncle Robert Schwab and his family. On my arrival I learned that he, whom I had not seen since his visit to Libau before the war, had just passed away. His Irish wife, Nellie, invited me to attend the church funeral. I was surprised but was told by her that he had converted to Catholicism. While visiting Latvia in the late 1930s to explore the possibility of living in the Baltics as head of Shell Oil (which he declined), he had told my parents that even though he had married a Roman Catholic, that he would not convert. Uncle Robert was an obsessive penny pincher; his frugality was so severe, according to Nellie, that at times he even managed to get his three children—David, Amalia, and Bernard—to return the allowance that he had grudgingly given them. I was also taken aback by the meager house in which the family lived. Way back, Nellie told me, he even had a paramour until Nellie spied on him and managed once and for all to put an end to his infidelity.

In London I also visited our dear family friend Helen Usiskin who lived with her family in a spacious and elegantly appointed one-family home. On returning to Paris, I forgot on the train my Leica M3 that mother had given me as a gift. In January I finally left for New York aboard one of the Queens. Denise, Pamela, and Hans-Joachim Arndt saw me off on the train to Cherbourg.

Unlike the meals on the French ocean liner on which I had sailed to Europe, the food was simply terrible. After ordering calves' brain sauce vinaigrette, for much of the rest of the journey, I suffered mightily from indigestion. I soon learned of similar complaints from fellow passengers.

Mother was at the pier welcoming me with open arms. At first I did not dare tell her of the fate of the Leica M3, but, when I finally did, she said not to worry. "We have lost much more in life and this is only a matter of money. Next time you are in Germany, please buy another one."

Chapter VII
ROAD TO THE BEGINNING OF A CAREER—TEACHING

Financially things were improving. In addition to some of the prewar funds we had in Europe, German restitution payments also helped materially so that at last we no longer had to count pennies. In the mid-1950s, mother moved us into a decent and comfortable four-room apartment on West 99th Street off Riverside Drive. It did not take long to furnish it. The living room had a huge Persian carpet; a very comfortable couch; on the wall above hung a large impressive painting by the American Michael Lenson depicting triplets—the brothers playing chess and the sister kibitzing; on the other wall hung watercolor costume designs by the Russian artists Alexander Benois and Sergei Soudeikine—both were closely associated with Sergei Dhiagilev. In addition, we had a coffee table and several comfortable and inviting chairs among other accoutrements that she mostly obtained at auctions. My bedroom, which doubled as a study, had a semi-antique Persian Kashan carpet; a large bronze sculpture by J. J. Jacquet, the Rodin of Belgium, which mother placed atop a handsome old bookcase; a large old desk; a remarkable piece of furniture that contained a radio and a high-fi set; and a wonderful couch that doubled as a comfortable bed. The walls, too, were decorated with watercolors—mostly by Benois and Soudeikine. These she had purchased from our good friends and neighbors Vladimir and Mathilde (née Nieburg) Hessen. They, in turn, had acquired the Russian works from their émigré friends in Paris, including from Benois and his family. Later on, Mstislav Rostropovich and Latvian-born Mikhail Baryshnikov, among other Russian notables, became friends and clients of the Hessens. Mother's bedroom was also her sitting room that, in addition to a Persian carpet, had a comfortable couch that could easily be turned into a bed; a large television set on a semi-antique table; a coffee table; and several chairs. The small dining area with a table and eight chairs was an extension of the kitchen.

To live as normally as possible was mother's aim. Hence, she began to entertain at home with porcelain settings, silver utensils, and crystal—things she slowly began to acquire some years after we landed in New York. That such socializing was on a much smaller and considerably more modest scale than before the war was irrelevant.

On weekends, cousins Elie and Nuta Bruskin with their children Sam and Eve would drive in from West Hartford. Aunt Ida, Gerri Samuelson, cousins Ellen and Harry visited us from Brooklyn as did Marcia and Bernie Schwartz who drove in from Long Island, and Raya and Gustav Smith, who would walk over from West 86th Street. Regulars among friends included, among others, the Hessens, Fira and Boris Rosovsky, and when gin rummy was not the order of the evening also Selig and Sonia Rosovsky. With relatives the lingua franca was German as it was with mother's friends from Libau— Betty Feiges Rosengartem and Helen [Hilda] Krom Usiskin who visited us from London—and with her Viennese girlfriend in New York—Frances Steiner. With most of the others, the lingua franca was Russian. What I enjoyed most were their reminiscences of the culturally rich lives they and their parents had enjoyed especially in St. Petersburg prior to the Great War and in Latvia before the Second World War. Reliving the wonderful past was infectious—so much so that evenings I often stayed home to listen to their reminiscences.

After an incredibly rich and intellectually rewarding trip to Europe, I continued with my research and prepared for the Ph.D. oral examination, but I did not neglect my social life. For the latter, mother was delighted to prepare delicious hors d'oeuvres for my occasional wine and champagne soirees, and she always greeted my guests and then left to meet friends with whom she usually played gin rummy and, on occasion, frequented the theater, Carnegie Hall, the opera, and ballet.

However much I loved mother, I felt the need for some privacy. So I rented, with a fellow Columbia University graduate student, a small basement flat in Greenwich Village. On my allotted part of the week I had parties and, in general, enjoyed a Bohemian way of life. When not partying downtown, I would go home evenings as I did not want mother to be alone. Among my friends, regulars at either place included, among others, Sandy Saideman, Wlado Nenoff, Klaus Pringsheim, the Gelbs, Rizel Pincus (GDS companion), Walter Goldstein, Alex Groth, the Plottels, Adam Kanarek, and Barbara Schwartz—a young woman who was madly in love with Klaus, an emotion not reciprocated. For my soirees she would send a case of champagne on the condition that Klaus would attend. As one who enjoyed the delights of life, Klaus never missed a beat. Among others who frequented my uptown gatherings was Macha de Gunzburg—a woman on whom I had developed a crush at Columbia; she did not feel the same, however.

Despite the delights of my current life, the deep scars of the Holocaust were always there. According to mother, nights were the worst. I, at least, managed to sleep well. When in New York, I always accompanied mother to the very well-attended annual memorial services for the Jewish survivors of Latvia that Max Kaufmann organized. With fellow survivors, friends, and acquaintances we reminisced about the war years and desperately tried to gather information about those we loved and had presumably lost. Never hearing positive news about Bubinka and any other of our relatives and friends, we always returned home dejected—vowing never to forget what the Germans and their collaborators had perpetrated against our people. But a miracle did occur. After years of searching, by way of the Red Cross, mother found out that her sister Hermine was alive. She had spent the war years in Russia and had married a relative of ours, Leo Scher. Following the war, they returned to Riga, where he obtained a job in his profession: architecture. As soon as it became possible, we sent them parcels, which I continued to do after mother's death.

In one of the letters that reached us from Riga, Aunt Hermine mentioned that we would soon receive a letter from a distant relative— Abrascha Jevelson—who, with his wife, Etel had recently left Riga and settled in Munich. In a letter from them that followed, he mentioned that a first cousin, Mary Rosenwald (née Kurtz), had, before the war, married William Rosenwald, a Sears Roebuck heir, and that they resided in New York. Abrascha asked mother to please contact her. Mother replied that she had no clue of who she was or how to contact her and that she was about to leave for Europe on an extended trip and would visit them in Munich.

Following mother's stay in Berlin, she did proceed to Vienna by way of Munich and visited the Jevelsons. There she learned that his second wife, Etel, was from Vienna, and thus an Austrian citizen, and had received permission to leave Soviet Riga with him. Mother had known his first wife, Lydia Jevelson (née Feiges), well and also their daughter Zina, who had been a sometime playmate of mine. After their divorce, Lydia and her daughter moved from Riga to Libau, and mother often played tennis with her—a real pro. Both, Lydia and Zina perished in the Holocaust. Mother was most impressed by his second wife, a delightful Viennese with a good head on her shoulders, who exuded the charm characteristic of the people of that city. Her impression of Abrascha was that of a truly nice human being who was lucky to be married to Etel. On leaving Munich, mother promised to do her best to locate Mary Rosenwald, who, like mother, was born in Jelgava (Mitau in the German), once the capital of the Duchy of Kurland. I, in the meantime, had spent some weeks with Schmitt in Germany and, on my way to Vienna to meet mother, traveled to meet the Jevelsons as well. My impression of them was similar to mother's.

Prior to my arrival in Vienna, mother met father's cousin Lionel (Leiba) Galgut and his second wife, Asia, who had come from Johannesburg to visit her. (I subsequently welcomed them in New York.) His first wife, Fanny, my father's sister, had recently passed away. The first cousins married in Libau, and mother accompanied them to Danzig from where the newlyweds sailed for South Africa.

In Vienna mother met me at the station and insisted that I quickly drop my luggage at the hotel across the street, which a few years before had served as the headquarters of the French occupying forces. As it turned out, she was eager to take me to a specialty restaurant in the center of the city that, according to mother, served the most delicious duck and goose—favorites of mine. The following morning we took a train to Baden bei Wien where mother was staying and enjoying various medicinal baths for which Baden was well-known. As there was very little for me to do—except take long walks with her, inhale fresh air, drink bitter water, and enjoy good Austrian cuisine, and in cafés listen to orchestras playing mostly light Viennese music—I was bored but did not admit it to mother.

From Baden we made our way back to Vienna and, on the following morning, we took the scenically beautiful train ride to Venice. There I served as a tour guide for mother, taking enjoyable gondola rides, dining on exquisite Italian cuisine, and swimming in the Adriatic at the Lido Beach. Many years later, after mother's death, I learned from Aunt Hermine that mother, at age seventeen, was scheduled to travel with the orchestra to Venice but could not do so because she had recently married my father.

From Venice we proceeded to the resort towns of Rimini and Brindisi on the Adriatic, where we spent a week with the Sobotkas (Mia, my late brother's wife; her second husband Genek; and their son Sam), who arrived from Stockholm to meet us. I was happy to see mother relaxed and enjoying swimming in the Adriatic. The Sobotkas persuaded the two of us to return with them to Stockholm, which we did via Copenhagen and stayed with them in their apartment in the suburb Bandhagen. The weather was excellent and during the day we swam in Saltsobaden, near Stockholm.

Notwithstanding that mother had handsomely furnished our new apartment, she went on a buying binge in Paris, Berlin, Vienna, Venice, Rimini, Copenhagen, and Stockholm: Baccarat crystal; a fish set by Christofle; a Rosenthal dinner set; Meissen and Augarten porcelain dishes; a large silver fruit bowl in the form of a gondola; 18-karat gold jewelry in Rimini on the advice of Mr. Sobotka, who was in the jewelry business; Royal Copenhagen figurines and a tea set for six; and two engraved and signed Orrefors crystal vases.

Back in New York after several months, mother telephoned a relative by marriage, Dr. Henry Reichlin, originally from Vienna who had moved to New York in the early 1930s. As he was in finance as was Mr. Rosenwald, he provided details on how to contact the Rosenwalds. Because mother was not yet proficient in English she asked me to telephone Mrs. Rosenwald, which I did.

I introduced myself on the phone. She reluctantly acknowledged in a delightful Russian accent that she remembered her cousin, Abrasha Jevelson, from way back when her family lived in St. Petersburg and from the time after the Revolution when the family fled to Riga before settling in Berlin. She told me that Jevelson was a nice guy but basically a good-for-nothing. After asking how he was related to us, she invited me to lunch on the coming Sunday when we could continue our conversation.

I appeared promptly at noon at 895 Park Avenue and the door was opened by a butler in uniform. Mary Rosenwald descended the stairs from the duplex apartment, something new to me, and led me into the living room that had oil paintings by Picasso, Chagall, and Cezanne. Although tense, she was attractive, charming, and almost immediately began calling me by one of my Russian diminutive names Georgik. After briefly chatting about my Latvian Jewish past and the Second World War, she again lashed out at Jevelson, calling him her good-for-nothing cousin who had not raised a finger for her family when they fled St. Petersburg after the Revolution, arriving in Riga with little.

I told Mrs. Rosenwald that both mother and I had visited the Jevelsons in Munich and found them to be lovely people. I related to her some of his wartime experiences in Soviet gulags and that his daughter Zina had perished in the Holocaust. He obviously did not have an easy life, but now that he is a free man in the West, the couple needed help and mother, with her limited financial resources, was helping them as best she could. Although I did not ask for help outright I, nevertheless, planted a seed and this conversation ceased with the appearance of Mr. Rosenwald, who was followed by their three daughters: Nina, Elizabeth, and Alice.

After brief introductions, lunch was announced and we moved into the dining room where I was struck by the formidable Renoir hanging within.

Luncheon was served by two uniformed housekeepers, while the butler poured the wine. Mr. Rosenwald was quiet most of the time while the three sisters tried to impress me and vice versa. We all hit it off very well and I was invited to lunch on the following Sunday as well. After lunch, Mary and I went into the library and after a short tirade about her useless cousin, she consented to send him a monthly allowance of five hundred dollars—a lot of money in the late 1950s.

Because of the age difference, I could not fully involve Nina and Elizabeth in all my social activities. I was very fond of Nina and looked upon her as the sister I never had. Elizabeth fascinated me for her "intellectual" brashness, despite the fact that she often did not know what she was talking about but was absolutely convinced that she was in possession of the monopoly of truth. Nevertheless, she had a genuine appreciation of good art as did I. Alice was still a young kid who liked to assume a rather affected manner. I was convinced that she would grow up to become an actress.

Over the years I developed very warm feelings toward Mary. I not only continued to be invited to the weekly Sunday lunches but also to join the family in their chauffeur-driven limousine at dinners on Sundays at exclusive restaurants, including, among others, The Forum of the Four Caesars, Les Pavillion, and the Blue Angel. Summers I was often invited to their estate in Byram, Connecticut, where I swam in the pool to my heart's delight. Bill Rosenwald tried to interest me to the world of golf. After one lesson on his golf course on the estate, he gave up on me and I on golf. The family also took me along to luncheons and dinner dances at the Century Club in Purchase, New York—a club founded by German Jews. Mary made fun of the fact that the club had been "invaded" by two eastern Jews—herself and David Sarnoff, head of RCA. Mother was very grateful that the Rosenwalds reintroduced me to an economic and cultured upper-class milieu.

At my soirees at home, Nina and Elizabeth met, among others, my dear friends Sandy Saideman, Wlado Nenoff, Jeanine and Roland Plottel, Klaus Pringsheim, and Jim Barros. In due time, Nina fell in love with Sandy and had hoped to marry him and vice versa. Her mother was not enthusiastic, however. At one point she told me point-blank that it is I who should be marrying Nina. My reply: "I love her as a kid sister." Nina's sumptuous wedding to Sandy was soon held in the grand ballroom of the Plaza Hotel.

In these exciting and fruitful years of my life, I continued to take working trips to Plettenberg, combining them with trips to Paris, Copenhagen, Munich, Vienna, Venice, and Paris. I also passed the Ph.D. oral examination without a hitch. Following the examination, I was invited by the Burgess Professor of Public Law and Government Lindsay Rogers to visit him in his office. "Not bad, Schwab," he said while reading a journal. "Not bad at all." Standing almost at attention, I replied: "Thank you, sir." "What are your plans?" he asked. "I am anxious to complete the research for and the writing of the dissertation," I replied while he continued to read. "This is not what I mean. Have you entertained the idea of teaching?" "Not really, but I would not mind trying," I replied. "Very well. Please see the secretary [Ms. Black], I have arranged for you to teach a course at the college." "Thank you very much, sir," and I went next door with my mind exploding about teaching at Columbia University, a world-renowned institution of higher learning. I thought of mother, father, and Bubi. In my mind I was realizing my father's dream of a university professorship. On telephoning mother with the news, she was nearly in tears congratulating me and saying how proud papinka and Bubinka would have been of me.

Teaching turned out not all that easy. I was assigned to teach the fourth semester of Columbia University's famous Contemporary Civilization course. Although I was generally acquainted with the material dealing with European civilization and culture from roughly the end of the Middle Ages to the present—in those days Freud and Sartre among others—preparing for the fall semester entailed a tremendous amount of in-depth reading, which left little time for working on the dissertation.

As a junior and Jewish member of the overwhelmingly Wasp faculty, I, at times, felt ill at ease. At the weekly faculty luncheons at the Faculty Club during which specific intellectual topics were discussed, junior members were expected to be seen but not heard—a custom I was unaware of until I expressed my views on a particular subject. I got chilling looks from the others. Both Jim Barros and I dubbed the Faculty Club "the enemy camp," and began greeting senior members of the faculty with a nod we called "professional courtesy."

Eager to complete the research for and the writing of the dissertation, I declined the offer to continue teaching and spent considerable time at Columbia's Butler Library and the Public Library at 42nd Street. At the latter, I kept running into my former City College professor, Edward Rosen. He was always curious about my progress toward obtaining the Ph.D., and, after a good number of months, he asked whether I would like him to recommend me for a teaching position at City College—although he warned me that a recommendation from him could be the kiss of death. This reminded me of the adage that the fierceness of academic infighting is in inverse proportion to the smallness of the stakes. Rosen was appalled by the poor scholarship of some of his colleagues, including that of the department chairman Professor Wisan and that of Professor Snyder, who taught the history of modern Germany. As I was making progress on my dissertation and thought of Rosen's analysis, I thought I had nothing to lose and said "yes."

To my surprise I received a phone call from City College's history department inviting me to come for an interview with Professors Wisan and Snyder. It went well and, unexpectedly, I received an invitation to join the department in the fall of 1960 with a pay per course considerably above that of Columbia's.

On coming home with my first paycheck, I proudly announced to mother that from now on I will pay half the rent of the apartment—about $60 per month. Mother objected. I insisted and prevailed.

Chapter VIII
DISASTER AT COLUMBIA & AT HOME

As I progressed with my dissertation, I gave Herbert Deane chapter after chapter to review and incorporated most of his suggestions. He encouraged me to proceed with the good work I was doing. But clouds had begun to gather over my work after a pre-1933 Schmitt student and even a friend, Otto Kirchheimer, was hired by Columbia's political science department. I was looking forward to meeting him; I had been told that he had received his doctorate under Schmitt. I sent him my manuscript, and not long thereafter he invited me to visit him in his office. In a friendly manner, he informed me that I had failed to understand Schmitt and, in his view, I would have to rewrite the dissertation. He insisted that Schmitt helped pave the way for Hitler's victory and that he was already an anti-Semite during the Weimar period. I responded that I found no evidence in his writings to conclude that he had helped Hitler rise to power nor anything that smacked of anti-Semitism during the Weimar period. On asking him to enlighten me on both of his assertions, he merely said that I would have to read much more of Schmitt's writings, as well as of those of others who had dealt with the subject. But, he added, he would only have one vote following the defense of my dissertation.

Perturbed by the visit, I informed Deane, who assured me that I had nothing to worry about. Soon, the day came when I was to defend my dissertation. I entered the room of assembled examiners, including Professors

Deane, Neal Wood, Robert Cumming of the philosophy department, John Wuorinen of the history department, and one visiting professor from abroad.

The first hour and forty minutes of the defense went well and I gradually relaxed. I was easily able to answer a good number of questions, because I had anticipated some, including why I titled my study "The Challenge of the Exception: An Introduction to the Political Ideas of Carl Schmitt between 1921 and 1936" and why I considered my work to constitute a contribution to scholarship.

I had chosen the title because Schmitt was fascinated by exceptional situations. In numerous conversations with him, he had described himself as a sort of physician interested in diagnosing illnesses, and then determining how best to cure patients. As an example, I called attention to his book *Dictatorship* (1921) in which he drew a conceptual distinction between a state of exception and a state of emergency. The difference between the two, he noted, is that the former lends itself to overcoming a crisis (curable illness). In the instance of Weimar, for example, the sovereign authority needs to address a crisis by temporarily invoking Article 48 of the constitution, which would enable him to suspend in part or entirely basic rights provided for in Section 1 #2. Once successful, the constitution, as a whole, is restored to its normal status. This form of rule Schmitt called "commissarial dictatorship." A state of emergency, on the other hand, constitutes an extreme crisis (terminal illness) that cannot successfully be addressed by invoking the existing constitution. The crisis thus provides the sovereign authority or a revolutionary movement the opportunity to bring forth a new constitutional order that Schmitt called a "sovereign dictatorship." An example was what transpired during the Russian Revolution.

Deeply concerned by the Weimar crisis of the early 1930s, Schmitt was convinced that if President Hindenburg were to properly utilize Article 48, he would go a long way toward eliminating the centrifugal forces attacking the Weimar state. Toward that end Schmitt argued in *Legality and Legitimacy* (1932), it was important to thwart a Nazi or Communist victory at the polls by not permitting them to participate in the electoral process. Both movements, as was well-known, were intent on destroying the existing constitutional order. Their goal justified Schmitt in arguing that permitting them to compete for political power at the polls would be a violation of the spirit of the Weimar constitution as embodied in its Article 1: "The German Reich is a Republic." I also pointed out in this context that Bonn's post–Second World War Basic Law incorporated Schmitt's idea that the equal chance to compete for political power can only be extended to parties that subscribed to the spirit of the constitution.

Notwithstanding the danger that the Weimar state faced, Schmitt had been severely rebuked by liberal democrats for advancing an idea that was not in accord with the belief that every political party be given an equal chance to compete for power.

Answering the second question, I noted that my study of Schmitt's political ideas is the first in the English-speaking world, and I immodestly noted that I had discovered numerous discrepancies between what Schmitt said in his writings and references appearing about his works in the literature available in English, errors I had corrected in my dissertation. Replying to a question about his anti-Semitism, I noted that I had not encountered any references to it prior to 1933. Further, I noted that he had dedicated his *Constitutional Theory* to his close Jewish friend Fritz Eisler, who was killed during the Great War, and had praised Hugo Preuss, who was Jewish and a father of the Weimar constitution. I had also learned that he had helped obtain a Rockefeller Foundation grant for Leo Strauss to leave Germany so he could complete his work on Thomas Hobbes and that Franz Neumann was also in close touch with him as was Kirchheimer, even after he received his degree.

I concluded by noting that Schmitt's embrace of Nazism after January 1933 was purely opportunistic, and his newly acquired anti-Semitism, though not in the racial sense of the word, was bizarre and repugnant.

While answering questions I, from time to time, glanced at Kirchheimer and noticed that he was uncomfortable, fidgety, and was moving back and forth in his chair. This made me a little nervous, but things were going well. When Kirchheimer's turn to examine me finally came, he mercilessly attacked my work. He accused me of having "turned Schmitt on his head" and that "this is no way to write about him." However one looks at

Schmitt, he continued, he was among the most prominent gravediggers of Weimar. Schmitt had not only critiqued the Weimar constitution but actively undermined it, according to Kirchheimer, adding that I completely misunderstood Article 48.

I was astonished, ruffled, and intimidated by his raising his voice to a feverish pitch. Nevertheless, I proceeded to the best of my ability to defend the results of my research. On Schmitt being a prominent gravedigger of Weimar, I repeated Schmitt's concept of the equal chance and noted that Schmitt favored strong presidential leadership based on a latitudinarian interpretation of Article 48. I also brought up Schmitt's close association with Chancellor Kurt von Schleicher, whose well-known aim was to thwart Hitler's ambitions to power. One who held views like those of Schmitt cannot be accused of torpedoing the constitution. Yes, I said, he critiqued it as did many others, and I gently pointed out that Kirchheimer (who paraded in the U.S. as a staunch defender of Weimar) published an essay in 1930 under the provocative title "Weimar—And What Then?" in which he went beyond the Weimar constitutional order from his perspective—which was left wing but I made no mention of this political fact. At this he nearly exploded and, with saliva spewing from his mouth, almost shouted "of all my publications you had to single out that one." Based on my argument that Schmitt was not a gravedigger of Weimar and in view of Kirchheimer's outburst, I thought I had scored a major point with the examiners.

After the two hours were over I was asked to leave the room and waited outside for about twenty minutes until Deane emerged and nonchalantly informed me that I had failed the defense. Shocked and stunned by Deane's matter-of-fact attitude, I asked for an explanation. After all, for seven years he had encouraged me and my work, and now he merely said, "Who are we to challenge Kirchheimer? He is the expert in the field." My interpretation: to camouflage his anti-Weimar past, Kirchheimer—an "interesting Marxist literateur" as Schmitt liked to call him—invoked the well-known adage "the best defense is a good offense" to browbeat clueless American scholars about the intricacies of Weimar's history. (On learning how Kirchheimer assessed my work on him, Schmitt, even months prior to my defense, refused his request to be received by Schmitt. Kirchheimer, in 1949, reestablished contact by visiting him in Germany.)

As I left the building, I felt that my world had collapsed once more. How will I face mother, my friends at Columbia and outside the university, and colleagues at City College? Walking home on Riverside Drive, I kept thinking how best to break the news to mother. She opened the door and before I could say a word she congratulated me, kissed, and hugged me. For the celebratory occasion, she had prepared some of my favorite dishes: a juicy roast veal with roast potatoes, a good red Beaujolais, and a light chocolate mousse. After the embrace, I told her what had happened, and she immediately soothed me and reminded me of my poor school performance in Libau, and how far I had gotten since the end of the war. At least on the surface, she took my failure well and viewed what had happened as a temporary setback. "Remember Zockele," she said, "given your credentials, the world is wide open to you." Nevertheless, when mother saw how deeply troubled I was she tried to comfort me more by putting things in perspective. "Look Georginka," she said, "we have lost so much during the war, we have gone through hell, and you get upset about failing an exam. Were you to decide on an academic career, "the worst that can happen is that you will become a professor one day later," and she repeated a Russian proverb: The slower you will walk the further you will get. How right she was.

Soon the phone began to ring. Family, friends, and colleagues called to congratulate me and were stunned by the news. Sandy, the eternal pessimist, said that he was not surprised in view of all I told him about Kirchheimer. Others were shocked not so much by Kirchheimer's performance, but mostly about Deane—who for years had encouraged me to work on Schmitt and then stabbed me in the back. At City College on the following day, I informed the department's chairman, who did not seem perturbed. My former professor and now colleague in the department and good friend Edward Rosen counseled me to go into the field of ancient history, a subject I liked very much. Professor Lindsay Rogers of Columbia invited me to his home on Riverside Drive and counseled me to be calm and, surprisingly, said "don't give up on the Nazi pope. He has interesting things to say."

In the midst of all this, I tried to phone Deane about what had happened. On finally reaching him, he was cold and suggested that I look for another topic and should, perhaps, consult Kirchheimer. Noting Deane's reaction, I decided to no longer be in touch with him. Seeing him walk on upper Broadway in the Columbia area, we simply exchanged superficial nods. I also wrote Schmitt to tell him what had happened; he was stunned. When I visited him in Germany he said, "I have supervised many doctoral dissertations in my life, and however much I disagree with some of your conclusions, you have reached them on the basis of having read and studied the material. The treatment you received was not deserved and that he [Schmitt] no longer wanted to have anything to do with Kirchheimer."

With the typical stupidity of youth coupled with my belief that my scholarly assessment of Schmitt's works was correct and that I had fallen prey not to scholarly issues but to ideology and, perhaps, a personal vendetta, I went to see Kirchheimer—thinking that it might be better to work with an enemy you know rather than another Deane-like individual. He greeted me in a matter-of-fact fashion and immediately told me that he is neither my enemy nor foe. The subject of publication of my dissertation had come up at my defense, and, I informed the board of examiners that it had been accepted for publication by Duncker & Humblot, one of Germany's oldest and most prestigious publishing houses. Later, when I visited Kirchheimer, he strongly counseled me to keep it from publication. On a subsequent visit to Schmitt, I once more met Professor Roman Schnur, who told me that what had happened at Columbia was widely discussed in Germany and that Professor Carl Joachim Friedrich of Harvard had told him some time ago that he would see to it that nothing about Schmitt would appear in English. What had been also widely talked about in Germany at the time was that refugee professors in the United States who had formerly been associated with Schmitt, including Kirchheimer and Neumann, "borrowed" freely Schmitt's ideas in their writings without acknowledging him or turned his ideas on their heads. Although not a refugee from Hitler and not Jewish, but as one who was also intellectually indebted to Schmitt, Friedrich was also guilty of the same charge.

Kirchheimer and I finally settled on a Ph.D. topic: neutral countries and nuclear weapons, a case study of neutral Switzerland. That country had recently gone on record indicating that it might acquire tactical nuclear weapons in order to effectively defend its sovereignty from the Soviets. This caused an uproar in Switzerland, and citizens launched two initiatives prohibiting the government from introducing such weapons into its military arsenal. Both initiatives were defeated at the polls, thus clearing the path for the government to introduce such weapons.

As a straightforward case study, I thought I could do it quickly as I was working on nervous energy. Hence, as soon as the semester was over, I left for Zurich and rented a comfortable room for much of the summer in the Hotel Franziskaner, which was in walking distance of the *Sozialarchiv* and the university's library. To my astonishment and delight, I found at the archive manila folders neatly arranged according to subject matter. And there was plenty on the nuclear weapons issue, including newspaper clippings from the Swiss press, sparing me days and weeks of time in the stacks. I worked quickly and thoroughly from the minute the archive opened until it closed for lunch at noon, which enabled me to go for a swim in Lake Zurich, have lunch at Mövenpick on the Parade Square or Sea Street, and back to the archive by 2:00 p.m. Half an hour after the archive closed at 5:00 p.m. I was on the dance floor in the garden of the elegant Hotel Baur au Lac on the lookout for female companionship. As the dollar was very strong, I could afford to dine alone or with a companion at one of the many good restaurants. Cheese raclet with a good dry white wine or Wiener Schnitzel were among my favorite dishes. Café Sprüngli on Bahnhof Street had the best pastries in town, and I sometimes visited the place more than once a day. If I was up to it, I would return to the Baur au Lac's grill room for at least a drink late in the evening, as it was the only place in Zurich to the best of my knowledge where one could still dance. On weekends, I would take long walks and explore the sights of Zurich and environs.

At one point Ernst Hüsmert visited me with his wife and daughter, and was horrified to meet my German girlfriend who, it turned out, was a niece of one of the leading SS generals—Karl Wolff. He had been Himmler's liaison officer with Hitler until 1943, subsequently serving as German military governor of north Italy and plenipotentiary to Mussolini. Unaware of all this until Hüsmert's visit, I quickly disengaged myself from this relationship.

Toward the end of the summer, Nina and Sandy came to Zurich. There, at the Baur au Lac, her uncle, the conductor Efrem Kurtz, arrived from Gstaad with his wife, the renowned flutist Elaine Shaffer; we visited for several hours at the hotel. (I, who considered myself an expert at gin rummy, subsequently lost $80 to Efrem in New York in less than an hour. For me this was a lot of money at the time.) After a few days together in Zurich, Nina, Sandy, and I flew to Nice for a ten-day vacation on the Riviera. There we had such a good time driving around in a rented car. Lunch and dinners at the best restaurants, including La Bonne Auberge, La Chaumiere, at the Carlton in Cannes, where I enjoyed the best quail ever, and, of course, lunching and dining the at the Hotel des Paris in Monte Carlo. We also visited Saint-Tropez, including the nudist *Plage* Tahiti. We did not undress but simply walked and watched. Men and women in motorboats and yachts cruised not far from shore, peeping with binoculars. Suddenly the police arrived, and, with the speed of light, nudists turned on their stomachs so as not to expose pubic hair and those who strolled hit the sand. With nearly $1,000 still in my pocket, I tried my luck at roulette at the Monte Carlo casino and within an hour or so had lost nearly half of my money while Sandy was winning. I learned from him not to select numbers at random but to cover parts of the board and to stick with it. In the course of nearly a week, I won almost all of my money back at the Palm Beach Casino in Cannes. At Cannes and Nice, we swam in the Mediterranean. Unlike the beach at Cannes, the beach and the water at Nice were full of pebbles. As Sandy was unable to return to shore on the slippery pebbles, I had to go out and rescue him. On the Riviera we also met Eddie Kurtz, Nina's uncle, a professional cellist who had a summer home in the nearby hills. With his encyclopedic knowledge of jokes he had us in stitches. A distant relative by marriage, Dr. Reichlin, had insisted that we also visit the Ephrussi-Rothschild Museum at Cap Ferrat. He was somehow related to the Ephrussi family.

On the way back to New York by way of Paris, I introduced Nina and Sandy to the painter Georges Dayez whose works I was by then collecting.

At his studio, they bought a large and stunning oil on canvas titled *Baou de Saint-Jeannet* painted in 1961. I also took Nina and Sandy to the studio of Camille Hilaire who was out of town but his daughter Christiane received us. There Nina and Sandy bought a large and impressive oil on canvas depicting an orchestra and I bought a large oil on canvas depicting a jazz quintet. In the evening, we took Christiane out to dinner and dancing at Maxim's. On another evening, Nina, Sandy, and I went to the Crazy Horse Saloon where, for the first time, I saw breathless-looking topless dancers performing interesting skits—some of which even had a modicum of intellectual merit.

Back in New York, we were welcomed at Idlewild (later renamed Kennedy) airport by mother and Mary Rosenwald and had a wonderful time relating our experiences while comfortably ensconced in a limousine to Manhattan. As in the past, on Sundays I continued to be invited to lunch at the Rosenwalds and, from time to time, to join them for dinner at some of New York's exclusive restaurants.

By the time I left Zurich I had a rough draft of the dissertation, but so as not to arouse Kirchheimer's suspicions about my having written a first draft in only a few months, I decided to submit only the first chapter in late September. About a month later he left word that he would like to see me. He thoroughly critiqued it, and I proceeded to rewrite according to his comments and instructions. This took several weeks. When I visited him once more, he critiqued the revisions. On reviewing them carefully, I soon discovered that he wanted me to largely restore the original version. Without arguing, I complied and he did the same again, that is, for me to restore them roughly to the second version. I soon realized that I was being whipsawed and that Kirchheimer was determined to torpedo my obtaining the degree—apparently in the hope that my Schmitt manuscript would be relegated to the dustbin of history and Kirchheimer's reputation as a defender of Weimar would remain intact.

I simply began to mark time, not really knowing what to do. Under my carefree veneer I was truly despondent as I was unsure of how much longer I would be able to retain my position at City College without a Ph.D.; I even contemplated changing careers—perhaps law or the stock market.

Marriage and children were out of the question, and, at this time, I was given my walking papers from my semi-companion Paula. She was moving on to greener pastures but, not wanting to leave me in the lurch, introduced me to her friend Hannah with whom I had a tumultuous relationship for several years. At about the same time, another bombshell struck.

Mother, visiting a cousin in Florida, Rosa Vovsi Armel, fell ill. The diagnosis was muscular dystrophy according to Dr. Wlado Nenoff, who told me confidentially that there is no cure. As this illness usually strikes young people, and because no one in the family ever had suffered from it, the case was considered unusual. Obviously, I never breathed a word to mother and, through her Russian-speaking friends, I secured Maria, a religious Russian-speaking housekeeper, for five days a week.

As the illness progressed slowly, mother enjoyed visits from relatives and friends. Nuta and Elie would drive in from West Hartford almost every second Sunday. My cousin Harry Schwab came at least once a week, as did cousin Ellen, her husband, my Aunt Ida, and the Rosovskys, among others.

Living on nervous energy and averaging not more than five or six hours of sleep a night I accomplished much: taking care of mother the best I could (I would not hear of putting her in a nursing home), preparing my lectures, and seeing Hannah who lived one block away. She was understanding of mother's condition and did not press me to spend much time with her. From time to time I even managed to do some work on my new dissertation in the hope that one day I might still succeed. One of my proudest moments was when I learned from family and friends that mother had called to tell them that she did not realize what a wonderful son she had.

Mother passed away on June 22, 1964, the day Germany had invaded the Soviet Union in 1941. Her departure was excruciatingly painful, not only because of the human factor and what she was forced to endure in life and how she "nursed" me back to "normality," but that she departed this world leaving behind her Georginka after all that he had endured during his lifetime.

Chapter IX
MARRIAGE

On returning home on a Thursday from City College in mid-December 1964, my cleaning woman, Maria, informed me that a woman had phoned and that she would call again in the late afternoon, which she did. She introduced herself as Eleonora Storch of Stockholm, and I welcomed her to New York and said I hoped to meet her soon. The thought had crossed my mind that I had, perhaps, met her in Stockholm in 1959, when mother and I visited the Sobotkas with whom we had recently spent time vacationing in Rimini and Brindisi in Italy. When Eleonora learned that I had no clue about who she was, she was upset and told me that she had been given my phone number by her father, who had received it from a Mr. Sobotka. The Sobotkas had apparently failed to inform me of Eleonora's impending visit. After chatting for some minutes, I told her that this need not preclude us from meeting for lunch at the Plaza Hotel the following Tuesday at 1:00 p.m. After she had agreed to meet, I asked how I would recognize her in the lobby of the hotel's 5th Avenue entrance? She assured me that she would be wearing a red coat.

Arriving about 15 minutes early, I sat down in one of the hotel's very comfortable armchairs, observing the strikingly beautiful women entering and leaving the hotel. At about five minutes past the hour, a very beautiful and well-dressed young woman entered in a dark coat and sat down on the round sofa under the chandelier. I wished then that the one in the red coat not show up, which would enable me to introduce myself to this young lady. After about ten minutes, I walked over and innocently asked whether she happened to be Eleonora Storch? She jumped up and said, "Yes." (Many months later I asked why she had failed to wear a red coat. She replied that she "did not want to meet an old and gray-haired professor with a beard. Seeing a handsome young man, I was delighted that the blind date was with you.")

We had lunch at the Palm Court, where I was impressed by her British accent, meticulous European table manners, charm, and grace. All in all, everything about her was ladylike. I suggested that we walk over to the Marlborough Art Gallery on East 57th Street and from there to Sotheby's on Madison Avenue. After leaving the auction house, Eleonora was eager to return to the apartment on Park Avenue and 85th Street where she was staying with relatives. I agreed to walk her home. On leaving Sotheby's we turned left on Madison Avenue. Eleonora protested and insisted that we had to turn right. We made a bet that if I were correct, she would return to Stockholm from Los Angeles—where she was to visit relatives—via New York and not fly directly from California. At the corner we asked a mailman who was emptying a mailbox the way to East 85th Street. Of course, I won the bet. In the meantime, I also learned that before heading to Los Angeles she would be visiting friends in Montreal.

On New Year's Eve the phone rang at about 6:30 p.m., as I was about to leave to meet Hannah for the New Year's festivities. On the phone was a Mr. Meier Segals of Montreal, originally from Latvia, who insisted that I immediately take a plane for Montreal with all expenses paid to attend a New Year Eve's party in Eleonora's honor. This was obviously impossible, and I would not stand up Hannah, even though I was about to end my relationship with her. Eleonora came to the phone and said, "You are coming, of course."

I explained that there was no way I could be in time for the party as in New York it now was 6:30 in the evening. Subsequently, I learned from her that Mr. Segals and his wife Henrietta had rounded up eligible bachelors in Montreal, including one of the Bronfmans, to be introduced to her. She did not care for anyone and whispered to Mr. Segals that she had met someone in New York she would like to be with. Hence the urgent invitation.

As agreed, after visiting Montreal and Los Angeles, Eleonora returned to New York in January 1965. Here, I introduced her to Sandy and Nina who had invited us for drinks; they then took us as their guests to the Metropolitan Opera's staging of Donizetti's *Lucia di Lammermoor*, with Joan Sutherland. Both Sandy and Nina were impressed by her and urged me to get serious. I needed no convincing. As time progressed, my esteem for her grew—she spoke French, knew some German, and even had a smattering of Russian. Her looks, her long hair, and warm personality greatly endeared her to me. Further, I was convinced that Eleonora would be a loving wife and a wonderful and warm mother.

We fell in love and decided to get married. Eleonora wanted to do so immediately—she did not appear eager to return to Stockholm. I, on the other hand, insisted that she return home and that I would follow shortly to introduce myself to her family.

In Stockholm I was warmly welcomed by her parents, her brother Marcus, and her sister Ruth and Ruth's husband Jan. The nine-room apartment on Norr Maelarstrand overlooking the river was typical of an upper-middle-class European bourgeois style with all that that implied, including numerous works of art, antique furniture, Persian carpets, silver, and so on. The atmosphere was warm, and I felt that I had acquired a new family and even began to address my in-laws-to-be as mother and father. That we all were Jews from Latvia helped. Eleonora's parents hosted a family dinner, and, on the following afternoon, a champagne engagement reception attended by the Sobotkas and other of their elegantly attired friends.

After four days, I returned to New York as I did not want to miss my lectures at the college; Eleonora followed several weeks later. My future father-in-law telephoned several times to make sure that I was well. We were married on February 27, 1965, at the home of the noted Rabbi Joachim Prinz. He hailed from Berlin and was a friend of my father-in-law from the days when both had served on the executive board of the World Jewish Congress and knew my Aunt Hermine in Berlin. The wedding was attended by my cousins the Bruskins, Sandy Saideman (recently separated from Nina), relatives of Eleonora—Mr. and Mrs. Meilach—and Wlado and

Lydia Nenoff (we were married one week apart). Neither Eleonora's parents nor siblings were able to attend. Following the ceremony, we dined at the exclusive French Colony restaurant in Manhattan.

The loss of my mother continued to be a sorrow and my precarious situation at City College a steady concern. Nevertheless, the months following our wedding and the summer were devoted to attending dinners and receptions in our honor, and we hosted a good number of receptions at home. I did the best I could with my students at City College. We visited cousin Nuta and Elie Bruskin and their children in West Hartford, and, in the summer, we decided to honeymoon by traveling to the West Coast by way of Salt Lake City—visiting my cousin Manya and her husband David Alder there. They hosted a reception in our honor and took us sightseeing in the handsome city and on excursions to the incredibly beautiful mountains surrounding the city.

In Salt Lake City, Eleonora and I rented a car and Manya and David mapped a route for us to take on our way to California. We stopped to visit Las Vegas where Eleonora won one hundred silver dollars at the slot machines, and I lost about the same amount—Sandy's formula did not work because of the double zero at U.S. roulette tables. Neither of us cared much for the gaudiness of the casinos, which certainly could not compare with the elegance of their European counterparts. But the disappointment with Las Vegas was more than offset by the breathtakingly beautiful scenery of the Grand Canyon, Bryce and Zion parks, and Jackson Hole, among other tourist spots. At one of them, we had a bear come to our bungalow looking into the window but was satisfied and left after having pilfered the contents of a garbage can on the porch.

In Los Angeles, we visited a relative of Eleonora's on her father's side—Dr. Simon Shubitz and his wife Helen. He and Helen received us graciously and also hosted a reception in our honor. From Los Angeles I telephoned a cousin of my father, Chaliapin's accompanist Max Rabinovich, in Laguna Beach. I succeeded only in reaching one of his former wives. In San Francisco, we again met up with Manya, David, and their daughter Mascha. They introduced us to the remarkable sights of that city and its environs and to exquisite restaurants.

What an exquisite and warm honeymoon it was. We swore never to be apart even for one day. From San Francisco we flew back to New York, looking forward to the forthcoming visit of Eleonora's mother. The visit turned out to be a disaster. In New York, she revealed herself to be the exact opposite of the woman who had warmly welcomed me to Stockholm.

We picked her up at Idlewild; in the taxi to Manhattan, she began to mildly castigate me for not yet having my doctorate and why it was taking me so long. She insisted that I obtain my degree as quickly as possible and begin to finally start earning real money. Had she been married to me, she added, she would have taught me lessons and "counted my ribs"—a colloquialism I had not heard before. Her reply to my response "I would do my best" was "that this is not good enough." Eleonora did not dare say a word but at home, when alone, she counseled me not to take mother seriously as no one in Stockholm did.

The critiques increased rapidly, centering mostly on money, squandering it by buying books, and wasting time reading and scribbling. All that I was doing was—*nicht aktuell* — irrelevant, a favorite expression of hers. Basically, she considered me a good-for-nothing and insinuated that the time had come for Eleonora to terminate the marriage after, of course, taking me to the cleaners. Money being uppermost in her mind, she insisted that I reveal the funds I had in bank accounts. Further, Eleonora tipped me off that she insisted that Eleonora take her to our safe deposit box from which I, in the nick of time, removed important documents and my mother's jewelry. With the help of Mrs. Meilach, she secured a copy of my mother's will in order to find out how much I had inherited. In regard to her verbal attacks, which usually began as soon as I returned home from college, I eventually asked her to hold off with the theatrics for ten minutes—until I managed to at least wash my hands. Eleonora, who was frightened of her, would usually leave the room.

In addition to being *Geld verrückt* (money crazy), a signature trait for which she was also legendary, as I learned, was her inability to distinguish fact from fiction. When she manufactured stories about me, attributing them to people she knew, stories that reached my ears, my practice was to telephone them to set the record straight. Without exception, they would laugh and say, "Who does not know the liar Anya?" Even though people confronted her about the bizarre tales she was spreading, she was unable or unwilling to change—apparently secure in her conviction that she could continue to fool people. Unable to achieve her goal of Eleonora leaving me, she concluded that "two idiots had found each other."

On one of her visits to New York in the late 1970s she said, "I have lied once in my life and was caught." I told her that she "misspoke. What she meant to say was that once in her life she told the truth and was caught." Her compulsive lying reminded me of the German proverb *Wer lügt der stielt* (He who lies steals).

Never in peacetime did I encounter another individual like that. It even affected my health. I was diagnosed with ulcers, but was quickly cured by my loving Eleonora with her unique medication: love, warm milk, and honey. Once my mother-in-law returned to Stockholm after several weeks, the relief was great and life returned to normal—reading, teaching, working on the dissertation on and off, and socializing.

In the weeks and months that followed, I learned that the elegant apartment in Stockholm was the façade for a severely dysfunctional home from which the three children left as soon as possible. For years her children would have nothing to do with their mother. I also realized why Eleonora had been eager to marry immediately in New York without first returning to her abnormal Stockholm home. Further, she endlessly quarreled with her husband mostly over money and spoke poorly of him—even detested him and, on numerous occasions, would lock him out of the apartment. Out of pure desperation to get into his home, he even called the police. From time to time she would leave home and check into the Grand Hotel or leave the country.

Eleonora introduced me to some of her mother's cousins in New York, Paris, and Israel. In contrast to Anya, they were educated, cultured, and sophisticated and had as little to do with her as possible. In her defense, however, I must say that in moments of sanity she could be funny, entertaining, charming, endearing, and even generous. Perhaps feeling guilty about how she has treated Eleonora over the years, she, in 1980, promised and even delivered from her Swiss bank account funds, "appropriated" from her husband, amounting to one-third the cost of our Riverside Drive cooperative apartment in New York City; it overlooks Riverside Park, the Soldiers and Sailors Monument, the Hudson River, and New Jersey. Nevertheless, from the time I met her until her death in the mid-1980s, I doubt that I exchanged more than 2,000 words with her—mostly about the weather.

Eleonora's father usually excused his wife's behavior, attributing it to nervousness due to the loss of her family during the war and the recently diagnosed illness of their daughter Ruth. I, of course, expressed my sympathies but made perfectly clear that her behavior and language were beneath contempt. He did not appreciate my outspokenness. Nevertheless, on occasion, he admitted to me that her lunatic behavior was largely responsible for his inability to concentrate on his businesses; such lack of attention ultimately led to several bankruptcies. Despite occasional digs at me, our relationship was basically correct; I respected him for his work on behalf of Jews during the Second World War. Early in 1945, he had even established contact with Himmler that materially contributed to the rescue of Jews. Eleonora loved and adored her father and vice versa. And this did not sit well with her mother.

Chapter X

FATE OF THE REJECTED PH.D. DISSERTATION ON CARL SCHMITT

Convinced that my dissertation on Carl Schmitt was scholarly—researched and written without passion and hatred—I decided not to abort the rejected thesis. Hence, as soon as it became evident that I would not encounter difficulties with my second dissertation (see below, chapter XI), I gave the publisher the green light to publish *The Challenge of the Exception: An Introduction to the Political Ideas of Carl Schmitt between 1921 and 1936.* After a delay of eight years, the first edition appeared in 1970, with a second edition in 1989.

As anticipated, ideologues cloaked in scholarly garb had a heyday denouncing the work, one even going so far as to claim that I had endorsed Schmitt's anti-Semitism. The first edition was initially largely ignored, even though a favorable review by Robert Lougee had appeared in *The American Historical Review* in 1971. But by the time the second edition was printed in 1989, serious Schmitt studies and commentaries had begun to appear with my study widely cited. In his endorsement of the second edition, G. L. Ulmen stated: "The burgeoning of Schmitt studies in the United States today is no doubt due primarily to Schwab, who virtually alone has pioneered that effort"; according to Professor Joseph W. Bendersky, "*The Challenge of the Exception* is a truly pioneering work by a student who dared to take a detached scholarly approach to Schmitt"; Professor Ellen Kennedy noted that "*The*

Challenge of the Exception was the first book on Carl Schmitt's thought to appear in English. It is not likely to lose its place as the first source for work on this important thinker"; and, according to Professor John Stroup, "The work of Professor George Schwab, which, while once highly controversial, is now widely accepted by Schmitt specialists." In 1997, Professor John P. McCormick noted in his *Carl Schmitt's Critique of Liberalism: Against Politics as Technology* (New York) that "Schwab's *Challenge of the Exception* ... [is] most frequently and violently criticized as apologetic, yet [he] does not in fact promote Schmitt for any political ideology." (15) Discussing *The Challenge of the Exception* in 2012, Bendersky stated that "Schwab's pioneering work initially had no impact and was relatively neglected, only to be belatedly acknowledged in subsequent decades a historiographical milestone." ("From the Führerstaat to God and Abu Ghraib: The Strange Path of Carl Schmitt in the English-Speaking World" in *Revista de Ciencias Sociales—Valparaiso* [Chile, 2012], 41).

The second edition of my Schmitt study was translated into Chinese in 2011—twenty-two years after it first appeared. The first edition of the work appeared in Japanese translation in 1980, and the Italian translation in 1986, with an introduction by the noted Italian sociologist Professor Franco Ferrarotti.

To cement my scholarly credentials in the sphere of Schmitt studies, I, in addition to having written a number of articles—some of which have also appeared in translation—have also translated three of Schmitt's works, each of which included my introductions and notes. These were: *The Concept of the Political*, which was originally published by Rutgers University Press in 1976; in 1996, it was published by the University of Chicago Press. Without taking account of the sales by Rutgers, the Chicago Press informed me that close to 50,000 copies have been sold between 1996 and 2017—a figure that is hard to believe. *Political Theology: Four Chapters on the Concept of Sovereignty*, originally published by The MIT Press in 1985 with a second printing in 1988, the Chicago Press informed me that close to 20,000 copies have been sold between 2005 and 2017. *The Leviathan in the State Theory of Thomas Hobbes: Meaning and Failure of a Political Symbol* was originally published by Greenwood Press in 1996 and subsequently by the University of Chicago Press in 2008. This publication was the fruit of a year-long tutorial with Erna Hilfstein, a graduate student, that I held at the Graduate Center of the City University of New York. According to the Chicago Press, sales figures in the nine years are over 3,500 copies. The three translations with Chicago contain forewords by Professor Tracy B. Strong.

By way of G.L. Ulmen in the early 1980s, I brought my work on Schmitt to the attention of Paul Piccone—founder and editor of the intellectually challenging quarterly *TELOS*. A year has not passed since then without Schmitt appearing in the pages of the journal. By now it would not be an overstatement to note that a Schmitt craze is taking place at American institutions of higher learning. One may only speculate where this may end.

Chapter XI
BIRTH OF A FAMILY AND VICTORY AT COLUMBIA

Three days before my birthday on November 25, 1965, the phone rang at about 7:30 in the morning. My friend and City College colleague Professor Edward Rosen was on the line congratulating me. Still half asleep, I remember mumbling something to the effect that my birthday is on the 25th of November. "This is not the reason I am calling ... Did you hear the news this morning?" "No," I answered. "Your problem at Columbia is solved," said Rosen. He had just heard over the radio that Kirchheimer had dropped dead on a flight from Washington, D.C., to New York. What a curious birthday gift, I thought.

The news of his death spread quickly, and I began to receive congratulatory phone calls from, among others, Sandy Saideman, Klaus Pringsheim (whose daughter Erika is my godchild), Wlado Nenoff, and Jim Barros, who, in his inimitable colorful way, urged me to "get your ass moving" by going to the political science department and requesting reassignment to a new reader, which I did with alacrity.

I was assigned to two gentlemen scholars, professors Dankwart A. Rustow as my first reader and Philip E. Mosely as the second reader. As I was telling Rustow my story about Deane and Kirchheimer, he asked me not to brood over the past and to forget Deane, "a spineless wonder of the world"—an expression I was not familiar with. He urged me to shape the new dissertation into a presentable form. Professor Mosely was on the same wavelength, suggesting that I show him whatever Rustow had read and commented upon.

With Kirchheimer out of the way, I could now peacefully focus on completing the new dissertation, which was critical for obtaining tenure and advancing at City College. I now felt more secure about my professional future but decided to hold back publishing the Schmitt study lest it cause another bump in my quest to obtain the Ph.D. Going over the new dissertation, what soon became clear was that I would need to incorporate the material that had appeared since 1962. This necessitated me returning to Switzerland. Hence, Eleonora and I began making plans to leave for Europe sometime in June 1966.

Our first stop was Paris, where I introduced her to Georges Dayez, his companion Marie, and his daughter Anne. Eleonora's warm personality and worldliness were, to my delight, heartily welcomed. Studying his art in the studio on numerous visits on this trip, she became deeply impressed by it; ultimately, Eleonora dramatically changed her mind from her first encounter with his art when she had visited me in my apartment and thought me to be crazy. Finally, she confessed that she no longer could live without his works.

From Paris we proceeded by train to Plettenberg, where I introduced her to Schmitt, Anni Stand, and the Hüsmerts. As in Paris, Eleonora was warmly received. I brought Schmitt up to date regarding the publication of my Schmitt study and the status of my new dissertation. I told him that my first reader would be Dankwart Rustow—who had told me that his late father had been impressed by Schmitt's Weimar writings. Schmitt, in turn, told me that he knew Rustow in Berlin and regarded him highly.

From Plettenberg, we took the train to Zurich. Both Eleonora and I looked forward to a quiet period—away from New York's hectic pace of teaching, researching, socializing, and "perpetually" honeymooning.

In Zurich, I continued with my research at the *Sozialarchiv* and at the university and city libraries. Following a quick swim in Lake Zurich, I would meet Eleonora for lunch; late afternoons we would often go dancing at the Baur au Lac followed by walks and dinner. Weather permitting, weekends found us on the ferry to nearby Küsnacht, where we swam and lunched at a wonderful restaurant on the banks of Lake Zurich. On the return trip, we snacked aboard the ferry and, on arriving in Zurich, called it a day. From time to time we would also travel to Interlaken, where we swam in the public pool or took the train to the top of the Jungfrau by way of Grindelwald.

Not knowing anybody in Zurich, we were alone much of the time until the spell was broken by the simultaneous arrival of Sandy Saideman and Sally Wechsler from New York and the Laus, who drove in from Munich. Together we had much fun, visiting art galleries, the museum, Café Sprüngli for excellent desserts, lunch at the elegant Dolder Grand Hotel, dancing at the Baur au Lac, and dining at the exclusive art-filled Kronenhalle restaurant. This was often followed by a nightcap at the Baur au Lac Grill.

Shortly after they had all departed, we left for Bern where I did additional research at the military library. Bern was just about the dullest place I had ever been—Eleonora felt the same. For the ten days we spent there, evenings, after dinner, and before calling it a day, we usually went to say good night to the bears. Shortly after returning to Zurich, with my research still not complete, we left for New York.

Back home, I was busy preparing lectures, spending much quiet time at Columbia's Butler Library and the Fifth Avenue Library reading, researching, and writing and rewriting parts of my new dissertation. I was optimistic, largely because the chapters I had submitted to my readers came back with constructive criticisms. Eleonora, after sitting in on some of my history classes for entering students, decided to enroll at Hunter College and registered for liberal art courses for credit. She also began to work at The College Entrance Examination Board. We became very close friends with her boss Lillian Robbins and her husband Lew. They followed in our footsteps and began collecting art, including works by Georges Dayez, André Lhote, Russian costume and stage designs, and Yugoslav naïve art.

Despite our busy schedules, we socialized and also attended concerts, the opera, and ballet. Sandy had been deeply hurt by his divorce; in 1965, I introduced him to a very intelligent and beautiful former student of mine, Rochelle Nitzberg. After a tumultuous courtship, they finally married in 1970.

In 1968, a week or so before the eruption of student unrest at Columbia, I successfully defended the new dissertation. Professor Mosely suggested that it be published in book form. I demurred as I was utterly bored by the subject but did not tell him so. Nevertheless, he insisted that I, at the least, submit two chapters with his recommendation to the University of Pennsylvania–based foreign policy quarterly *ORBIS*. To make absolutely sure that the two chapters he designated be up to date, I thought another research trip to Switzerland was in order.

A highlight of that summer was our journey to Moscow and Leningrad, where we met my favorite aunt, Hermine, and her second husband Leo Scher, who happened to also be related to mother's side of the family; while there, we also visited with Eleonora's uncle, Mulya Storch, who had traveled from Riga to meet us in Moscow.

We had hardly entered our hotel room at the Metropole when Hermine and Leo arrived, greeting us in German, while Aunt Hermine simultaneously pointed her finger to a listening device clumsily hidden in the living room's chandelier. Not having seen them since 1940, we had much catching up to do, which we did while taking long walks. The food at the hotel's dining room was good; Eleonora gorged herself on the Beluga caviar present on every table.

From Hermine and Leo we learned much about their war years in the Soviet Union, the horrors of the war, and life in totalitarian Stalinist Russia. Not to endanger her life, when fleeing Riga for Russia with Leo, Hermine destroyed letters her late father-in-law (Xavier's father) had received from Chancellor Bismarck when he was China's envoy to Germany as well as her Chinese diplomatic passport. Shortly after the war, they had returned to Riga but she dared not enter the apartment at 11 Elizabetes Street.

While Hermine worked in a factory during the war, Leo fought at the front. Fluent in Russian and German, he was often summoned by the higher-ups to interrogate German prisoners of war. Back in Riga life was difficult but at least Leo occupied a high position as a professional architect; he had been an architect in Berlin until the mid-1930s.

From Eleonora's uncle, Mulya, we learned of his travails in Russia during the war and in postwar Riga. He spoke much about Eleonora's father—

especially of their close relationship in prewar Riga—and of her father's largesse after the war, which enabled Mulya to purchase a small house with a garden in the outskirts of Riga.

Mulya was eager to find out why his brother had suddenly ceased to be in touch and stopped helping him. We did not mention that he had encountered financial difficulties, although Mulya hinted that his sister-in-law probably had a hand in it and noted that she had a difficult personality. Eleonora and I promised to send him a few parcels and $25.00 a month until her father would once more be in a position to help.

In Moscow and subsequently in Leningrad, Leo and Hermine succeeded in getting tickets for the opera and ballet. I remember Hermine at one point turning to me at the ballet saying, "You see, Georginka, I now live in the Soviet Union without staff and driver and life goes on and I am quite happy." In Leningrad, we met up with remnants of mother's family—the Gerschkewitch clan originally from Porchov, some of whom had been living in St. Petersburg since the turn of the century. As the German armies were approaching Riga during the Great War, the Jacobsons left for St. Petersburg, where they lived with relatives in a sprawling apartment off the Newsky Prospect. Mother's cousin Fira invited us for tea—for fear of her being reported to the secret police by the families now living in this apartment in which Fira had just one room, we had to sneak into her room where we met some other relatives who had survived the war in Leningrad.

We stayed in a suite at the Hotel Astoria. The entrance hall sported a Persian carpet as did the living room, which was furnished with antiques and a refrigerator. As in Moscow, one could easily spot listening devices. The bedroom was relatively modern; the bathroom boasted a few small Persian carpets. Unlike at the Metropole, the Astoria did not liberally indulge guests with caviar of any kind.

As in Moscow, Eleonora, Hermine, Leo, and I would take walks in parks where we met some of my other relatives—others sent regards as it was too risky to meet because of their positions. The parks were obviously not "bugged," and we could speak openly of, among other things, the conditions in the Soviet Union and the prospects for the country. Although conditions had improved considerably since the days of Stalin, the Soviet Union was still very far from a free society, with little hope that one day the Soviet Union would implode. When Eleonora asked one Gerschkewitsch relative, who had played a considerable role in the theater world before the revolution and in Soviet Russia, to whom in the family he belonged, he replied with a smirk: "I belong to the state."

After our week in Leningrad, Hermine and Leo departed for Riga, and Eleonora and I for Zurich where, as already mentioned, I intended to update the two chapters Professor Mosely insisted that I publish. We anticipated meeting Sandy Saideman in Zurich, and, together, we planned to drive to St. Moritz and Pontresina.

Working at the *Sozialarchiv,* I managed to update the chapters in about a week. Toward the end of the week, Sandy arrived—pining for Rochelle but not yet able to make up his mind about marrying her for fear of another marital disaster. Once married, they had three children: Lewis, Mara, and Seth—my godson.

With my work done, I rented an Opel Kapitän shift car. Although I had learned to drive on one, the two cars I owned in New York (Buick Specials) had automatic shifts. The drive to St. Moritz nearly ended in disaster. An inexperienced shift-car driver, I often stalled on the way up the mountainous, very narrow two-way winding road that appeared to me to be never-ending, with me trying to avoid looking down thousands of feet. Every time I stalled, Sandy, who sat next to me, covered his eyes but Eleonora in the rear was stoically quiet. At last we arrived at Pontresina by way of nearby St. Moritz. There we checked into the luxurious Kronenhof Hotel.

The carefree week was spent hiking, lunching usually at the Kronenstübl; from time to time, we would drive to St. Moritz for lunch or dinner. The U.S. dollar was still king. The return trip to Zurich was uneventful. Driving the winding roads down I rarely stalled. Because considerable stretches of the road were on the side of the mountain, I was spared from looking down thousands of feet.

From Zurich, the three of us flew back to New York. There Sandy often invited us to accompany him on his weekends at the Century Club in

Purchase, New York, where we swam, played tennis, and Sandy also played golf.

With the Ph.D. dissertation out of the way and several publications in the pipeline: "Switzerland's Tactical Nuclear Weapons Policy," on the conceptual distinction between "enemy and foe," and my failed Ph.D. dissertation, I was, as noted, optimistic about my academic future. The time was at last ripe to enlarge the family. From the outset, the two of us were clear that, come what may, we would do our utmost to counter my wartime experiences and Eleonora's dysfunctional family legacy and bring the children up as normally as possible.

As Eleonora had difficulties conceiving, she received fertility injections and, on August 14, 1969, gave birth to non-identical quadruplet boys—Adrian, Clarence, Claude, and Solan—at the Children's Hospital of Columbia University. The news of the birth was widely reported here and abroad, in the print and on radio and TV newscasts. Most unfortunately, Adrian lived for only three days. The rest of the brood grew up with distinct personalities and were handsome, highly educated and cultured, and successful.

To say that Eleonora's pregnancy was difficult is an understatement. We obviously had to considerably curtail our social activities but, on her insistence, we still managed to host a cocktail reception in honor of Georges Dayez and, from time to time, we continued to accompany Sandy to the Century Club. Toward the very end, as I was getting ready to rush Eleonora to the hospital, we received a phone call from Dr. Pete and Rhoda Reichman (née Galgut)—a distant cousin of mine. They had just arrived from South Africa and were eager to meet us for the first time. As normal family life was dear to me and to Eleonora, she did not wish to be rushed to the hospital as Dr. Solan Chao had insisted be done when he discovered three weeks before her due date that Eleonora would be having quadruplets, not the expected triplets. I promised her that I would meet the South African relatives and explain why we were not able to even invite them for a drink. Eleonora reluctantly consented. A few days later, I met them at the Frick Museum and a long friendship ensued. In addition to being a highly accomplished radiologist, Dr. Reichman was also a novelist; he wrote a long article about the new-found relatives for the *South African Jewish Times* (Oct. 1970).

Some hours after our sons were born, I went home to get some sleep. But to no avail. Relatives and friends phoned and the media pestered for news. Unable to fall asleep, I returned to the hospital and found Eleonora tired with rosy cheeks and very content. She informed me that her brother had called to offer congratulations as well as her sister and father; she had even exchanged a few words with her mother, who, upon being informed that Eleonora was pregnant, had insisted that it was nothing more than propaganda.

At the time of the birth we lived in a large one-bedroom apartment in Lincoln Towers on West End Avenue and 69th Street. While the babies were still in incubators, we purchased three cribs that we placed in our bedroom; we slept on a very comfortable couch in the living room. We were very fortunate to have had a most wonderful part-time housekeeper, Regina, from Santo Domingo, who used to be a cook for the American ambassador. She warmly welcomed each child as he was brought home from the hospital, and she remained with us for years.

Chapter XII

TORTUOUS ACADEMIC ROAD BUT WONDERFUL FAMILY EXPERIENCES

Overwhelmed by Eleonora's difficult pregnancy, delighted by the material enlargement of the family, and proud of my scholarly achievements, I did not pay close attention to the student unrest in the country and closer to home at City College; this turmoil was engendered by the Vietnam War, race riots, and student unrest at colleges and universities across the country. The explosion in the Spring 1969 semester at the largely white and elite City College (known as the Poor Man's Harvard) was aggravated by its location in Harlem. Black and Puerto Rican students had taken over City College's south campus, demanding greater access for minorities; the college's decision to close the south campus for a number of weeks led to unanticipated consequences. In response to the upheavals, the City University's Board of Higher Education, during the summer of 1969, announced a new entrance policy: Open Admissions.

The university's junior colleges were compelled to accept all New York City high school graduates applying for admission—irrespective of academic preparedness or qualifications. Standards for the senior colleges were somewhat higher, which was not saying much, given the poor academic record of a good number of New York City high schools. By materially degrading admission requirements—and by abolishing the two-year core curriculum that students had been required to complete—the result was that a degree from City College would become suspect.

I returned to the Fall semester with a heavy heart, both to a college that was about to be transformed and to a History Department already burdened by personality conflicts and issues of scholarship of some members. Because the full impact of the open admissions policy was not immediately felt, I was hopeful that the college would be spared its worst aspects.

In principle, I was not opposed to the new policy, because City College all along had a similar policy—according to which afternoon and evening classes were open to non-matriculated students (those who had failed the entrance exam). These students could matriculate provided they achieved a B average after completing 30 credits or a C average after 60 credits. I had hoped that a variation of that policy would become the norm and the reputation of the college preserved. My hopes were soon dashed.

A year after the open admissions policy began to be implemented, a noted physicist, Robert E. Marshak, was appointed as president at the college. Given his academic credentials, many of the faculty at the college could not imagine that he would be lax on standards. But, after a meeting between Marshak and Professor Howard L. Adelson, the chairman of the History Department and a well-known medievalist—Adelson was uncertain that Marshak, assurances notwithstanding, was truly committed to maintaining academic standards. From statements the president began to make, what soon became clear was that he was more committed to aiding the socially disadvantaged and, hence the, in general, academically unprepared students than to maintaining standards. Obviously naïve or clueless about how to reconcile the City College tradition of (and former commitment to) high standards for the matriculated and non-matriculated, Marshak soon revealed that his priority was the hard sciences—he had little interest in the social sciences and the humanities.

Although the effects of the new policy were not immediately felt, the divisions in the History Department began to deepen dramatically in response to the new policy and the abolition of the core curriculum. Two major camps emerged: the political left that sympathized with the New Left, including, among others, Professors Joan Gadol, Dante Puzzo, and Emanuel Chill; and the right of center that included, among others, Professors Adelson, Edward

Rosen, Stanley Page, Henry Huttenbach, and George Schwab. We also had colleagues who occupied the middle ground—some of whom congratulated me for my stand on standards but could not say so publicly because of the positions they occupied in the department or at the college. The political left and New Left sympathizers favored the social engineering policy, with the latter often being referred to as elitists, racist, and even fascists. *New York Post* reporter Joseph Berger noted that "Dr. George Schwab . . . says that because the college is not adequately preparing students who take his classes he has had to trim his reading lists and water down his coursework to the detriment of his better students." He proceeded to quote me: "If I were to maintain the same standards I maintained 10 years ago, I would have to fail 75 percent of my students. ... [In] the early '60s I was considered a Communist because I made my students read Marx and Engels. Now I'm considered an elitist because I demand standards." (December 18, 1974)

The division in the department was further aggravated by the arrival in 1972 of a new chairman: Herbert Gutman. Like Marshak in his field, Gutman was a well-known social historian. His decisions soon made clear that he entertained sympathies for the political left and acted accordingly. With political lines drawn in the department, promotions were recommended in accordance with ideological loyalties at the expense of scholarly achievements and ability to teach.

Because incoming students were no longer required to enroll in the two-year core curriculum, ethnic study programs and remedial courses flourished. Traditional students able to leave the college left, and a decline of registration in history courses resulted. At one point, I was reassigned to teach a remedial course in which I had to introduce students to the study of the social sciences. One assignment every week was for students to read the "Week in Review" section of the *New York Times* (a good number of students had never heard of this daily) and then be prepared to discuss the lead article. After taking the attendance in the pot-smelling classroom, I called on a student to answer the assigned question. He correctly replied that it dealt with the possible partition of the Holy City of Jerusalem. Another student with a raised voice asked "Hey, what's Jerusalem?" A third one called out in a loud voice, "Don'cha know? That's where God dropped Jesus." At the end of the semester, I had no choice but to fail a majority of students. This did not sit well with the supervisor of the program whose name, I believe, was Nancy Lay. She noted that I was not "sufficiently sensitive" to the needs of students; I was then dropped from teaching the remedial course.

At another time, I was asked to teach an M.A. course on the Second World War and the Cold War. Assuming that graduate students were appropriately prepared to take a course on the recent past, I was in for another shock. Even though the course dealt with the roots of the Cold War and the Cold War itself—a period in which we were living every day—a good number of the students at least knew that it had something to do with the United States, the Soviet Union, and the atomic bomb. That's all. After that, I declined to teach graduate courses at the college.

Complaining bitterly of what was happening at City College, Harold Proshansky, at the time the president of the university's Graduate Center, invited me to apply for an appointment to the Center's History Department, which I did; I was accepted after delivering a lecture on Carl Schmitt. Together with the provost, Hans Hillerbrand, I was given the opportunity to develop a series of conferences on history and politics. At about the same time, City College granted me a semester sabbatical (September 1973– January 1974—the only one in 40 years). We used this opportunity to travel as a family to South Africa (see page 211).

On returning to New York, I had phoned a few of my colleagues at City College to find out what was going on and was told that the college continued on its downward spiral; nothing further needed to be said about the incompetently administered open admissions policy and ideologically deeply flawed Marshak administration. I also soon learned that a good part of my time would be taken up with the case involving my friend and colleague Henry Friedlander; with defending myself against charges of obstructing administrative justice in the department; and with issues around my promotion to full professor.

Henry Friedlander, a Holocaust survivor fluent in German and widely known in the field as an outstanding twentieth-century German historian and as a pioneer in the relatively new field of Holocaust studies, had been with the college's History Department. Not affiliated with either faction but sympathetic to the one I belonged to, he had been outmaneuvered by the political left and not reappointed to his position, thus ending his career at City College. Because of the public outcry that this case engendered, he was transferred to the Jewish Studies Department. There, the recently appointed chairman, Rabbi Irving Greenberg—widely known as a left sympathizer— pretty much from the outset worked to deny Friedlander tenure. Ultimately, Friedlander was informed of the decision by the Department of Jewish Studies to not reappoint him for a sixth year (1975–1976), thus denying him tenure, which meant losing his job. It was in this context that Friedlander approached me to help him file a grievance against the decision. I readily accepted the challenge and invited Professor Martin Tamny of the Philosophy Department to help me prepare a brief, which he did.

The hearing was held at the university's headquarters — the Board of Higher Education. In my presentation, I stressed Friedlander's scholarly credentials as noted by, among many other leading scholars in the field, Professors Fritz Stern of Columbia University, Otakar Odlozilik of the University of Pennsylvania, Stephen Ambrose of Johns Hopkins University, Lucy Dawidowicz of Yeshiva University, Randolph Braham of City College, and Elie Wiesel of the Department of Jewish Studies at City College (whom I met for the first time while preparing the brief and with whom I became good friends). With variations on a theme, the letters stressed Friedlander's extraordinary scholarship in German history and Holocaust-related studies. Even though Henry was a Holocaust survivor, including of Auschwitz, he never let this cloud his writings and teachings.

Reliable sources had informed me that Rabbi Greenberg was eager to teach the Holocaust. I pointed out that in this context, "Professor Greenberg's qualification in the [Holocaust] field are dubious: His training was in American history, and his doctoral dissertation, completed in 1960, was in this field, namely, *Theodore Roosevelt and Labor 1900–1918*. Since then, he has not published any scholarly works on either the Holocaust or the fate of European Jewry." I noted that Rabbi Greenberg was undoubtedly concerned about the implications of the Holocaust for Jewish theology and modern European history, but that that cannot be "mistaken for training and experience as an [Holocaust] historian."[1]

I further stressed that Friedlander's credentials as a classroom teacher were exemplary from the perspective of his knowledge of the material and usually fully captured the attention of his students according to many faculty observers.

The last point I made in the grievance proceedings was that denying Friedlander tenure had nothing to do with his accomplishments as a scholar and teacher and was based on political considerations and that Greenberg's lack of credentials to teach the Holocaust was self-evident. I noted that the facts presented constituted a violation of Article 8.1 of the agreement between the Board of Higher Education and The Professional Staff Congress, which states that "Neither the Board or the Union will discriminate in respect to hire, tenure of employment or any terms of conditions of employment of any employee covered by this Agreement because of sex, race, national origin, religion, political belief or membership in or lawful activity on behalf of the Union."[2]

Apparently despondent by now, Rabbi Greenberg noted that Professor Friedlander had a raspy voice—as did Henry Kissinger, I responded.

The outcome of the grievance was a compromise: Greenberg won; Friedlander would not be retained by the Jewish Studies Department. Friedlander won by obtaining tenure and was transferred to the Jewish Studies Department at Brooklyn College. City College thus lost an outstanding scholar and teacher and the university retained an internationally renowned scholar. At the end, I walked over to the rabbi and extended my hand to him and said it was a fair proceeding. He refused to extend his hand and said: "When I will need someone to represent me, I will know to whom to turn."

The upheaval in the History Department caused the university president to appoint an investigative committee composed largely of academics from outside the college. The committee's recommendations failed to fundamentally diagnose correctly the issues ailing the department and the college. Reasoning that the History Department issue was an internal college matter, Marshak decided to form a new committee consisting of three City College professors and two outsiders, including Professor Donald Koster of Adelphi University, who was to head the investigation to once and for all bring an end to the conflict. Because of the presence of City College faculty on the investigating committee, the notorious five (Adelson, Rosen, Page, Huttenbach, and Schwab) or, in the words of Nat Hentoff, "the obnoxious five," (*Village Voice,* January 6, 1975) refused to cooperate by not testifying before the Koster committee. As anticipated, the committee recommended to the Faculty Senate that the five be censured and, in addition, that Professor Stanley Page be brought up for disciplinary reasons largely because he was the most contentious of the group; such disciplinary action could result in his being expelled from the college.

Professor Michael Arons, chairman of the Faculty Senate Executive Committee and a Marshak lackey, convened the Faculty Senate. As I was not certain what this would entail for me legally, I asked my friend Sandy Saideman, a Harvard-trained attorney, to accompany me to the hearings at which I was charged with obstructing the Koster investigation by refusing to appear before that committee. Not only did he quickly agree to accompany me to speak on my behalf, which was denied, he laughed his head off at the proceedings wherein Arons acted as judge, prosecutor, and jury. I was worried about the bitterness of these hearings and my reasons for refusing to cooperate with them. Sandy kept assuring me that I had nothing to worry about as the proceedings from a legal perspective were a farce. How right he was. Under the spotlight of the media, professional organizations, and the City University union, plus faculty pressure from around the country, the fraud that had been perpetrated against the "obnoxious five" was fully exposed and all charges, including the extra one against Professor Page, were dropped.

Things began to calm down after Herbert Gutman was transferred to CUNY's Graduate Center full-time in 1975. Under the stewardship of Professors Arthur Tiedemann, Irwin Yellowitz, and Joel Wiener—all political centrists and scholars—what once more became possible within the department was to channel more energy to where it truly belonged at the college.

Still, the issue of my promotion to full professor was not resolved until the end of the 1970s. As one of the so-called troublemakers, I was anathema to the political left—in part because of my work on Schmitt, they were determined to thwart my promotion. Thus, before leaving for the Graduate Center, I received from Herbert Gutman a threatening memorandum dated February15, 1974. In it he stated that a *New York Times* reporter "asked me for information regarding the alleged irregularities concerning your promotion. . . . I declined to discuss [this] matter with him. . . . I hope that for your sake . . . the story makes no mention of [this] allegation. . . . . I have no desire at this time, or in the near future, to make public any of the materials surrounding your promotion."

With my conscience completely clear, my scholarship solid, and my teaching abilities not disputed, I did not fear Gutman's threats and continued to speak out about the politicization in the History Department and the incompetent Marshak administration's implementation of open admissions.

As I was getting nowhere regarding my promotion, I seriously entertained the idea of suing the university for $2 million and so informed CUNY Vice Chancellor Julius Edelstein (he happened to have an office next to mine at the Graduate Center). A gentleman to the core and a proponent of the open admissions policy, he listened carefully to my story (of which he was already partly aware from the media) and asked that I not proceed with the suit and wait for his answer following some inquiries he would make at the Board of Higher Education. I agreed. In the meantime, it was announced that Marshak would be leaving City College in 1979 and that Professor Alice Chandler would become acting president. Edelstein came back with the following message: that I should lie low until Chandler assumes her new office and my promotion will go through as she is fully aware that the whole affair in my case was purely political. And so it was.

Teaching demands and academic disputes notwithstanding, Eleonora and I made sure that my troubles would not adversely affect our considerably enlarged family's life. Although Eleonora bore the brunt of the work, especially in the 1970s, she never made me feel that I did not do my part.

I got up at about 3:00 in the morning to help Eleonora feed the babies. We were also fortunate to have excellent help. I have already mentioned Regina, while my in-laws sent Lotta from Sweden. Later on, we had a wonderful babysitter and playmate—Amy Nammack, a neighbor at Lincoln Towers.

When the triplets were born, we still lived in a one-bedroom apartment in Lincoln Towers on West End Avenue and 69th Street in Manhattan; we soon moved to a two-bedroom apartment in the same complex and, finally, in 1978, to a three-bedroom apartment on Riverside Drive, which continues to be the Schwab family headquarters. Between the time they were born in 1969 and the fall they left for college, we lived a rich and varied life with our sons —exposing them to the many resources that New York had to offer to children.

A highlight of my semester's sabbatical was our trip to South Africa where I had many relatives I was anxious to meet. The immediate excuse for the trip was to attend the marriage of a distant cousin, Jessica Reichman, to Howard Deutsch, a former star student of mine at City College. I had introduced them while Jessica was staying with us for some weeks in the early 1970s. As the triplets were eager to fly to Johannesburg by way of London (and to stop over in that city to experience the thrill of riding on double-decker buses), this was also an opportunity for us to see our dear friends, Sue and Joel Wiener and their children. Joel happened to be on leave from the History Department and was teaching at the University of York.

In my correspondence with him, I focused on how the open admissions policy was unfolding: decline of standards, politicization of the department in general and the faculty promotion process in particular, and good students able to transfer leaving for other colleges and universities. The visit would thus enable me to bring Joel up-to-date, for, in his letters to me, he had indicated that he simply could not believe what I was describing. Our stay in London was brief and fruitful for Eleonora, me, and the children. On relating what was happening at the college, I remember Joel nodding, as if to agree with me. Joel, who was a scholar to the core, truly did not seem to be able to believe or accept the unbelievable, especially that the Harvard of the Poor was on the road to becoming little more than a remedial institution.

Because of our triplet sons, the flight from London to Johannesburg was a truly sensational experience. The South African airline told us that it had not been privileged to host triplet boys. Although we flew economy class, we were truly pampered. At the stopover in Kenya, the airport's toilet attendants' tasks included buttoning or zippering boys' trousers. On landing at Johannesburg, I noticed in the distance an elderly couple waving nonstop. Not recognizing them, I initially ignored them but, after a few minutes, I pointed a finger at myself, acknowledging their greetings. I was surprised to learn that my father's cousin Ann Joffe (née Galgut) and her husband Harry had flown to Johannesburg from Cape Town to welcome us at the airport. Also at the airport were Rhoda Reichman and her mother Becky who, during our visit to Johannesburg, turned over to us her apartment in the Linksfield section of the city, with her housekeeper, car, and driver. Rhoda had in the meantime secured for the triplets an unbelievably wonderful nanny.

The wedding, held close to the waterfall pool and the nearby tennis court in the garden of the Reichman home in the Senderwood section of the city, was nothing short of spectacular. All three boys were part of the wedding procession. At this wonderfully warm home we spent many a day swimming, dining, and playing. We also met Jessica's brother Myrone, with whom we also spent time. On many mornings on the way to court from Pretoria to Johannesburg, Supreme Court Justice Oscar Galgut, another relative, would pick me up; I was deeply impressed by his bearing and verbal facility in both English and Afrikaans.

While I was observing in court and when the children were not swimming in the pool, the driver and nanny showed Eleonora and the boys the highlights of the city. Eleonora and I also visited Pete's radiology office in town and met with a few Latvian Jews who were friends of the Reichmans. In the afternoons, Rhoda, Eleonora, and I usually had tea at one of the luxurious hotels. Evenings we were invited to visit the Reichmans' friends, had dinners with the Reichmans or in restaurants with the Joffes. This hospitable couple invited us to be their guests in Cape Town and we accepted with pleasure. The nanny was so competent that we were easy in our minds leaving the children with her, thus giving us some free time to enjoy ourselves. In New

York, before and after this trip, I made sure, whenever possible, to be home for dinner with Eleonora and the children.

While in Johannesburg, we met more relatives from the Galgut side of the family. Three sisters, Fanny Levin (whose son, Aaron, headed the pediatric cardiology department at Cornell Medical Center in New York and lived with his family in Larchmont, N.Y.), Polly Yawitch, and Bessie Mizroch. They invited us to tea in the afternoon, which we enjoyed immensely as we listened to family stories. Toward the end of our visit, Fanny was hospitalized with a heart condition; Eleonora and I visited her in the hospital, and subsequently we met her in New York when she was visiting her son and his family.

In the meantime, the Joffes left for Cape Town and we boarded a small plane for Mala Mala, an exclusive safari resort. Together with the boys, we enjoyed immensely the experience of being driven in daylight and late evenings throughout in the huge park—observing animals roaming freely unlike in zoos; we also enjoyed the near-midnight dinner in the open feasting on impala.

At one point, Solan removed one of his shoes and put his foot into a lake that had some hippopotamuses. One swam toward him. Luckily Eleonora saw what was happening and quickly grabbed him by the collar and pulled him back.

Back in Johannesburg, the Reichmans took us and the kids to a huge stadium where African dancers performed. We enjoyed it greatly and were struck by the enormous talent of the indigenous people. Before leaving for Cape Town, the family toured Soweto. Although some Africans lived there extremely well, overall it was a sorry sight to see how Africans were compelled to live in a ghetto—even though it was a far cry from a German Nazi ghetto. To me and to Eleonora, racial discrimination was anathema. While the family stayed in Johannesburg, I flew for a two-day visit to Bulawayo, Rhodesia, to visit Raya and Gustav Smith who had moved from the United States to live near her brother.

Slowly we began to prepare for the trip to Cape Town. Somehow Pete Reichman had managed to obtain permission for our African nanny to accompany us on the plane—a very happy development as we truly loved her. At the airport in Cape Town, we were welcomed by Ann and Harry Joffe and were then driven to their large, handsome apartment overlooking the Atlantic Ocean on Beach Road in the Sea Point section of Cape Town. Eleonora and I were struck by the handsome works of art by African painters that adorned their walls. After a while, we were driven to the Ritz Hotel, also located in Sea Point, where we stayed for ten days. During our visit, we met their children: Henry Joffe and his wife Lorna, and Myra who was married to Dr. Gerald Sutin; Dr. Sutin had worked with Dr. Christiaan Barnard—the surgeon who had performed the first-ever heart transplant surgery. We also met the Sutins' children (Linda, David, and Claire); and we were introduced to another relative, Myna Dennis, born a Galgut.

Every day without fail, Ann Joffe fetched us from the hotel at 10 in the morning and drove us around Cape Town, showing us, among other places, the point at which the Atlantic Ocean met the Indian Ocean. We also had the thrilling experience of having baboons follow our car and even jump on it. For years, the children talked about this unique experience, telling it time and again to their friends. We also had lunch several times at the top of Table Mountain, which was in the center of the city. Ann, Eleonora, and I also had tea several times at the luxurious Mt. Nelson Hotel. Ann also drove us to the wine country Muizenberg and Stellenbosch; in Stellenbosch, we visited its university.

On returning to Johannesburg, we gradually began to prepare for our return to New York. It was difficult to say good-bye to Ann and Harry with whom we had truly bonded and the Reichmans. In fact, the Joffes surprised us by coming to Johannesburg to bid us farewell. We soon learned that they had established a fund for our children's education. Because of transfer restrictions we, for many years, were able to receive only the interest. To acknowledge in part all this extraordinary hospitality, Eleonora and I invited the Reichmanns and the Joffes to a farewell dinner at the Langham Hotel.

As Eleonora was interested in visiting her family in Stockholm, she then flew with the children to Sweden while I returned to New York. Eleonora stayed with the boys at her brother's home. On visiting her parents, her mother asked whether she had come to Stockholm to find out what her inheritance would be. Also on this trip, Eleonora's mother locked her four-year-old grandson Clarence in a closet for having applied some of her rouge to his face. I subsequently told her how lucky she was that I was not there, for I would have done the same to her. She just stared at me. The boys adored their warm-hearted and loving grandfather. After returning to New York with the children, Eleonora needed weeks to recover from the snake pit that was life in her former home.

Shortly after Eleonora and the triplets returned, she discovered a lump in her breast, which turned out to be malignant. We consulted specialists and decided that she should have a mastectomy at Columbia-Presbyterian. We were assured by the surgeon that the cancer had not spread and that there was no necessity for radiation or chemotherapy. Some weeks after the operation, her mother decided to visit New York. I was civil but largely ignored her.

From early on in the lives of our sons, I attempted to inculcate the importance of work. Thus, when, in the wee hours of the morning the triplets would jump into our bed wanting to play, I would inform them that I soon would have to get up to go to work; they insisted on doing likewise. So, we began to prepare them for the time that they, too. would go to work; they looked forward to going to work at the Lincoln Square Synagogue's nursery, a stone's throw away from where we then lived. Their greatest thrill was for us to leave for work together—they to their nursery and I to City College; toward the end of the day, we often compared notes.

Strong believers in a thorough and structured education, we enrolled all three at the Lycée Française de New York on East 72nd Street (a school to which many UN diplomats sent their children). In those days, a graduate of the Lycée usually received up to two years of college credit at American colleges and universities. The school considered English a foreign tongue, which was taught once a week; we, however, lived in the United States, so Eleonora and I decided after six years to transfer the boys to an outstanding American private school. Browning, a small, highly regarded boys' school, was strongly recommended to us.

Following the thorough education that Clarence, Claude, and Solan had received at the Lycée, they considered the coursework at Browning easy. After three years at Browning, Clarence was fed up with what he considered ghetto life, took the exam for the competitive Bronx High School of Science, and was accepted. There, he informed Eleonora and me, he, for the first time, saw what life really was and would give his lunch to poor kids; he also informed us that we had no clue of what life outside the ghetto was really like.

Clarence excelled at school and, upon graduation, continued his education at Columbia and Harvard universities. Neither Claude nor Solan entertained the notion of going to a public school no matter how prestigious. They remained at Browning, where they were permitted to establish the French journal titled *En Avant*—a publication that continues to thrive. Upon graduation, Claude continued his education at the University of Pennsylvania; after graduation, he pursued two graduate degrees at Columbia and at the University of Pennsylvania. Solan went to the University of Chicago and Georgetown Law.

Even during the difficult 1970s and 1980s, we spent many summers in the United States and in Europe. In the summer following the birth of the triplets, for example, the parents of Eleonora's friend Gaby Hammer insisted that we spend that season at their summer home in Croton-on-Hudson, which was surrounded by acres of land and had a large pond. Years later, my cousin Aaron Levin and his wife Lenore invited us to spend about four weeks house-sitting in Larchmont, New York, while they were away visiting their families in South Africa. There we often swam in the nearby Long Island Sound and explored Westchester. At times, we rented a house in the Catskill Mountains that belonged to Max and Erna Hilfstein. (She was a former undergraduate student of mine at City College and later at CUNY's Graduate Center.) We also spent time with Victor and Renia Gelb at their summer retreat in Freedom, New Hampshire. The children also went to Camp Hillard day camp and, for two summers, to Brantley, a sleep-away camp in the Adirondacks close to the Canadian border. In New York, when not abroad in the 1970s and 1980s, we frequented the Atlantic Beach Club in Long Island in the summer. We had been introduced to the club by Amy Nammack's mother.

Amy, who was about five years older than the triplets, was also a student at the French Lycée and often babysat for them; she adored the boys. The triplets considered her to be their older sister and the adoration was mutual. At the club, we did a lot of swimming in the ocean and the pool; the children also took tennis lessons. A regular guest of ours at the club was Wlado, with whom the children enjoyed playing tennis. He was a real pro.

A number of summers we also spent with the family of Eleonora's brother in Stockholm and at their summer home on the island of Rådmans (some 50 miles from Stockholm), where the cousins—Tobias and Elisabeth (Flisa) and our sons played with one another. My brother-in-law Marcus and I played gin rummy for hours on end to the annoyance of his wife Gunilla and Eleonora. In Stockholm, our children played with aunt Ruth's (Eleonora's sister) children: Robert and Nina. The triplets also enjoyed exploring Stockholm, especially visiting the Vasa maritime museum and, with their grandfather, a casino located inside the Sheraton Hotel in the center of town. In the summer of 1976, we visited Paris, where I introduced the children to Georges Dayez and his daughter Anne (whom the children had already met in New York when she stayed with us). Clarence in particular was eager to meet Mr. Dayez as he was convinced that he could paint and draw at least as well as the artist. Thus, before leaving for Paris, I informed Georges that he would be meeting a competitor and that he should be prepared to engage him in a match. As we were walking toward his studio, Clarence began to have cold feet and wasn't sure whether we should abandon the visit. As the die had been cast, I told him we had no choice but to proceed. Dayez was prepared for the three of them to do some drawings on his huge desk and we all had fun. We were also warmly received by Joseph and Shulamit Grynholc. She was a cousin of my father, which I discovered when the family visited Johannesburg. After touring the usual sites in Paris and Versailles and where I used to live when I studied in Paris, we flew to Munich to visit the Laus and introduce the children to the Jevelsons. We also visited the Laus' summer home in Ambach where we explored the beautiful surroundings. In

1980, our friend Gwendolyn (Gwennie) Chabrier, who much later wrote a novel about my war years (*Behind the Barbed Wire*), invited us to spend part of the summer at her vacation residence in the French Alps, which we gratefully accepted. From New York, we flew to Geneva and from there in two taxis proceeded to Megève where Gwennie had a duplex apartment in a residential hotel that also had a swimming pool. There we, for the first time, saw topless women—a sensation for the children. About two weeks after our arrival, Claude came up to me and said that the triplets were bored and that we should leave Megève for the French Riviera. On asking him why they were bored, he confessed that he and his brothers learned from one of their French playmates that on the Riviera the women were also bottomless. Eleonora and I did not heed his request.

In addition to doing a lot of swimming and hiking every day, the children did some horseback riding and Solan jumped off his mount as the horse was galloping toward a lake; he proceeded to explore on foot the village and environs and enjoyed French cuisine.

As the dollar in relation to the franc was at all-time low, I began to run out of cash and left for Zurich to fetch money from my late mother's account. In Zurich, I met Jimmy and Barbara Lau who had driven from Munich to meet me; together we drove back to Megève[3] for a wonderful reunion. There we were also visited by Bernard and Eleonor Brown who usually spent summers in France.

After celebrating the children's birthday in Megève, we departed for Paris and visited the Grynholcs and George Dayez. Once again, we took the children on sightseeing trips to the Eifel Tower and Versailles and the places I had lived; we drove to La Baule where the children went to a day camp; on the way back to Paris, we drove through chateau country. Thanks in large measure to Gwennie, we had an incredible summer.

Angry at the low dollar exchange rate, I felt I had to console myself and bought a very large oil painting by Dayez titled *The Bathers*, which had been exhibited at Artcurial in Paris in 1978 and reproduced in the catalogue. Dayez rolled it up in a huge tube, which the children carried aboard the plane and which the crew dubbed "the bazooka."

Passovers we usually spent with the Saidemans, Sutins, Levins, or Wieners. On Thanksgiving, we were usually invited by the Plottels to watch the Thanksgiving Day parade from their Central Park West window. As both Eleonora and I enjoyed entertaining, we often hosted dinner parties and receptions at home.

On our return from France in 1980, the children began to prepare for their bar mitzvah in 1982. A triplet bar mitzvah was a sensation. To perform the ceremony, the charismatic Rabbi Shlomo Riskin of the Lincoln Square Synagogue postponed his move to Israel by about six months. The cantor for the day was none other than the celebrated Sherwood Goffin. Well over a hundred relatives and guests were on hand; they hailed from all over, my in-laws from Sweden, other relatives and friends from Israel, South Africa, England and, of course, the United States. On the following day, Eleonora and I hosted a reception in our home. It was this bar mitzvah that inspired Gwennie to write the novel about me.

Notes

1. "The Case of Professor Henry Friedlander: Department of History, 1970-1972;." Department of Jewish Studies, 1972. The City College of the City University of New York (Spring 1974), p. 25.
2. Ibid., p. 40.
3. Barbara Lau recently reminded me in New York that upon arriving in Zurich we went straight to the bank. Because of a holiday, the bank was closed and I could not access my mother's account. I was fortunate that the Laus were able to help me until it reopened.

Chapter XIII
NATIONAL COMMITTEE ON AMERICAN FOREIGN POLICY (NCAFP)—HIGHLIGHTS

One morning in Megève, in July1980, I picked up the *International Herald Tribune* and learned to my shock that Professor Hans J. Morgenthau (author of *Politics Among Nations*—bible of students of international relations)—founder of the NCAFP in 1974—had died at age 76. Only a month or so earlier, he had attended one of our dinner parties in New York, where he met and took a liking to Gwennie; she did not reciprocate.

I had met Hans J. Morgenthau in the early 1970s after he had retired from the University of Chicago and had joined CUNY's City College and Graduate Center's political science departments. He had read my book on Carl Schmitt, and, at a series of luncheons, he made no bones about his dislike of Schmitt and that he disagreed in particular with my conclusion that Schmitt's anti-Semitism was opportunistic—seen in his writings only after Hitler's accession to power in 1933. I told Morgenthau that in Schmitt's writings prior to 1933, I had found no evidence of anti-Semitism. Further, I noted Schmitt's influence on and association with, among others, Otto Kirchheimer, Franz Neumann, and Leo Strauss—as previously noted, Schmitt had helped obtain a Rockefeller fellowship that enabled Strauss to complete his study of Hobbes in France and England. Also, Schmitt dedicated his *Verfassungslehre* (1928) to his bosom friend Fritz Eisler who had been killed during World War I.

Intellectual disagreements notwithstanding, Morgenthau in passing had mentioned on several occasions that he had been approached by a number of people suggesting that he become head of a think tank currently in formation. Unlike other think tanks, for example the Council on Foreign Relations, this one would formulate foreign policies based on principles of political realism, which were planned to be submitted in the name of the organization to our government and the public. I, too, I said, have heard something to that effect at City College but that Morgenthau's name had not been mentioned. "Would I, in principle, be interested in joining such an organization?" he asked. "Yes," I replied.

How could I have said no to Morgenthau—a towering intellect? As a Cold War warrior deeply concerned by the global aspirations of the Soviet Union whose policies continued to be underpinned by militant Marxist-Leninist ideology, I was influenced by Morgenthau's balance of power concept as a means of avoiding major conflicts. So far as the Soviet Union was concerned, I also subscribed to the concept of containment as articulated by George F. Kennan. To counter Soviet propaganda on the merits of the dictatorship of the proletariat, the United States must strengthen its global reach by stressing the values of liberal democracy as practiced in the United States that includes inalienable rights, religious and political toleration, freedom of speech, the separation of powers, and the rule of law.

The new organization was born in response to the disarray in U.S. foreign policy caused by the Watergate scandal, anti-Americanism in Europe, the Israeli-Arab conflict, and the bitter debate over the so-called policy of détente (lessening of tensions) in Europe vis-à-vis the Soviet Union. Next, I was told that a meeting would be held at the home of Ambassador Ira Hirschmann in New York, who, working on behalf of the War Refugee Board during the Second World War, had used bribes to rescue countless numbers of Jews from Romania, Hungary, and Bulgaria. I was invited to attend this meeting, which would constitute the official launch of the think tank to be known as the National Committee on American Foreign Policy (NCAFP). A conflict with my teaching schedule prevented me from attending, however. Despite my absence, I was made a co-founder of the NCAFP in 1974 and a member of its Board of Directors.[1]

In regard to the so-called policy of détente, the United States had hoped that the lessening of tensions in Europe largely as a result of the two Germanys reaching agreement in 1973 that recognized the fact on the ground that they are, for good, separate entities. As there was no lessening of tensions elsewhere between East and West, I could not conclude, based on my extensive readings of Marxist-Leninist literature about tactics, how best to maneuver in the struggle to acquire political power. Accordingly, I was under no illusion that Moscow was prepared to pursue genuine détente. So far as I was concerned, Moscow considered détente nothing more than one of the instruments in its toolbox aimed at destabilizing Western Europe and undermining NATO—a "salami slice" tactic of divide and, ultimately, rule. At NCAFP conferences and at press briefings in New York and Washington, Morgenthau, too, argued that détente in Europe with the Soviet Union, however positive, would be more meaningful if it were indivisible—that is, applicable everywhere. Stated succinctly, I argued that détente in Europe is more than questionable so long as the Soviet Union continues to pursue its aggressive policies in the Middle East, Africa, Central America, and elsewhere. The bankruptcy of U.S. policy was exposed in 1973, when Egypt and Syria—with up-to-date Soviet weaponry—attacked Israel, the only liberal democracy in the Middle East.

The controversy surrounding the U.S. policy of détente reached feverish heights, until President Ford in 1976 forbade his speechwriters to use that word. At the NCAFP we celebrated this event as our first material input into U.S. foreign policy.

Not long after the birth of the NCAFP, I was approached by Jac Friedgut, an officer, who suggested that I become the editor of a newsletter that would "serve as the Committee's face to the world." I accepted the offer with alacrity. By way of the power of the written word, I was convinced, I could continue to help reverse the ill-conceived U.S. foreign policy toward Soviet Russia. Further, it would also enable me to reinforce the message of liberal democratic America constituting a beacon of light to the world.[2] The first issue appeared in November 1976, with the lead article by Hans Morgenthau titled "Enduring Realities and Foreign Policy." As I became more active in the NCAFP, Morgenthau said to me: "I [Morgenthau] am the chairman of the NCAFP, but you will do the work." (Little did I realize then that this would be the case until I retired from the presidency of the NCAFP at the end of January 2015.)

Given the disarray in our foreign policy, I, director of CUNY Graduate Center's Conference on History and Politics, organized a conference on "United States Foreign Policy at the Crossroads" in 1980. In my presentation, titled "Toward an Open-Society Bloc," I spoke of the need for much of the world to confront Soviet aggression by forging a global counterforce. My thought was that countries genuinely committed to liberal democratic values should constitute the core of countries of an open society defensive bloc. Like-minded but legally neutral countries, for example, Switzerland, could gravitate toward the bloc as an associate country. Countries that were not yet liberal democracies, for example, Argentina, could, in turn, gravitate toward associate and core countries in designing strategies and tactics to thwart aggression. Given the variety of sovereign states, the best that could be hoped for is agreement on fundamentals.[3] I was delighted, of course, that the NCAFP embraced the idea—which did not come as a surprise. In 1982, Secretary of State Alexander M. Haig, in the context of a more limited framework, coined the phrase "strategic consensus," which appropriately captured the idea of an open society bloc.

With variations on a theme, the concept I advanced was later discussed by the Council on Foreign Relations in the United States and by think tanks in Canada and Western Europe. Further, The University of Freiburg in Germany and the military academy near Hamburg invited me to speak on my concept. It may also be argued that the Partnership for Peace (PfP), which was formed in 1994 in the midst of the Balkan crisis, may to an extent also have been inspired by the concept of the open society bloc. Its purpose was for Euro-Atlantic countries to bilaterally strengthen security relationships as well as with NATO. (Neutral Switzerland, too, became a member.)

A material turning point in the fate of the NCAFP, and to an extent in my life, came about circuitously. In the mid-1980s, Elie Wiesel—a member of the NCAFP board—invited me to become an adviser in the development and building of the United States Holocaust Memorial Museum in Washington, D.C. I agreed, and he assigned me to serve on the Collections and Acquisitions Committee (on which I continue to serve). Soon thereafter he received, in 1986, the Nobel Peace Prize; with the prize money, he established the Elie Wiesel Foundation for Humanity and appointed Sister of Mercy Dr. Carol Rittner as the first director of the foundation. I bonded with her as did Eleonora and our sons (whom she hired as interns during the summer). She became a regular guest at our home, meeting friends (including Gaby Schiff and Anita Warburg who were also members with me of the American Federation of Jews from Central Europe). From time to time, she slept over in Clarence's bed; he was proud to tell his friends that not many people could claim that a nun had slept in my bed.

In 1988, Elie, jointly with President François Mitterand of France co-hosted at the Elysée Palace in Paris a conference of more than 70 Nobel laureates to discuss "Facing the 21st Century: Threats and Promises." Elie invited me to be his adviser on issues pertaining to disarmament and peace. Toward that end, Sister Carol asked that I come to Paris to assist her with the organization of the conference and, subsequently, I returned to be at Elie's side.

The conference, as I understand it, was underwritten by the Wiesel Foundation, President Mitterand, and William J. Flynn who, at the time, was chairman of the Board and Chief Executive Officer of Mutual of America in New York.

The day preceding the conference a good number of participants accepted the suggestion by President Mitterand that we visit Auschwitz-Birkenau. On landing in Cracow, we were welcomed by Lech Wałęsa, head of the Solidarity movement—the first independent trade union established in a country in the Soviet orbit. In a long procession of cars, we first visited an old synagogue that had not been destroyed by the Germans and the Jewish cemetery next to it. From there, we proceeded to Auschwitz-Birkenau.

There we said Kaddish, of course, and proceeded to familiar sights: barracks and crematoria. Reliving on-site the horrors of an extermination camp as was Stutthof—the reason I never visited it after the war—I could not wait to return to Paris.

The overall tone of the conference regarding the coming century was optimistic. Bearing in mind the recent end of Mao Zedong's bloody Cultural Revolution, the ascendancy of Deng Xiaoping with his gradual modernization reforms in China in the late 1970s, and Mikhail Gorbachev's more recent *glasnost* and *perestroika* policies in Soviet Russia—respectively, the increased transparency in government institutions and activities and economic reforms loosening central control, even allowing some private ownership—hopes were high about the further democratization of the Communist system with all that that implied. Of special concern were human rights and the elimination of the scourge of nuclear terrorism. The SALT I and SALT II treaties signed by the United States and the Soviet Union in 1972 and 1979 were good beginnings in limiting the nuclear arms race.

Throughout the conference I could not help but think of the horrors that Auschwitz-Birkenau symbolized with the dreamlike setting of the Elysée Palace: the furniture, chandeliers, champagne receptions, gastronomic feasts of which the French are masters, and spending time with Nobel laureates were experiences never to be forgotten (comparable, but on a smaller scale, was a Nobel laureate dinner in Stockholm in 2009 to which Sheila Johnson Robbins and I were invited by my brother-in-law, Marcus Storch, who was chairman of the Nobel Foundation). Also, in Paris, Sister Carol introduced me to William Flynn, with whom I developed a warm relationship and who expressed interest in joining the NCAFP, which had, as I will relate below, far-reaching results.

Following our return from Europe, Bill Flynn began to attend meetings of the NCAFP, was impressed by our public programs, and became a member. What he did not know was that the NCAFP's finances were more than strained, despite the committee's president, Ambassador Francis L. Kellogg (with his wife Mercedes) being a prominent member of New York society, which opened doors to the city's social elite. Sister Carol, too, was impressed with the work of the committee and did not want to see the organization fail; so she engineered an invitation from Mr. Flynn to have me, Eleonora, herself, and two Mutual of America executives—Stephanie Kopp and Linda DeHooge—join him for an evening out on the town. Sister Carol insisted that this would be a fine opportunity to approach Mr. Flynn about our shaky finances and ask him to help me save the organization. Bill Flynn invited us to a wonderful restaurant in the West 40s that had a large dance floor and an orchestra. We all had a wonderful time and Mr. Flynn whirled Eleonora around the dance floor more than once. I was unaccustomed to asking for money, but Sister Carol was insistent, kicking me under the table and saying *sotto voce* "ask already." I kept saying, "I can't." At last I gathered my courage and said: "We at the NCAFP are facing a financial crisis." He listened and asked me gently how much it would take to keep the think tank going. My reply: $10,000, but with $20,000 we would be in heaven. With a smile on his face, he looked at me and said: "In the morning you will have a check on your desk in the latter amount." What a relief that was. (The unswerving support the NCAFP has received from Mutual of America is unprecedented. I wish to acknowledge and thank Bill Flynn, Thomas J. Moran, and John R. Greed.)

Although I was pushed to become president of the NCAFP by the mid-1980s, I did not feel I was up to it. I was comfortable to be the intellectual guide of the organization. Further, I was afraid that it might adversely affect my university duties. All in all, I was comfortable with what I had been doing, namely, guarding Morgenthau's legacy by way of publications, conferences, and continuing to identify, articulate, and help advance American foreign policy interests from a non-partisan perspective within the framework of political realism.

Upon assuming the presidency in the early 1990s, at about the same time Bill Flynn had become NCAFP chairman, he suggested that to save money the NCAFP move to the Mutual of America headquarters at 666 Fifth Avenue, which we did. He also suggested that we take the initiative to bring the warring terrorist parties of Northern Ireland to the table. However challenging and intriguing the idea was to a former Sternist, I needed a rationale to justify the Committee's becoming involved in a sectarian conflict between Catholics and Protestants, a conflict far removed from global political power rivalries.

Although my knowledge of the conflict in Northern Ireland was cursory, I was fortunate to have had Edwina McMahon, a specialist on Ireland and former assistant of mine at CUNY's Graduate Center, as my associate editor. Over the years she had talked to me and written for our publications about the conflict and Britain's involvement in Northern Ireland. This provided me the hook with which to present the issue to our executive committee.

As Britain was in a deep economic slump, I argued that she could ill-afford to spend billions of pounds annually on Northern Ireland (population about one and a half million people) without it affecting our mutual security interests in Europe, the Middle East, and elsewhere. After all, like-minded Great Britain was our closest military ally. Following spirited discussions ably led by Bill Flynn and with the support of Ambassador Angier Biddle Duke (a former president of the NCAFP), and myself, the executive committee finally supported the idea.

With the committee's support behind him, Bill Flynn sprang into action. He argued that the U.S. could play a material role in bringing about peace in Northern Ireland. The immediate issue centered on how to bridge the gap between the political stances of Catholic republicans and Protestant unionists. Flynn used the Downing Street Declaration of 1993 (drawn up by Prime Minister John Major of Britain and Prime Minister Albert Reynolds of Ireland, it proclaimed the right of the people of Northern Ireland to self-determination) as a starting point.

Flynn's idea was to host a conference on Northern Ireland at New York's Waldorf-Astoria to which the NCAFP would invite leaders from both sides. Invitations were sent to Gerry Adams, president of Sinn Fein (the political arm of the IRA); James Molyneaux of the Ulster Unionist Party; the Reverend Ian Paisley, head of the Democratic Unionist Party; John Hume, leader of the Social Democratic and Labour Party[4]; and Dr. John Alderdice, leader of the Alliance Party. Paisley and Molyneaux refused to attend because Adams (allegedly a former IRA operative) had been invited. Adams accepted but was denied a visa by the State Department. Flynn, not one to take "no" for an answer, mobilized his vast contacts in the American Irish community and friends, including, among others, Senator Edward Kennedy; Jean Kennedy Smith, U.S. ambassador to Ireland; Tony Lake, President Clinton's national security adviser; and Nancy Soderberg, his deputy, to counter the State Department's refusal to give Adams a visa by appealing directly to President Clinton. As I saw the process moving very slowly and the conference was about to start at the beginning of February 1994, I suggested to Flynn that we call off the gathering as without Adams there could be no deal. He did not concur and he was right. Seeing the merits of such a conference, President Clinton at the last minute overruled the State Department and ordered the issuance of a 48-hour visa to Adams. This caused an uproar at the State Department and at 10 Downing Street. The *Daily Telegraph* described the decision as "the worst rift since Suez."

As Adams was about to arrive at Kennedy, Bill Flynn asked that I, as head of the NCAFP, and Sister Carol be the ones to welcome him at the airport and we did. A huge press conference took place at the airport followed by our trip back to Manhattan with the driver and Bill Barry, Flynn's security agent, in the front and Sister Carol, Gerry, and me in the back. I introduced myself to Gerry as a former Sternist and indicated that we were both fighting the British. We became so engrossed in our conversation that Bill Barry interrupted us and said to me, "Please let Mr. Adams see something of New York." Upon arriving at the Waldorf-Astoria, we checked Adams in under the name Shlomo Breznitz, a very well-known Israeli scholar.

Demonstrations for and against the conference across the street from the hotel did not prevent the conference from convening the following day. As at the airport, the open-door gathering was flooded by the media. To add both pizzazz and gravitas to the conference, Flynn and I agreed that Ambassador Duke should be the conference's moderator. I also arranged for a photographer to photograph Adams with my friend and colleague Professor Arthur M. Schlesinger, Jr., dean of American historians. Duke welcomed Flynn, me, and the speakers, making introductory remarks that were followed by presentations by Alderdice, Hume, and Adams.

For the first time the United States and not just the American Irish community was made aware of the reasons behind the conflict that had taken the lives of many thousands. Stated succinctly: the largely Protestant majority was committed to remaining part of Britain in contrast to the Catholic nationalist or republican position that was intent on ridding Northern Ireland of British control and, eventually, joining Ireland. The three speakers did agree on the need to remove the gun from Irish politics and that the conflict could not be resolved by military means. The Downing Street Declaration was, more or less, accepted by the three speakers as a working document. And all three agreed on the principle "from many we are one." In the words of John Hume, "The essence of unity is the acceptance of diversity."

Adams was concerned about the absence of details. Hence, he questioned whether Britain was truly prepared to give up control of Northern Ireland. His problem with the declaration was that it notes, "processes, measures, and steps envisaged. . . .The declaration is described . . . as the 'first step.' What then is the second step? Or the third step." In other words, Adams questioned "the real motives of the British government."

What we had hoped for from Adams did not materialize, namely, a commitment from him as head of the political arm of the IRA to urge it to cease its terrorist activities in Northern Ireland and in England. But all was not bleak. On the way back to the airport, I asked Gerry where do we go from here? He said, "George, I promise you that we will not go back to the old ways."

The enormous publicity that the conference had engendered took Paisley by surprise, and he did not want to be left out. At Bill Flynn's urging, we re-invited him and he accepted, arriving in New York with his associate, Peter Robinson and the Reverend William McCrea in mid-April. Known for his bombastic anti-Catholic speeches, Paisley did not disappoint the audience.

Paisley blasted the Downing Street Declaration, calling it "a phony peace process inspired by Prime Minister John Major of Britain and Prime Minister Albert Reynolds of the Republic of Ireland." He maintained that by selling out the Protestant majority of Northern Ireland and by implicitly condoning terrorism in Northern Ireland by the left-wing Marxist fanatic "Gerry Adams... the godfather of terrorism in Northern Ireland," the British government was in the "business of surrender and betrayal."

Attacks against the Downing Street Declaration notwithstanding, Paisley did leave room for negotiations between Northern Ireland and Ireland, so long as "Dublin [is] prepared to spell out that it accepts Northern Ireland's status as an integral part of the United Kingdom both de facto and de jure." He reminded the audience that the majority consider "themselves as British. Their lifestyle, their culture, their history, their identity... hinge on the long gestation of Britishness." Paisley's deputy, Peter Robinson, was just as adamant that Northern Ireland must be part of the United Kingdom.

Realistically, we could not expect the friction between the two sides to dissipate overnight. But what impressed the Northern Irish leaders was the NCAFP's evenhandedness; we thus gained their trust.

To show their gratitude for materially helping the opponents to remove the bullet from these very fraught politics, the Irish Republican Army announced on August 31, 1994, the complete cessation of military actions. The Loyalists followed suit on October 13, 1994. They even invited Bill Flynn, a Catholic, to be present when they made their announcement.

The removal of the bullet from politics opened the door to further negotiations. We knew that years would be needed to heal wounds and that the NCAFP would have to continue to play a material role in the confidence-building process. As a prime mover in bringing the opposing parties to the table, Bill Flynn continued his shuttle diplomacy. On several occasions I, among others, including Thomas J. Moran, accompanied him to Belfast and Dublin. Bill Flynn and I were also invited to 10 Downing Street in London.

It was heartening to hear Gerry Adams state in New York at an NCAFP conference in September 1994 that "Ireland would not be Ireland without our Protestant brothers and sisters." The words of David Ervine, head of the Progressive Unionist Party and a former Loyalist terrorist, at an NCAFP conference in October 1994 were also encouraging: "Let us firmly resolve to respect our differing views of freedom, culture, and aspirations and never again permit our political circumstances to degenerate into bloody war."

The publicity that the 1994 conference engendered strengthened contacts that we had with Washington in general and with the White House in particular. The Clintons even hosted a reception in honor of Gerry Adams to which Bill Flynn and I were invited. Our new-won prominence was not lost on the People's Republic of China (PRC). As may be remembered, in the mid-1990s, the PRC was on a serious collision course with Taiwan—the Republic of China (ROC)—over the issue of the ROC hinting that it might declare de jure independence; the PRC strenuously objected to this because of the PRC's insistence that Taiwan is part of China. To show its seriousness, China even fired missiles off the coast of Taiwan in March 1996 and threatened to attack the island were it to declare de jure independence. An attack on Taiwan could bring the U.S. into the conflict because of the Taiwan Relations Act of 1979, which noted that the U.S. would come to Taiwan's aid were China to attack Taiwan. Because of the growing relationship between the U.S. and China, despite China's aggressive behavior toward Taiwan, tensions in the region could explode—which would not serve the U.S. national security interest.

Due to our new-won prominence and because Secretary Henry A. Kissinger was the NCAFP's honorary chairman, I began to be courted by, among others, Guo Changlin of the PRC Mission to the United Nations. It soon became evident that his assignment was to sound me out about whether the NCAFP could play a similar role in defusing tensions between the two sides of the Taiwan Strait as we did in Northern Ireland. To me it sounded very challenging—another Track I½ and Track II project—and Bill Flynn was supportive as was the executive committee, and Henry Kissinger asked to be kept informed.

As I was not conversant with the ins and outs of this issue, I approached a colleague at CUNY's Graduate Center, Professor Donald S. Zagoria. On asking if he would consider heading the project, he agreed. We titled it U.S.-China Relations and the Question of Taiwan. Changlin soon invited me to lead a fact-finding mission to Beijing. Prior to embarking on our first trip to both sides of the Strait, Changlin arranged for me to have a private meeting in Shanghai with the esteemed Wang Daohan, president of the Association for Relations Across the Taiwan Straits (ARATS) and former mayor of Shanghai who had convinced party officials to name his protégé, Jiang Zemin, a future president of China. Changlin also told me that arrangements had been made for me to meet privately in Taiwan with Wang Daohan's counterpart, Koo Chen-fu, head of the Straits Exchange Foundation (SEF).

When I met Wang Daohan, a charming gentleman, he asked me to extend his greetings to Mr. Koo—for whom he appeared to have warm feelings—and to suggest that they continue their conversations, which had been interrupted because of political tensions between Beijing and Taipei. As an incentive, he suggested that I hint that the principle of the "1992 Consensus" (that Taiwan is part of China) could be tweaked.

"The 1992 Consensus" is a concept that was floated by Taiwan and states that both sides of the Taiwan Strait belong to One China but that each side of the Taiwan Strait interprets its particular political system. Whereas the Mainland had no problem with the One China part of the concept, the second part was a nonstarter. Hence, what did Wang Daohan mean by "tweaking" the "1992 Consensus"? In the following years of the NCAFP's fact-finding missions to both sides of the Strait in which we endeavored to bring about the lessening of tensions between the two sides of the Strait, which would serve U.S. national security interests, I kept meeting with Wang Daohan and Koo Chen-fu. It soon became clear to me that Beijing could passively accept a de facto Taiwan but that the lawful seat of government of the One China is in Beijing. Full stop.

For years I considered myself to be a messenger boy between Wang Daohan and Koo Chen-fu. But it was not in vain. Under President Ma Ying-jeou of the Kuomintang Party (KMT) relations between the two sides of the Strait improved dramatically. He was not offensive toward the Mainland, which was reciprocated. Trade between the two sides of the Taiwan Strait increased materially as did tourism. Even President Ma's predecessor, Chen Shui-bian of the more aggressive Democratic Progressive Party (DPP), admitted that "the National Committee on American Foreign Policy's program is the best Track Two effort that exists in contributing to the stability in the Taiwan Strait." According to Dr. Kissinger, no organization has achieved more proven positive results in its Track I½ and Track II diplomacy with China and Taiwan than has the National Committee on American Foreign Policy.

Gradually the NCAFP's mandate expanded beyond U.S./China/Taiwan relations to also include U.S. security relations with Japan and the Koreas, which took my delegations to Tokyo and Seoul. Because of the enlarged mandate, we renamed the project to Forum on Asia Pacific Security (FAPS). Thus, in addition to our fact-finding mission to China and Taiwan, in New York, I also began to host Track I½ round-table discussions with North Korean delegations that included First Vice Minister Kim Kye Gwan, Ambassador Ri Gun, Mrs. Choe Son Hui, and Mrs. Hwang Myong Sim. Though the "New York Connection"—as our line of communication is known—continues, the NCAFP's noteworthy success was accomplished in New York in 2005 when North Korea agreed to return to the Six-Party Talks in Beijing. For that accomplishment, the NCAFP has "received what, in diplomatic circles, can only be called rave reviews," according to the fall 2005 issue of the *Carnegie Reporter*.[5]

Flashback to Mikhail Gorbachev's accession to power in the Soviet Union in 1985, which was followed by his introduction of *perestroika* and *glasnost*. At last I began to sense that things would change in the domestic Soviet arena but not necessarily in traditional Soviet foreign policy. In my wildest dreams I could not have imagined Soviet Russia collapsing. How wrong I was, and, as we all know, Gorbachev's reforms culminated in the collapse of the Soviet Union in 1991 followed by the dissolution of the Soviet empire. The death of militant Marxist-Leninist Soviet Russia obviously meant the end of the lethal Soviet aspiration of global domination. But the new Russia, though at bay, was still a nuclear superpower and an enormously large country with vast natural resources that still needed to be harnessed. Hence, it was only a matter of time, I was convinced, before Russia would reassert its traditional pre-Soviet age-old national interest in "extending" its borders as a means of protecting its homeland. This, at least, meant spheres of influence at Russia's periphery.

Following the collapse of the Soviet realm, debates reminiscent of the controversies surrounding the policy of détente erupted on both sides of the Atlantic. A school of thought gained traction mostly in Western Europe that centered on NATO. The argument advanced was that the danger the world once faced was gone and that NATO had become irrelevant and needed to be dissolved. Largely lost in the debate was that Russia was a sleeping giant. Hence, under my initiative, the NCAFP went on record as strongly opposing that view. Just as NATO had largely safeguarded peace in Europe since the end of the Second World War, it could do so in the future in the face of a reinvigorated traditional Russia, which was bound to happen sooner or later, and also guard against out-of-area threats emanating from the wider Middle East, most seriously, militant Islamic fundamentalism.

The anti-NATO chorus in Western Europe overlapped with widespread anti-Americanism largely attributable to envy that the United States had emerged from the Cold War as the sole superpower. Europeans also critiqued the U.S. for being trigger happy in its pursuit of narrow and largely irrelevant foreign and security policies. Europeans argued that the U.S. should, instead, follow the European model and concentrate on the process of negotiations and seek economic solutions to problems.

Alarmed by the possibility of the dissolution of the trans-Atlantic partnership, I invited noted personalities to address the NCAFP to counter the Europeans' myopic view. Thomas R. Pickering, then U.S. ambassador to Russia, noted, at the Inaugural Angier Biddle Duke Lecture in 1996, that, given the plight of Russia following the collapse of the Soviet Union, a "resurgent and aggressive Russia is unlikely to materialize in the near term." At the Fourth Angier Biddle Duke Lecture in 1999, General Brent Scowcroft observed that "The North Atlantic alliance is vital to the United States and I hope to Europe. Absent NATO, there is no automatic way for the United States to be part of European security." Speaking on "NATO and the Importance of the Transatlantic Link" (2002) at the NCAFP's Annual Board and Membership meeting, General Wesley K. Clark noted "that despite the demise of the Soviet Union, real security challenges would lie ahead . . . [for example] regional instability in the Balkans and around the periphery of the former Soviet Union."

To deepen our understanding of the ailing transatlantic security relationship, I invited Professor Bernard E. Brown, a leading expert on

Europe, to establish at the NCAFP a transatlantic project. At a series of meetings at NATO headquarters in Brussels, where we met with R. Nicholas Burns, our ambassador to NATO, in Geneva, and round-table conferences in New York, American and European participants largely agreed that a weak NATO would not serve the security interests of the members of the alliance as well as non-NATO members in Europe. To reinvigorate NATO, participants argued that to overcome anti-American sentiments and to an extent anti-European sentiments in the United States, a prerequisite would be to materially deepen relations between and among NATO countries in general. In the words of Ambassador Robert Hunter, the United States and the European Union (EU) should form a "natural community, the common interests and values of which should be institutionalized in a nonmilitary organization that could operate in the realm of economics, politics, society, and culture." Ambassador Herman J. Cohen spoke about the need to form a "clubhouse" of transatlantic democracies. These and similar suggestions are reminiscent of the concept of the open society bloc.

True that 9/11 jerked NATO into unanimously supporting the United States and awakened the West to the dangers that militant Islamic fundamentalism posed. But the individual who rapidly awakened the West to NATO's *raison d'être* was no other than Vladimir Putin when he became president of Russia.[6]

From its inception, the NCAFP's Middle East project took a strong position on the relevance of Israel to the United States—not always shared by some in the Washington foreign policy community. At conferences and press briefings in New York and Washington, Morgenthau and I stressed that Israel was the only like-minded country in the region and, as such, was a natural friend and ally of the U.S. as well a strategic asset to the U.S. in its confrontation with Soviet Russia. The decisive victories Israel won over Arab aggressors in 1967 and 1973 whose militaries were well equipped with Soviet weapons displayed how Israel, small in size and population, could hold her own against and defeat her far larger foes.

Later, I was fortunate to have been able to recruit Fereydoun Hoveyda, a renaissance intellectual, to head the NCAFP's Middle East project. Hoveyda was the last of the Shah of Iran's ambassadors to the United Nations; his brother, Abbas, was also the Shah's last prime minister. From Hoveyda I learned much about Islam in general and Arab Islam in particular.

Convinced that there can be no genuine peace between the Muslim world—especially the Arab Muslim world—and Israel and, by extension, the West—Hoveyda, early in the new century, organized a round-table conference titled "Can Muslims Accept Israel in Their Midst?" What made the proceedings so compelling was that most of the panelists were not Western experts but originally hailed from the region and had taught or were teaching at U.S. institutions of higher learning.[7] The presenters' consensus: "that a non-Muslim state will not be tolerated in the long run in the Middle East." For Israel to be accepted in the region and, by extension, for genuine peace between the Arab Muslim world and the West, would require Arab states to endorse "democracy, human rights, and cultural diversity." (Of interest: the demand for the 1,500 copies of the conference proceedings that were printed was so great that a second printing of 1,500 had to go to press shortly thereafter.)

As previously noted, Hoveyda also argued that there can be no genuine coexistence between the Arab world and the West so long as the Muslim mindset remained stuck in the Middle Ages. What was needed, according to him, was to bring that mindset into the twentieth century. In other words, the mindset had to be reeducated. Toward that end, Hoveyda organized additional groundbreaking conferences titled: "Reform and Human Development in the Muslim World"; "Democratic Reform and the Role of Women in the Muslim World"; and, "Arab Women and the Future of the Middle East."[8]

The word that became the focus of the gatherings was "reform." To bring the Muslim world into the twentieth century could only be brought about by the reformation of the mindset. This would entail on the part of the West to materially expand the use of cultural and other soft power tools, including mobilizing the media, calling on Muslim countries to adhere to the Universal Declaration of Human Rights, which members of the United Nations have signed, and highlighting those countries that refuse to do so. There is no doubt that the NCAFP gatherings and the summaries that were printed and widely disseminated contributed to igniting the Arab Spring in 2010.

Prior to Hoveyda's death, he asked that I appoint Amir Taheri as his successor, which I did. By and large he followed in Hoveyda's footsteps, but because of Iran's growing regional threat, which had implications for U.S. national security interests, the accent shifted to militant Shia and Sunni fundamentalism, Iran's drive to acquire nuclear weapons and become a nuclear proliferator, its aspiration to become the region's hegemon, and Iran's and Arab Islam's ambition to destroy Israel. Time and again the NCAFP went on record as favoring the destruction of militant Islamic fundamentalism, preventing Iran going nuclear and from acquiring biological and chemical materiel. Checking Iran's nuclear and non-nuclear ambitions, I argued that the U.S., with friends and allies, resort to imposing severe sanctions. In the overall context of the geopolitics of the greater Middle East, the Israeli-Palestinian conflict, though important in and of itself, was basically a regional irritant. The NCAFP has gone on record favoring a two-state solution. But so long as the Palestinians are divided and do not come to the negotiating table, Israel takes advantage by expanding its territory in the West Bank.

Because militant Islamic fundamentalism had infected parts of the African continent, I considered the NCAFP's Africa program—originally led by Peter Pham followed by Herman J. Cohen—an extension of our Middle East program. The grave threat that this disease presented was well captured by Cohen in the title of an article written for the NCAFP's *American Foreign Policy Interests* (vol. 35, no. 2, 2013): "Al Qaeda in Africa: The Creeping Menace to Sub-Sahara's 500 Million Muslims." Speaking about al-Qaeda at an NCAFP round-table on "The Greater Middle East: The New Political Landscape" (2012), Eva Sohlman noted that Yemen is its home, finding fertile ground there in 2009 after decades of civil war, tribal conflicts, terrorism, and the influence of the conservative school of Salafi Islam."

Perhaps because of the NCAFP's reputation as an activist think tank that articulates and supports realist policies and has influence in Washington, I was approached early in the new century by Kazakhstan officials. They were convinced that their geographic location in Central Asia made them vulnerable to China and Russia, and this fact should be a security interest to the United States. Even though Kazakhstan had voluntarily destroyed more than 1,000 nuclear warheads, delivery systems, and chemical weapons inherited after the collapse of the Soviet empire, the country was on the backburner of U.S. foreign policy concerns. I was also reminded that the country is pro-Western with a secular Muslim population and could serve as a model for the region and beyond. In short, the officials were eager for the NCAFP to send a fact-finding mission to study the situation. Toward that end, I invited Kazakhstan's Minister of Foreign Affairs H.E. Kasymzhomart Tokaev to address these issues in NCAFPs bimonthly *American Foreign Policy Interests*, which he did in the April 2004 issue.

Because I was largely uninformed about Kazakhstan and Central Asian countries in general, I consulted Professor Michael Rywkin—a world-renowned Russian and Central Asian scholar—and experts in and out of government, only to learn that the country and the region could potentially become an arena of contention between Russia and China largely because of its rich energy and mineral resources and strategic location as a land bridge from Europe to East and South Asia. I was soon convinced that the U.S. national interest would be well served by considerably enhancing and expanding relations with Kazakhstan; I received the green light from the executive committee to establish a new project.

In 2005, I invited Michael Rywkin to become the director of this project, which he accepted, and invited NCAFP Senior Vice President Donald S. Rice, Esq., to head a fact-finding mission to the country. Rice and Rywkin were joined by NCAFP Treasurer Richard R. Howe, Esq., Ambassador Peter Tomsen (ret.), and Professor Peter J. Sinnott, director of the Caspian Sea Project at Columbia University.

Gradually the NCAFP convinced the National Security Council (NSC), the Department of State, and the Pentagon of the relevance of Kazakhstan to U.S. security equations and recommended that the "United States increase its interactions and cooperation with Kazakhstan's military and intelligence agencies, support and encourage educational and cultural exchanges," and "facilitate regional cooperation between the Central Asian states," and be aware of the importance of the region to China and Russia with all that that implied.[9]

In 2010, with the consent of the executive committee, I helped to launch the cyber-security project. The seriousness of this issue was brought to my attention by NCAFP Trustee Edythe M. Holbrook. As a new and manmade domain of warfare (in contrast to land, sea, and air), cyber weapon-tools operating in cyberspace—a synthetic domain—have revolutionized warfare. In 2007, without firing a shot, for example, Estonia's infrastructure was paralyzed by a cyber attack; the following year, malware infected a laptop belonging to the U.S. Department of Defense; and, in 2010, the Stuxnet computer worm severely damaged Iran's nuclear centrifuges at Natanz. It soon became obvious to me that cyber weapons have the potential to bring countries inexpensively to their knees in minutes, perhaps even seconds.

This entirely new type of warfare raises an overarching question: Does it destroy the Westphalian system that had gradually begun to emerge in the middle of the seventeenth century? Yes. As an official declaration of war that has traditionally preceded a conflict is not anticipated in cyber warfare, how can a cyberspace aggressor be pinpointed? Is the aggressor a state or non-state actor? Is the non-state actor acting independently or as a surrogate for a state? So long as these basic questions cannot be answered, how can the aggrieved country undertake countermeasures?

To address challenges that cyber aggressors pose and how to respond prompted Edythe Holbrook to organize round-table conferences, sometimes jointly with West Point colleagues.[10] Although progress has been made in the course of the last decade, much still remains to be done.

Even before becoming president of the NCAFP in the early 1990s, I am proud of having taken the initiative to establish awards honoring two outstanding individuals.

Following the passing of the founding father of the NCAFP in 1980, Hans J. Morgenthau, and with the unanimous approval of the executive committee, we established a commemorative award bearing his name. The encomium I composed reads: "The person to be so honored is one whose intellectual attainments and/or practical contributions to United States foreign policy have been judged so exemplary in the tradition of Professor Morgenthau as to merit this singular award." The first person so honored was Ambassador Angier Biddle Duke in 1981. The presentation was made by Henry Kissinger.

My second recommendation was Elie Wiesel—a NCAFP board member. I argued that he deserved to be honored for his courage to keep the past alive as a lesson for a future beyond hate, which was unanimously accepted by the executive committee. At a black-tie dinner in 1987, I presented the humanitarian award to Elie Wiesel. The citation I composed reads: "The Humanitarian and Peace Award was established in 1987 to especially honor Elie Wiesel for his extraordinary commitment to advancing human rights and peace in the world."

In 1994, I floated the idea of establishing an award bearing the name of Ambassador George F. Kennan—father of the doctrine of containment (whose first posting was in Riga where his daughter Grace was born—a future chairwoman of the NCAFP). My suggestion was unanimously accepted by the executive committee; the citation for The George F. Kennan Award for Distinguished Public Service reads: "This award, established in 1994 in honor of George F. Kennan, scholar, diplomat, and statesman, recognizes an American who has served the United States in an exemplary way and has made a seminal contribution to defining and illuminating the national interests of the United States." The first person so honored was Ambassador Kennan. It was NCAFP Honorary Chairman Henry Kissinger who made the presentation. (Kissinger was succeeded by Ambassador George F. Kennan who, in turn, was succeeded by the Honorable Paul A. Volcker.)

In 1996, the executive committee unanimously accepted my suggestion that the NCAFP establish an annual lecture to bear the name of Angier Biddle Duke—who had played a pivotal role in the formative years of the organization and had recently passed away. The first speaker was Ambassador Thomas R. Pickering, who was then our ambassador to the Russian Federation.

In 1997, the NCAFP at my suggestion established the Initiative for Peace Award to honor Chairman William J. Flynn for his "Decisive leadership and daring diplomacy in spurring two cease-fires and promoting the peace process in Northern Ireland." It was unanimously accepted by the executive committee; Mr. Flynn was the first recipient of this award. Renamed the William J. Flynn Initiative for Peace Award in 2001, the inscription reads: "The Award is presented to an individual who has worked tirelessly to resolve a conflict that has affected the national interests of the United States."

Further, early in the new century an anonymous donor in my honor established the George D. Schwab Foreign Policy Series at the NCAFP, according to which four public lectures had to be so designated. Shortly thereafter, an anonymous donor also established in my honor the George D. Schwab Fellowship in American Foreign Policy at the City University of New York's Graduate Center (and, in 2002, I was the recipient of Latvia's Order of Three Stars; in 1998, I was a recipient of the Ellis Island Medal of Honor; and, most recently, in 2018, I was the recipient of the Elie Wiesel Award).

In 2009, Trustees Grace Kennan Warnecke and Hatice U. Morrissey, with my encouragement, established the Young Leader Award. Later recipients automatically became members of the 21st Century Leaders Council, which had been formed by Trustee Edythe M. Holbrook in 2010. This award was created to recognize the achievements of young leaders "who display a serious commitment to furthering the United States national interests in accord with the principles of political realism." The first three recipients in 2009 were John Delury, Nathan Fick, and Joshua Cooper Ramo.

Shortly before I retired in January 2015, I suggested to the executive committee that we establish a soft power award focused on cultural diplomacy. My candidate for the inaugural award was Jo Carole Lauder. This finally came to fruition in 2016 when I was invited to present the first "Award for Excellence in Cultural Diplomacy and International Engagement" to her. The citation reads: "This inaugural award is presented by the National Committee on American Foreign Policy to honor the work of an individual, who through professional or personal endeavors, has exceptionally contributed to advancing the exchange of ideas, values, traditions, and other aspects of the culture of the United States to strengthen relationships, enhance socio-cultural cooperation and promote the national interest."

On my retirement I was succeeded by Ambassador Rosemary A. DiCarlo. I could not have hoped for a better successor. Ambassador DiCarlo is a career diplomat with a Ph.D. who has served our country with distinction in Moscow, Oslo, and in New York. In New York, she served as president of the UN Security Council. In 2018, Secretary-General António Guterres of the United Nations appointed Ambassador DiCarlo Under-Secretary-General for Political Affairs. She was succeeded at the NCAFP by Ambassador Susan M. Elliott, an equally illustrious personality. She has served our country with distinction in Dushanbe, Moscow, Belfast, and as deputy assistant secretary of state. When Ambassador Elliott introduced herself as the president of the NCAFP to the former president of Latvia, Vaira Vike-Freiberga, President Vike-Freiberga supposedly said to her: So, you are the new George Schwab.

Notes

1. The Board included, among other distinguished individuals, Saul Bellow, Bruno Bettelheim, Donald D. Brennan, Eugene Wigner, Michael Wyshograd, Howard L. Adelson, Henry Friedlander, and Eric Isaac. I also learned that two Israelis—the author Shmuel (Muhi) Katz and the concert pianist David Bar Illan—had also played a role in the formation of the NCAFP.
2. Gradually I assembled a coterie of impressive intellectuals who consented to write for the "American Foreign Policy Newsletter," including, among others, Arthur M. Schlesinger, Jr., John H. Herz, Gil Carl Alroy, Bernard E. Brown, Michael Rywkin, Rael Jean Isaac, Dankwart A. Rustow, Michael Curtis, Vojtech Mastny, Donald Rotunda, Giuseppe Amendola, and Donald S. Zagoria.
3. Presenters included, among others, Arthur M. Schlesinger, Jr., Vojtech Mastny; Walter LaFeber; Dankwart A. Rustow; Seymour Maxwell Finger; and, Kenneth and Beverly Thompson. The edited volume appeared in print in 1982, which I dedicated to Hans Morgenthau: "In Memory of Hans Joachim Morgenthau—Inspiring Thinker, Honored Colleague, Devoted Friend."
4. It took John V. Connorton, Jr., Esq., to convince future Nobel laureate Mr. Hume to accept the NCAFP invitation.
5. U.S. participants in the NCAFP's Track I½ and Track II work included, among others, A. Doak Barnett, Raymond Burghardt, Kurt M. Campbell. Ralph Cosa, Karl W. Eikenberry, Bonnie S. Glaser, Winston Lord, Douglas H. Paal, Nicholas Platt, Evans Revere, Robert A. Scalapino, Ezra Vogel, and Donald S. Zagoria.

NATIONAL COMMITTEE ON AMERICAN FOREIGN POLICY
(NCAFP)—HIGHLIGHTS

6. Participants at the numerous conferences included, among others (alphabetically): Giuseppe Amendola (U.S.); Inocencio F. Arias (Spain); Kenneth J. Bialkin (U.S.); Albert Bildner (U.S.); Donald Blinken (U.S.); Renate Bohne von Boyens (U.S.); Bernard E. Brown (U.S.); Steven Chernys (U.S.); Michael Curtis (U.S.); Viola Herms Drath (U.S.); Phillipe Errera (France); Steven Everts (U.K.); Julian Lindley-French (France); Richard N. Gardner (U.S.); Irene Finel-Honigman (U.S.); William Hopkinson (U.K.); Fereydoun Hoveyda (U.S.); Richard R. Howe (U.S.); Ephraim Isaac (U.S.); Dieter Kastrup (Germany); Hugo Kaufman (U.S.); Madeline Konigsberg (U.S.); Joseph LaPalombara (U.S.); Hatice Morrissey (U.S.); Christa Percopo (U.S.); Ann Phillips (U.S.); Donald S. Rice (U.S.); John B. Richardson (EU); Nina Rosenwald (U.S.); William M. Rudolf (U.S.); Michael Rywkin (U.S.); Martin Schain (U.S.); Nancy Soderberg (U.S.); Stefano Silvestri (Italy); Ronald Tiersky (U.S.); Kurt Volker (U.S.); Grace Kennan Warnecke (U.S.)

7. These included Nassir Assar; Ali Banuazizi; Peter Chelkowski; Bernard Haykel; Muhammad Musli; Amir Phares; and Amir Taheri.

8. Including, among others, Raghida Dergham; Mona Eltahawy; Ghida Fakhry; Irshad Manji; Bernard Haykel; Muktedar Khan; Sherifa Zuhur; and Mohammad Ja'far Mahallati.

9. Over the years, U.S. participants in round-table conferences and fact-finding missions included, among others, Zeyno Baran; Robert Blake; Stephan Blank; Richard Boucher; Matthew Bryza; Daniel Charap; Steven Chernys; Alexander Cooley; Evan Feigenbaum; John J. Fox; Blaine D. Holt; Roger Kangas; Mark N. Katz; Daniel M. Klippstein; Daniel Merkel; Matthew Nimetz; John M. Ordway; and Daniel Russell.

10. Edythe Holbrook was assisted by Camino Kavanagh. Participants in conferences included, among others, Dmitri Alperovitch; Giuseppe Amendola; John Brickey; John V. Connorton, Jr.; Nathaniel Fick; Melissa Hathaway; Jon Healy; Rhett A Hernandez; David P. Hunt; Igor Kharkov; James A. Lewis; Catherine Lotrionte; Joseph S. Nye, Jr; Harry D. Raduege; Rafal Rohozinski; William M. Rudolf; David E. Sanger; Marcus Sachs; David Scharia; Adam Segal; John N. Stewart; and Nicholas Thompson.

Chapter XIV
RETURNING TO LATVIA, TRAGEDY AT HOME, RENEWAL

The story of my return to Latvia antedates June 1990—the year I returned—when, to my great surprise and even shock, I blurted out to Per Ahlmark on an early morning phone call from Stockholm in June 1990: "Yes, I will go with you to Latvia." This, as earlier noted, after having sworn in August 1944 never to return to this blood-soaked country that had robbed me of my idyllic childhood and destroyed my family. How did my snap decision come about?

On our trip to Auschwitz-Birkenau, which preceded the conference of Nobel laureates in Paris, we truly bonded. (Eleonora, the children, and I had met Per in the Hamptons while he was vacationing with the Wiesels, where he had insisted on acting as a bartender.) During our days in Paris, he quizzed me about my experiences during the war and asked whether I had entertained the thought of visiting Latvia. My reply: "Never." Per brought up the subject again and again during long-distance phone conversations. I told him that this was not on my radar screen. Gentle person that he is, he told me that after many tries he had finally succeeded in persuading Elie Wiesel to visit his birthplace—Sziget, in Romania—with Per accompanying him. Per even said that it would be his honor to accompany me.

Although I was determined not to return to Latvia, Per did plant a seed in my mind. My endeavor to repress the war years had been successful only to an extent, because, deep down, I could not erase those awful years. The horrific past was brought back each year when I accompanied my mother to the annual Latvian Jewish memorial services in New York commemorating those we had loved and lost. These services were organized by Max Kaufmann, author of the 1947 eyewitness account, *Churbn Lettland: The Destruction of the Jews of Latvia.*

Further, it was Elie Wiesel in the mid-1980s who gently reminded me of my duty as a survivor who is articulate and writes well to record my past—a past that must never be forgotten. I told Elie that I could not live the way he does—thinking non-stop about the Holocaust; it would drive me insane, I said. He brought up the subject once more, during our visit to Auschwitz-Birkenau and in Paris. I nodded. In 1990, I caved into Per's urgings, and subsequently to Elie's entreaties, but did not put pen to paper for many years.

On the way to Latvia, I stopped off at Stockholm, where I stayed overnight in Per's apartment; on the following day, we flew to Riga. On arriving in Latvia's capital, a city and country that were then on the road to full independence from the Soviet Union, Per and I checked into Hotel Riga—we immediately noticed that the rooms were still bugged and quite clumsily. Across the street, I saw men in leather coats milling around. They reminded me of the Soviet secret police in Libau. Downstairs in the restaurant, I ordered a Russian chicken dish but was served a fish dish instead. As we soon learned, this was nothing unusual in the Soviet paradise.

My original intent was to show Per the places I had been incarcerated and where my father, brother, and relatives had been killed—and to say Kaddish at the killing grounds. Finding out the condition of Jews still living in Latvia was also on my agenda. Per thought that we should broaden the agenda to include discussions about the country's independence and emerging relations with the free world. Because Per was a well-known fighter for Baltic independence and a former Swedish deputy prime minister, we had immediate access to senior statesmen and politicians. My position as senior vice president of the National Committee on American Foreign Policy also helped.

Before getting down to essentials, I introduced Per to the Riga I remembered: where I had lived with Aunt Hermine at 11 Elizabetes Street and with another aunt who had lived with her brother around the corner at Vilandes Street. I noted that this section of Riga was known as the diplomatic district—the most exclusive part of the city. It was full of fantastic ornamental and decorative Art Nouveau buildings. Per was astonished by the beauty of the streets in that district and by Riga in general. I was surprised to see how little of the center of Riga had been destroyed during the war. Yet more than dozens of the architectural gems were run down—the price of fifty years of neglect. We also visited the Jewish Center—known as the Jewish club before the war—where we met with Gregory Krupnikov and Ester Rapina, the co-heads of the Jewish community. They briefed us on the condition of Jews in Latvia in general and in Riga in particular. Stated succinctly: gradually a cultural Jewish renaissance was beginning to reemerge. To bring this point home, we were invited to an extraordinary performance of the Kinnor Choir, a group of several dozen Jewish teenagers led by Michael and Fanny Leinwand and Ivar Brod.

The place I was most eager to visit, of course, was the Rumbula forest near Riga, where most Latvian Jews had been slaughtered and perhaps also my brother (some believe that Bubi may have been killed at Bikerniek forest). Per was always at my side, but at one of the mass graves he let me walk alone where I shed tears and said Kaddish. I assumed that my Riga relatives were killed there as well. A memorial commemorating the Nazi victims was at the entrance.

Thanks to Per's connections, we were received by, among others, Latvian Foreign Minister Janis Jurkans and Secretary of the Supreme Council I. Daudišs. I was pleasantly surprised as was Per by the openness with which Latvian officials and politicians admitted the sorry role some Latvians had played in the destruction of Jews during the war.

A result of numerous conversations with officials and politicians and of Per's writing about our visit in Sweden's largest daily *Expressen* and my doing the same in the *American Foreign Policy Newsletter*, the Latvian Parliament, in September 1990, passed a "Declaration" on the "Condemnation and Inadmissibility of Genocide and Anti-Semitism in Latvia." This declaration condemned the genocide of the Jewish people who, over the centuries, had materially contributed to "Latvia's economy . . . culture, science, and medicine," acknowledged that "some citizens of Latvia" had participated in the slaughter of Jews, promised to "immortalize the memory of Jews," and to create "favorable conditions for Latvian Jews to renew and develop their national institutions for culture, education, science, and religion." Further, the declaration stated that "Latvia will not tolerate any manifestations of anti-Semitism and national discrimination" and will consider them "incompatible with the traditions" of Latvia.

The acknowledgment that Latvians played an active role in the killing of Jews combined with the declaration helped me rationalize my return to Latvia. On subsequent visits, Per and I continued our conversations with Latvian leaders, and we closely monitored the progress being made on Jewish issues in Latvia as well as Latvia's emerging role in the free world. As previously noted, I became convinced that the Baltic States needed to become members of NATO and worked hard toward that end.

While in Latvia the first time, we were provided with an official car and driver. This facilitated our visiting Aunt Hermine's former apartment. In the seven-room flat three families now resided. I showed Per the terrace from where I heard Vishinsky address crowds that allegedly welcomed the Soviet liberation of the country. I also showed him the room I used to sleep in. On this trip we also drove to the Kaiserwald where the concentration camp had been located. No traces of the camp remained. We continued to Aunt Tanya and her mother-in-law's residence in Kaiserwald where they had moved from 11 Elizabetes Street. I remembered the villa but could not locate it.

At last we left Riga for my hometown Libau. In contrast to Riga, the center of Libau had been largely destroyed by the Germans in 1941. Riga was not a strategic target; however, Libau was because of its three ice-free ports. One port, known as Karosta (war port), was a major naval base for the Soviet, Nazi, and czarist Russia's Baltic fleets.

The house I was born in on 27 Graudu Street still stood and was now the headquarters of agriculture for the region of Kurzeme. The nine-room apartment was now divided: father's library, which had doubled as a waiting room, with its own entrance was separated from the rest of the apartment, as was my bedroom where the paint covering the former door was still clearly visible. I showed Per the apartment we had rented at 21 Kuršu Street after the Soviets had expelled us from our long-time residence. I also showed Per the women's prison where mother and I were incarcerated for several hours, the ghetto, the basement apartment we had lived in (but it was locked), the commandant's office where I was his runner, and the Fireman's Square where, as previously noted, Jews had to appear mornings to be assigned for work for the German military. Further, I showed Per the SD headquarters, the residence of Kügler's mistress, Mrs. Kronberg, where I had been hidden on occasion. From there we proceeded to the Lighthouse where my father had been shot dead at the end of July 1941—I said Kaddish there. I also managed to show Per the Jewish tennis club where mother, Bubi, and I used to play as well as the wonderful Libau beach.

As in Riga, during this time of transition toward independence, there was the beginning of a Jewish cultural revival. At the Jewish Center we met Vladimir Ban, the chairman, who brought us up-to-date on the few hundred Jews, mostly ethnic Russian Jews, who had moved to Libau after the war. At Skede, near Libau, where the majority of Libau Jews had been killed in December 1941, including Aunt Yette, I recited Kaddish. There was no monument commemorating the thousands of Jews murdered, rather one merely indicating victims of fascism. Soviet policy was to conflate all victims of fascism into one.[1]

Returning to Riga, we departed for Stockholm, where I said good-bye to Per and took a connecting flight to New York. I thanked him for having persuaded me to return to Latvia, and I promised myself to take a more active part in the activities of the Jewish Survivors of Latvia in the United States, which was, after Max Kaufmann's death, headed by Steven Springfield. In 1993, the Jewish community of sovereign Latvia organized a reunion of Latvian Jews and their descendants worldwide.

Eleonora and I in the company of Steven Springfield, his wife Muriel, the refusenik Julia Gindiga Robinson, Peter Springfield, Leo Kram, Jac Ratz, Shoshana Kahn, among others, from the United States and elsewhere, including Per who joined us from Stockholm as did Grischa Jacobson and some non-Latvian Jews who had been incarcerated in Latvia, including Professor Gertrude Schneider—met in Riga's by now considerably spruced up Jewish community center at 6 Skolas Street. We all were warmly welcomed by the co-chairs Gregory Krupnikov and Ester Rapina. In addition to all of us visiting the Rumbula forest, we also visited the Bikerniek forest where most of the German, Austrian, and Czech Jews had been murdered and Latvian Jews as well—perhaps even Bubi. From there, the buses took us to the Gogol Street Synagogue, which had been burned to the ground by Latvians with 300 Jews inside only a few days after the Germans had occupied Riga. Of course, prayers were said at all the sites. We also toured the Riga Ghetto. Many tears were shed and a few survivors even fainted.

Those of us from Libau boarded a bus in due time for our trip to Libau where we were welcomed by Mr. Ban at the Jewish Community Center on Kungu Street. All the sites Per and I had visited in 1990 we did again together—painfully. At the dinner, both Per and I were invited to address the survivors and their descendants. Not anticipating this surprise invitation, I was for a moment at a loss in which language to address the audience. Not wishing to hurt anybody's feelings, I hesitated to speak German, my Russian was too rudimentary, and very few understood English. My solution was to speak the rudimentary Yiddish I had acquired during the war. As I spoke, I became so infatuated with my command of the Yiddish tongue that I could not bring myself to end my remarks. Back in Riga at a Kinnor Choir performance followed by a farewell meal, Per and I were once more asked to make a few remarks. Sure of my command of Yiddish, I pontificated for more than ten minutes, receiving a hearty round of applause. On returning to my table, I was approached by a gentleman who congratulated me for "speaking such a beautiful German." I was thunderstruck, but Eleonora was certain that I knew I had spoken German.

I was pleasantly surprised by Eleonora's enthusiasm for being among the Jewish Survivors of Latvia on Latvian soil; she had been born in Riga and had heard much about Latvia and the fate of Jews in Latvia from her Latvian-born Jewish father. She had researched the addresses of the building where she had lived, which was not far from the Jewish Center—a solid middle- and upper-middle-class neighborhood—as well as the location of her father's office in the old part of the city. I also showed her where I had lived in Riga. She was overwhelmed by the beauty of the diplomatic district, by the numerous parks, and by the city in general. Upon returning to New York, she joined me in taking a more active part in the doings of the Jewish Survivors of Latvia, including hosting a number of gatherings in our home. She was also looking forward to returning to Latvia. This, unfortunately, did not come to pass.

Eleonora was once more stricken by cancer, which, this time, had spread to her lungs and brain. After eighteen months of struggle to contain and reverse this horrible illness, Eleonora was prematurely taken from us in October 1998—at the age of sixty.

With death around the corner, she on numerous occasions said how happy she was to have lived sufficiently long to have seen the children grow up healthy and happy. Time and again she talked about the bar mitzvah at Lincoln Square Synagogue and how lucky we were to have had Rabbi Shlomo Riskin and Cantor Sherwood Goffin perform the services, and how many people from different parts of the world had attended. She called friends[2] to brag about the triplets' having graduated with a combined seven undergraduate and graduate degrees from elite U.S. universities. She was also delighted to have met in her waning month Clarence's wife-to-be, Pamela Haas, whom he had met while both were studying at Harvard, as well as her very nice parents Susan and David.

In and out of the hospital, the children and I took turns visiting her at Memorial Sloan Kettering, her niece Elisabeth (Flisa) came from Sweden to help, and the children would literally call dozens of time a day at the hospital or at home. Solan still lived at home. At quiet moments, Eleonora and I spoke a lot about our past—the ups and downs largely because of her relationship with Sweden that had affected both of us and which we had agreed, not always successfully, not to speak about. She on numerous occasions said that she had always tried to be an exemplary daughter but was especially disappointed by her mother and, to an extent, also by her father whom she loved and adored throughout. Toward the very end she also told me that a day had not passed without her thinking how terribly they had treated me. But that was the past. Now she made me promise her that I would do everything in my power to keep the children together. In her words: "Together they will prosper, apart they will flounder." This was not always easy. I am, however, certain that she would be proud of the men she had brought into the world.

Shortly before her death, Eleonora was overjoyed to learn that I had been nominated to receive the Ellis Island Medal of Honor in 1998; it recognizes native-born and naturalized U.S. citizens for their material contributions to furthering America's greatness. Although she was no longer able to attend the ceremony, Clarence and Pamela did. Also, before her passing, Eleonora was proud to learn that Bel Kaufman (granddaughter of Sholom Aleichem) had invited me to become vice president of the Sholom Aleichem Foundation.

A strong believer in the Jewish tradition that life comes before death, Eleonora would certainly have been overjoyed by Solan's marriage to Lisa Davis in Las Vegas (where they both enjoyed gambling) in 1999 and her giving birth to twin boys—Jonah Eric and Michael Adrian—in 2002. Clarence followed suit in New York in 2000, with Pamela giving birth to Zachary Eli in 2002 and to Eleonora (Ellie) Cara in 2004. Claude was the laggard. At last, he settled down and married Diana Han in Santa Monica in 2017. She gave birth to Noah Alexander in that same year and, as I go to press, I am overjoyed to report that Diana just gave birth to a daughter by the name of Ava Eleana.

Following Eleonora's passing, I frequently met with Clarence, Claude, and Solan to celebrate the unusually warm mother she was, her sense of humor, her joy in entertaining, which extended to friends who regularly slept at our home, including, among others, Stephanie Collomb (who even lived with us for a while), Sister Carol Rittner, Joan Peters, and Mona Schlachter. Bearing in mind Eleonora's deep interest in the rich history of the Jewish people and the tragedy of the Holocaust, we explored ways in which we could immortalize this precious soul. An opportunity soon presented itself.

Our long-time friend Jeanine Plottel, a colleague at CUNY's Graduate Center, suggested in 1999 that I become a Library Associate of its Mina Rees Library, which I did. As the holdings of the library were rapidly expanding and the library was in need of financial support, I agreed to establish The George D. Schwab Family Fund with the proviso that the income be used to purchase books related to Jewish studies. The contract stated that "Bookplates, indicating that the books are from 'The Family of Professor George D. Schwab—in memory of Eleonora Schwab,' will be placed in each of the books." The Fund also gifted a student desk and a bookshelf.

At about the same time another opportunity presented itself. On my nearly annual trips to Latvia since 1990, I was pleased to note the extent to which Jewish activities had expanded at Riga's Jewish Center. As the written word and Jewish education in general have since time immemorial been integral to Jewish life, and because much of the prewar library at the center was neglected and publications decimated, there was now much talk about the need for renovating and enlarging the library's space and materially expanding its holdings. Hence, the moment was ripe for me to make a move.

Initially, with the help of my sons and friends, I offered to financially aid the renovation and enlargement of the space. I further committed myself to supporting the library financially and providing publications in English about the Holocaust and Jewish history. In return, it was agreed that the library would be known as The Eleonora Schwab Library.[3]

The library was officially dedicated by President Vaira Vike-Freiberga of Latvia in 2001—in the presence of my son Claude and many guests. According to the librarian Tsilia Raines in 2016, in fourteen years the library has grown from four thousand publications to over fourteen thousand in Latvian, Russian, English, German, Hebrew, and Yiddish. Every publication I provided contains a bookplate that says: "Eleonora Schwab Library given by George D. Schwab & Family." The Schwabs are especially grateful to Barbara Lau of Munich for her donation of publications in the German tongue and to Liat Sela Wexelman, deputy ambassador of Israel to Latvia, for donating books in Hebrew.

In the late 1990s, President Guntis Ulmanis of Latvia invited me to become a member of the President's Commission of International Historians whose mandate was to study Latvia's recent past—the two Soviet occupations and the Holocaust. I was reappointed by President Vike-Freiberga and continued to serve.

Largely because some Latvians had participated in the murder of Jews, on the one hand, and widespread anti-Semitism during the Nazi occupation largely due to the venomous Nazi propaganda that wedded despised Bolshevism with equally despised Judaism, on the other hand, research on the Holocaust in Latvia by Latvian academics was not always easy. The bulk of the research on the Holocaust that has been done in Latvia is, unfortunately, not available in English.

My friendship with Bel Kaufman goes back to the late 1950s—when I met her at the home of the Rosenwalds. Over the years we kept in touch and Bel kept telling me of her endeavor to keep the memory of Sholom Aleichem alive. As the years passed, Bel on occasion mentioned that the Sholom Aleichem Foundation—of which I knew nothing—needed to be reorganized. In passing she kept mentioning that once reorganized she would like me to become part of the new foundation. One day Bel phoned and asked me to join the foundation and that Elie Wiesel and Joan Peters had agreed to join as well. She reiterated the aim of the foundation, which was to further interest in the writings of Sholom Aleichem, keeping the Yiddish language alive, and convening annual memorial services in New York at which time selections of his writings would be read. Jokingly, she said, "there is much more to Sholom Aleichem than 'Fiddler on the Roof.'"

Bel even went so far as to suggest that I become the foundation's president. I, of course, thanked her for the honor and replied by noting that my Yiddish was rudimentary; I was dumbfounded to learn from Bel that her Yiddish, too, was elementary. Further, I told her why I could not accept the honor because obligations involved in running the rapidly growing National Committee on American Foreign Policy. Then, she said, "George, we are old friends, I really don't need you—but I need your name." My reply, please give me a title that would not entail me doing much work. She suggested that I become vice president, and I agreed.

Some time passed before I heard from Bel again. When, at last, I did assume my post of vice president, I was spared, as Bel had promised, from attending to daily chores, which her husband, Sidney Gluck, a humanitarian

Marxist, did very well. The foundation did indeed implement the vision as articulated by Bel. But gradually, Sidney began to politicize the foundation. Whenever possible he injected his ideology into the foundation, which made me feel uncomfortable as it did Joan Peters. She ultimately resigned from the board. I argued that a cultural foundation must not go on record promoting any kind of political ideology—but I did not prevail. I finally resigned. But this did not affect my friendship with Bel and Sidney.

The new century brought a change into my life, a woman I had casually met in 1986 at the United States Holocaust Memorial Museum meetings—Sheila Johnson Robbins.

At about the turn of the new century, Marion Wiesel had lunch with Sheila in New York. On informing Sheila that Eleonora had recently passed away, Sheila sent me a condolence letter in which she informed me that her husband, Lester, too, had passed away in 1996. Of course, I sent her a condolence letter in return. Not long thereafter I received from Sheila an invitation to a dinner party at her home in Manhattan. Because of a prior commitment I had to decline. In due time, I received another invitation, which I accepted.

On that occasion I took another look at Sheila. Born in Canada and living most of her life in New York, I noted that she was an attractive Scandinavian-looking woman and a seasoned hostess. She, like Eleonora, had class as we would say in Europe. As the evening progressed, I discovered that behind her commanding presence lurked what I sensed was a warm woman to whom I took more than just a liking. All in all, an interesting challenge to a European-oriented male not easily intimidated by strong American women.

I followed up by inviting Sheila to accompany me to Julia Robinson's inimitable New Year's Eve party, which Eleonora and I and at times also the children had attended for years. I came away that evening thinking that I would not mind having a short-term relationship with her. What impressed me as well was something very dear to me: though not Jewish herself, Sheila had a genuine interest in the fate of the Jewish people during the Second World War.

Well, here we are two decades later and Sheila and I are still together—or, as we say in America, we are a couple until she passed away in February

2020. I also had gotten to know her son, Peter, who is in the family's real-estate business and also teaches pottery, his wife, Page, a jewelry designer, and their two delicious sons—Harvest and Tobey.

In our extensive travels to Latvia, Sheila also began to support, among other charities in Latvia, the Eleonora Schwab Library and participated in Jewish events in Riga, Libau, and New York—where she got to know well, among others, Steven and Muriel Springfield, Gerta Feigin, Drs. Ivar and Bronia Brod, and David Silberman.

Over the years, she and I bonded in Riga with the archivist Rita Bogdanova (née Blumberg; whose mother, Bella, during the Nazi period, lived for a while in Libau with mother, Bubi, Mia, and me). Also in Riga, we became close friends with Olga and and Arkady Suharenko. He is the head of the Jewish community of Latvia and a very successful banker. In Libau we bonded with the inimitable Jewish leader Ilana Ivanova (née Zivcon). Her imaginative leadership and projects (supported by, among others, Arkady Suharenko, the Haas brothers [Raymond and Selwyn] of London and Jersey in the English Channel, the Libau tycoon Sergejs Zaharjins, Sheila Johnson Robbins, and me) have caught the attention of the world far beyond Libau—to as far as New York and Washington, D.C.

Further, when in Libau, our friendship with the Zaharjins became so close that I began to consider Sergejs my younger brother. Way back, their son Aleksejs (Alex) had studied in the United States. I used to invite him and his future wife, Svetlana, to some of the receptions I hosted in New York in honor of our dear friends, the Latvian president Dr. Vaira Vike-Freiberga and her husband, Dr. Imants Freibergs. Sheila has also hosted dinner parties in honor the Freibergs.

Because of the generous support provided by the Suharenkos, the Haas brothers, Sheila, and myself for the study of the Holocaust in Latvia and beyond, our names appear on Washington's Holocaust Museum's donor wall.

In her curiosity about my past, Sheila wanted to visit places I had lived in Europe after my liberation. Hence, we went to Neustadt/Holstein where we toured the former U-Boat school, the notorious red light Clemens Street in Lübeck, the Warburg estate near Hamburg, and Hamburg's red-light district—the Reeperbahn and in Berlin, the building where I met mother and the cafés on Kurfüstendamm and on Friedrich Street where I used to hang out with mother, and the apartment I was born in in Libau, among other sites. Over the years, we also visited the Laus in Munich; Zurich, where I had done a lot of research for my Ph.D. dissertation; Paris, where I introduced Sheila to the Distels—Anne was the daughter of Georges Dayez—from whom, over the years, she bought paintings by Dayez; the Philippe Massons, the Bertrand Collombs, and my father's cousin Shulamit Grynholc; London, where we visited Sheila's friend Susan Fischgrund (née Bloom), Oxford University where I read my chapter on the Second World War; Vienna together with the Ronald Lauders; and, at the invitation of the Chinese government and with the William Rudolfs and the Donald Rices, Beijing, Shanghai, and Suchow.

When not traveling in the summers, Sheila liked to spend time in her house in East Hampton, where I swam in the ocean and in the pool. There we have celebrated the birthdays of the triplets; in Manhattan I usually invited family and friends to celebrate my birthday at the end of November. While still president of the National Committee, I also annually hosted receptions for members and foreign policy gurus and salon evenings where distinguished guests would comment on burning national security interests affecting the United States.

Notes

1. Per, in his memoirs (*Gör inga dumheter medan jag är död!* [Stockholm, 2011]) speaks about some of our trips to Latvia.
2. Rochelle Saideman, Sally Wechsler, Barbara Advocate, Barbara Lau, Sue Wiener, Sister Carol Rittner, Marion Behr, Edith Rudolf, Ginger Runes Najar, Jeanine Plottel, Suzy Eban, Lillian Robbins, Julia Robinson, Eleanor Ripp, Mona Schlachter, and Ann Marie Morris among others.
3. The outpouring that the founding of the Eleonora Schwab Library engendered was astonishing. Contributors included: Manya Alder; Prof. Howard L. Adelson; Rachel Oestreicher Bernheim; Nuta Bruskin; Sol N. Bukingolts; Anna and Samuel Charney; Arnold Engel; Jewel and Joel Faerber; Gerta Feigin; Linda and Robert Fisher and Family; Marilyn and Leon B. Friedman; Renia and Victor Gelb; Jamie K. Ginsberg; Pamela Haas; Susan and David Haas; Ella Hirschhorn; Dr. Sarah and Prof. Morris Holbrook; Prof. Frances and Floyd Horowitz; Andrew C. Jacobs; Eve and Dr. Howard Kaufman; Selma Kon; Gregory Krupnikov; James and Dr. Barbara Lau; Samuel

Manevich; David Margolick; Ann Phillips; Liuba Rakhman; Edgenie and Donald S. Rice; Sheila Johnson Robbins; Alexander J. Ross; Reba I. Rottenberg; Dr. Margrit Rustow; Beulah and Reuben Saideman; Rochelle and Sanford Saideman; Esther Schwab; Lisa Schwab; Mona Schlachter; Prof. Johanna Spektor; Naomi and Peter Springfield; Steven and Muriel Springfield; Vera Stern; Karen S. Strand; Drs. Myra and Gerald Sutin; G.L. Ulmen; Suzanna and Prof. Joel Wiener; Barbara and Harry Wittlin; Gitta M. Wybou.

SELECTED BIBLIOGRAPHY

Anders, Edward, and Juris Dubrovskis. *Jews in Liepaja, Latvia, 1941-1945. A Memorial Book.* Burlingame, California, 2001.

Angrick, Andrej, and Peter Klein. *The "Final Solution" in Riga: Exploitation and Annihilation, 1941-1944.* New York and Oxford, 2009.

Barkahan, Menachem, ed. *Extermination of the Jews in Latvia, 1941-1945.* Riga, 2008.

Bobe, Mendel, ed. *The Jews in Latvia.* Tel Aviv, 1971.

Brown, Edward E. "The United States and Europe. Partners, Rivals, Enemies?" *American Foreign Policy Interests* 26, No. 2 (2004): 129-138.

Caune, Andris, ed. *The Holocaust Research in Latvia.* Vol. 12, Riga, 2004.

Cherries on the Elbe, The Jewish Children's Home in Blankenese, 1946-1948. Association for Researching the History of the Jews in Blankenese. Konstanz, Germany, 2010.

Cohen, Herman J. "Al Qaeda in Africa: The Creeping Menace to Sub-Sahara's 500 Million Muslims." *American Foreign Policy Interests* 35, No. 2 (2013): 63-69.

_____. "Managing Transatlantic Divergence: Lessons from Africa." *American Foreign Policy Interests* 25, No. 5, (2003): 395-404.

Davis, Ethel S. *Latvia's Haunted Secrets.* Sydney, 2013.

Drath, Viola Herms, ed. *Germany in World Politics.* New York and London, 1979.

Eliach, Yaffa, ed. *We Were Children Just Like You.* Brooklyn, 1990.

SELECTED BIBLIOGRAPHY

Ezergailis, Andrew. *The Holocaust in Latvia, 1942-1944. The Missing Center*. Riga and Washington, D.C. 1996.

Feigmanis, Aleksandrs. *Latvian Jewish Intelligentsia: Victims of the Holocaust*. Riga, 2006.

Gitelman, Zvi. *A Century of Ambivalence. The Jews of Russia and the Soviet Union, 1881 to the Present*. New York, 1988.

Hoveyda, Fereydoun. *The Broken Crescent, The "Threat" of Militant Islamic Fundamentalism*. Westport, Connecticut and London, 1998.

Jahn, Franziska. *Das KZ Riga-Kaiserwald und seine Aussenlager 1943-1944 Strukturen und Entwicklungen*. Berlin, 2018.

Kaufmann, Max. *Churbn Lettland: The Destruction of the Jews of Latvia*. Enlarged edition. Riga, 2019.

Kennan, George F. *Memoirs 1925-1950*. Boston, 1967.

LaFeber, Walter. *America, Russia, and the Cold War 1945-1992*. 7th ed. New York, 1993.

Lenin, Vladimir. *"Left Wing" Communism: an Infantile Disorder*. Whitefish, Montana, 2010.

Lower, Wendy. *Hitler's Furies, German Women in the Nazi Killing Fields*. Boston and New York, 2013.

Mastny, Vojtech, ed. *Power and Policy in Transition, Essays Presented on the Tenth Anniversary of the National Committee on American Foreign Policy in Honor of Hans J. Morgenthau*. Westport, Connecticut, and London, 1984.

Matthäus, Jürgen, and Frank Bajorh. *The Political Diary of Alfred Rosenberg and the Onset of the Holocaust*. Lanham, Maryland, 2015.

Michelson, Frida. *I Survived Rumbula*. Washington, D.C., 1979.

Morgenthau, Hans J. *Politics Among Nations: The Struggle for Power and Peace*. 4th ed. New York, 1971.

Nollendorfs, Valters, and Erwin Oberländer, eds. *The Hidden and Forbidden History of Latvia Under Soviet and Nazi Occupation, 1940-1991*. Riga, 2005.

Plavnieks, Richards. *Nazi Collaborators on Trial During the Cold War: Viktors Arājs and the Latvian Auxiliary Security Police*. London, 2017.

Press, Bernhard. *Judenmord in Lettland 1941-1945*. 2nd ed. Berlin, 1955.

Reichelt, Katrin. *Lettland unter deutscher Besatzung 1941-1944, det lettische Anteil am Holocaust*. Berlin, 2011.

Rittner, Carol, R.S.M., ed. *Elie Wiesel Between Memory and Hope*. New York and London, 1990.

Rywkin, Michael. "Russia's Foreign Policy at the Outset of Putin's Third Term." *American Foreign Policy Interests* 34, No. 5 (2012): 232-237.

Schneider, Gertrude, ed. *Muted Voices, Jewish Survivors of Latvia Remember*. New York, 1987.

_____. *The Unfinished Road, Jewish Survivors of Latvia Look Back*. New York, 1991.

Schwab, George. *The Challenge of the Exception: An Introduction to the Political Ideas of Carl Schmitt between 1923 and 1936*. 2nd ed. with a new introduction. Westport, Connecticut, and London, 1989.

_____. "Enemy or Foe: A Conflict of Modern Politics." *TELOS* 72 (1987 [1968]): 194-201.

_____. "The Quest for Peace, Bill Flynn, the National Committee on American Foreign Policy, and the Beginnings of the Northern Ireland Peace Process," in Irish America Heritage Series. New York (2008): 8-11.

_____, ed. "Toward an Open Society Bloc." *United States Foreign Policy at the Crossroads*. (Westport, Connecticut, 1982): 55-63.

_____, and Henry Friedlander, eds. *Détente in Historical Perspective*. 3rd printing. New York, 1981 (1975).

Schwarberg, Günther. *Angriffsziel Cap Arcona*. Hamburg, 1983.

Sohlman, Eva. "Women's Role in Syria's Uprising Obscured by War and Intifada, but Still Crucial." *American Foreign Policy Interests* 35, No. 2 (2013): 70-74.

_____. "Al Qaeda In Yemen Pushed Back, but Terrorism Threat Remains Strong." *American Foreign Policy Interests* 34, No. 5 (2012): 249-254.

Talty, Stephan. *The Good Assassin: How a Mossad Agent and a Band of Survivors Hunted Down the Butcher of Riga*. New York, 2020.

Zagoria, Donald S. *Cross-Strait Relations, Breaking the Impasse, an Interim Report on U.S-China Policy and Cross-Strait Relations*. New York, 2000.

INDEX

Note: Italicized page numbers indicate captioned photographs.

INDEX